CAREER OPPORTUNITIES IN ART

THIRD EDITION

CAREER OPPORTUNITIES IN ART

THIRD EDITION

SUSAN H. HAUBENSTOCK AND DAVID JOSELIT

KAREN BRESSLER AND ELISE ROSEN
GENERAL EDITORS

Checkmark Books®
An imprint of Facts On File, Inc.

To Edna S. Hirsh,
who cultivated our love of art

CAREER OPPORTUNITIES IN ART, THIRD EDITION

Copyright © 2001, 1994 by Susan H. Haubenstock and David Joselit

Checkmark Books
An imprint of Facts On File, Inc.
11 Penn Plaza
New York, NY 10001

Library of Congress Cataloging-in-Publication Data

Haubenstock, Susan H.
    Career opportunities in art / Susan H. Haubenstock and David Joselit.—3rd ed.
        p. cm.
    Includes index.
    ISBN 0-8160-4245-4 (alk. paper)—ISBN 0-8160-4246-2 (pbk. : alk. paper)
    1. Art—Vocational guidance—United States. I. Joselit, David. II. Title.

    N6505 .H35 2001
    702′.3′73—dc21   00-034584

Checkmark Books are available at special discounts when purchased in bulk quantities for businesses, associations, institutions or sales promotions. Please call our Special Sales Department in New York at (212) 967-8800 or (800) 322-8755.

You can find Facts On File on the World Wide Web at http://www.factsonfile.com

Cover design by Nora Wertz

Printed in the United States of America

VB Hermitage 10 9 8 7 6 5 4 3 2 1
        (pbk) 10 9 8 7 6 5 4 3 2 1

This book is printed on acid-free paper.

CONTENTS

ACKNOWLEDGMENTS

The authors gratefully acknowledge the assistance of the following individuals who provided information for this book:

Dave Almy, Joan Arenberg, Phyllis Barczak, Scip Barnhart, Barry R. Bauman, Sherry Berg, Peter Blum, Marilyn Bonoff, Valerie Bove, Ann Boyd, Terence Brown, Donna Cooper, John Curran, Jim Dady, Ninkey Dalton, Geri Davis, Georgia Deal, Lisa Ebel, Jeannie Englehart, Richard Flood, Hal Foster, Elise Frost, Karen Garamella, Gary Garrels, Earl Goldstein, Merrie Good, Susan Graham, Frank Green, Marcia Heimbinder, Chriss Holderness, Abigail Housen, Jennifer D. Josselson, Kathleen Sullivan Kaska, Patricia Kelley, Eileen Kinnaird, Jeffrey Kline, Peter Krueger, Diane Mandel, Bono Mitchell, Vicki Morgan, Kathy Morrill, Carla Munsat, Bill Neudorfer, Mike Pararas, Helaine Posner, Maureen Reier, Jill Schwartz, Sharon Siegel, Barbara Strongin, Michael Tarantino, Christian Thee, Clifford Tisdell, Margaret Ong Tsao, Bernard Ungerleider, Lis Wackman, Gloriah Walsh, Anne Young, William Zamprelli and Bob Ziembicki.

The authors of the revised edition gratefully acknowledge the assistance of the following individuals who provided information for this book:

Tamara Cannon, Public Information Officer, New York State Council on the Arts, New York City; Hope Daniels, Editor, *American Style* magazine, Baltimore, Md.; Tim Doyle, Director, Materials for the Arts, City of New York, Department of Cultural Affairs, Department of Sanitation, Board of Education; Nina Jensen, Director of Museum Education, Graduate School of Education, Bank Street College, New York City; Meredith Levy, New York City; Gregory P. Mango, Photographer, New York City; Karen Marks, Director, Bonnie Ruby Art Gallery, New York City; Museum Reference Center, Smithsonian Institution Library, Washington, D.C.; Caroline Owens, Adelson Galleries, New York City; Evie Porwick, For Position Only, FPO Creative Placement, New York City; Nathan Raisen, APF Master & Frame Makers, New York City; Vincent Verga, Art Renaissance, New York City.

HOW TO USE THIS BOOK

Purpose

Career Opportunities in Art is a comprehensive listing of jobs for people interested in the art world. Eight major categories of careers are presented, and 84 different positions are described. Job descriptions are detailed and include information on duties, salaries, prerequisites, employment and advancement opportunities, relevant organizations and special advice on getting into the desired field. The book is intended both for those who are seeking entry-level jobs and for more experienced people who are thinking of changing careers.

Sources of Information

Research for the book included numerous interviews with professionals in various fields, as well as information obtained from professional organizations, the federal government, and library research. In addition, coauthor David Joselit contributed his own experience and expertise as a museum staff member and art journalist.

The job descriptions are generalized from the many actual jobs we reviewed. Certainly, job content, salaries, and growth potential vary from one organization to another, based on the organization's size, geographic location, and philosophy; we have noted some of these variations within the job descriptions in this book.

Organization of Material

This book has nine sections. The first eight cover different fields that employ many people in art-related positions; the ninth consists of appendixes listing educational institutions, trade schools, scholarships, internships, organizations and associations, and a bibliography.

All the positions covered in the book are intended for people with studio art and/or art history backgrounds and interests, often combined with other skills. Many of the jobs described here have not been presented in other books on art careers, and we hope to give the reader new and different job possibilities to consider.

Explanation of Job Description

Each job description follows a basic format and is complete within itself, so the reader does not need to refer to other parts of the book to get a complete picture of a given job. As a result, the reader may note some repetition from job description to job description.

Jobs are listed by the predominant title, followed by a career profile that summarizes a job's major duties, alternate titles, salary range, prospects for employment and advancement, and prerequisites, including education, experience, and special skills. The career ladder diagram shows a typical career path, including positions leading to and growing from each job. If a job is at the entry level, "student" is listed as preceding it.

The position description notes the typical duties and responsibilities of the job and the environment in which the job occupant functions. The section on salaries explains income ranges and notes factors that may affect them, such as individual skills, size of the employing organization, or geographic location. Salary ranges are based on averages, and readers may find positions that pay more or less than the figures given in this book.

Readers should particularly note the sections on employment prospects and advancement prospects, which can lend some reality to the idea of working in an attractive but often overcrowded or underpaid field. Exciting-sounding jobs may be difficult to obtain, while jobs that are relatively easy to get may be dead ends. These are important considerations for a job seeker.

The education section describes the academic requirements of the job. These can range from no formal requirements to graduate degrees and specialized training.

The experience and skills section describes work experiences that are necessary in order to obtain the job and cites personal qualities and abilities that successful candidates should possess.

The section on organizations and associations suggests groups that might be useful to the job seeker by providing support, information, education, and the opportunity to make professional contacts. Where there are no relevant organizations or associations, there is no listing.

Finally, there are tips for entry, which consist of advice from professionals in the field on how to get a foot in the door of your desired career.

Appendixes

Appendix I lists 66 colleges and universities in the United States that offer programs in art therapy, arts administration, and museum studies. As noted in Appendix I, nearly all colleges in this country have courses of study in art and art history, so we have not listed schools with these majors; any good college handbook will provide this information.

Appendix II lists 114 trade, industrial, and vocational schools that train artists in studio art and design.

Appendix III contains information on art scholarships, fellowships, grants, and loans.

Appendix IV covers paid and unpaid internships offered by 55 organizations in various art-related fields.

Appendix V lists organizations and associations that can be useful to those wishing to pursue any of the careers covered in this book.

Finally, Appendix VI is a bibliography listing periodicals and books that provide additional information on the jobs described here.

INTRODUCTION
Finding a Career in Art

You enjoy art. You like the freedom to express yourself, and you are excited by the opportunity to create something new. You have taken art classes, you have mastered new skills and you have seen your own abilities grow. You have gone to museums and galleries and have been challenged and inspired by the work of other people.

You have decided to make your career somewhere in this world of art. Despite visions of penniless artists and warnings that you can't make a living at it, you believe that you can find a place in the art community.

And it can be done. With careful study and planning, hard work and determination, some flexibility and the right information, you can find a job in the art world and begin to build a career.

Romance vs. Reality

Certainly, you have chosen a difficult field. Many thousands of art graduates each year join the search for the dream job—a well-paid position at a prestigious museum, let's say, or the post of critic for an important art magazine. Those jobs are out there, of course, but the competition for them is fierce, and the salaries can be less than what one might hope for. The problem, then, at the beginning of your career planning is to take a clear-eyed look at what jobs are available and what kind of life you can expect to live while occupying such jobs.

There are many different aspects to consider. Exactly how closely related to art must the job be? Will you be happy only if you're a portrait painter? Could you enjoy teaching art, or writing about it, or selling other people's works? Would you be happy reviewing artists' grant proposals or selling art supplies? In general, it can be said that jobs that are less closely related to the act of creating art are easier to get. That is, it is generally easier to find work as a framer than as, say, an illustrator.

Income is another prime consideration. Are you willing to start at the bottom, in a low-paying job? If you begin as an art gallery receptionist, for example, you can get a foot in the door of the gallery business.

Upward mobility may be important to you. Do you hope to get into a career where there is a significant opportunity for you to be promoted to higher positions? If so, you might be interested in museum work or in a job with a funding organization, rather than in the fields of art therapy or conservation.

Some careers require lengthy preparation; an art history instructor, for instance, usually needs a doctorate. A framer, on the other hand, can train on the job and become proficient within months.

There are jobs in which it is important to be able to deal well with people, such as customer service positions in auction galleries. And there are jobs in which that ability is less important—say, as a preparator at an art gallery.

Finally, there are jobs that are best for risk-taking entrepreneurial types—freelance careers, for example—and jobs that offer more security, such as elementary and high school art teaching.

All these considerations—and perhaps more, based on your personal needs—are vital to your choice of the right career for yourself. It is important to learn as much as you can by reading material on career planning and on the art world in general, and by talking to people in your fields of interest. And it is equally important to listen to yourself and to be honest about your career wants and needs.

The Most Promising Fields

Because many art career areas are so competitive, it may be helpful to note where jobs can be found most easily. In general, the commercial, profit-making side of the art world is more open to newcomers than the nonprofit side. It is easier to find work in a gallery than in a museum, and it is easier to get a job at an auction house than in a school art department. Business-related art careers are more plentiful, especially with the ever-increasing popularity of the Internet. Most large corporations, small companies, and many individuals have their own web sites, so there is now a greater demand than ever for web page designers. Government agencies and museums depend on appropriations and donations for funds, and they tend to hire fewer people and to have less to pay them with.

It is a paradox that the image of the "artistic" person is of someone who is distant from the constraints of the business world, incapable of dealing with practicalities. In fact, even an independent fine artist needs practical, real-world skills to succeed at making a living in art. Everyone needs sales skills—to make contacts with potential employers or customers, to achieve a promotion, to get people interested in a new idea or pet program. Any background that combines art and business will likely provide good experience. And any "artistic" person who can appreciate and master some basic marketing and other business skills will have a lifelong advantage over those who don't have such skills.

The Importance of Focus

Regardless of what career you eventually choose as your goal, you can improve your chances of entering the career you want by focusing your energies on it. It really is unimportant how competitive a field is; if you focus your effort on becoming the best prepared, most qualified candidate for the job, your prospective employer will have no choice but to hire you.

How do you achieve this? The first step is to research the careers that interest you until you can make an intelligent choice. Your research should include plenty of reading about the career and the people in it; check books, periodicals, and newspapers. In addition, you should check with organizations and associations of people in the field for information they can provide. Attend meetings of such organizations and speak to people in your area of interest; they can give you the best and most current information on the field and how to enter it.

Through your research you will learn how other people have prepared to enter the career field to which you aspire and what qualifications employers seek when they are filling jobs. Then your mission is simple: to focus your efforts on becoming the best candidate for the job you want. It may require formal education or an apprenticeship; it may steer you toward a certain volunteer or summer job rather than another one. It may help you to select business courses as electives while you major in art; it may lead you to look for a specific part-time or summer job to get some experience. The bottom line is to know what you want and to set out in a determined way to get it.

Flexibility

What if you just aren't that focused on a specific career? There is something to be said for flexibility, too. Perhaps you feel that you want to work in the art world in some way, but the specific job is not that important to you. Without a strong focus, you may feel a bit adrift, but you have the advantage of being able to select from a wide variety of possibilities.

You might choose a line of work, such as art journalism, and just take any entry-level opening that comes up—perhaps something in the circulation department or in advertising sales. Or you might take a secretarial job in an art-related business in order to learn more about it and see if it's right for you.

Freelancing

Another way to look at the career picture is to consider self-employment or freelancing. It takes a certain kind of outlook to feel comfortable working for yourself; many people prefer to get some experience working for others before setting up on their own. It may take some money to get started in a business. A freelancer can have dry spells between jobs, and income may be erratic. But there are numerous people who enjoy working for themselves, setting their own hours (to some degree) and choosing the assignments they take on (once they become established).

Several art careers lend themselves to freelancing. A fine artist, for example, is really a sort of freelancer. Illustrators, independent curators, art consultants, art journalists, conservators, and preparators can all work on a freelance basis. Self-employment is the norm for gallery owners, print publishers, art school directors, and custom framers, among others.

A Note on Geography

It is important to consider where you can find art jobs. Many of the positions art graduates seek are available only in large cities—particularly in New York, which is the art capital of the United States. The largest number of art galleries, auction houses, museums, and funding organizations is in New York. Other important cities for art jobs are Washington, Boston, Chicago, Atlanta, Houston, Dallas, Los Angeles, and San Francisco.

But many art-related jobs are available in a wide variety of communities. Art galleries exist in numerous small towns and resort areas. Quite a few museums are located in smaller cities. Art teachers work in schools throughout the country, and framers can be found in most towns.

Geography should be an important issue for you to think about. The major cities offer more art positions and have more workers in the field of art, while the smaller towns may provide equally good jobs with less competition and a more relaxed lifestyle.

Accepting the Challenge

The same qualities that attracted you to the world of art in the first place can be channeled to help you find the career you want. Use your vision to choose your goal, and use your creativity to make your way toward that goal. You have chosen a challenging and exciting field; challenge yourself to do your very best to find the right job and go after it with everything you have. This is the only way to achieve the satisfaction of working in the fascinating and inspiring art world.

ART AND DESIGN

ADVERTISING ARTIST

CAREER PROFILE

Duties: Create designs for advertisements

Salary Range: $20,000 to $55,000

Employment Prospects: Good

Advancement Prospects: Fair

Prerequisites:

Education—Art school background or bachelor's degree in art or design

Experience—Internship at an advertising agency or a design studio

Special Skills—Working knowledge of computer design software, creativity, communications skills, design sense

CAREER LADDER

```
┌─────────────────────────────┐
│        Art Director         │
└─────────────────────────────┘

┌─────────────────────────────┐
│      Advertising Artist     │
└─────────────────────────────┘

┌─────────────────────────────┐
│      Studio Assistant       │
└─────────────────────────────┘
```

Position Description

The Advertising Artist uses graphic design skills to develop artwork for use in advertisements. The Advertising Artist may work for an advertising agency or a publication. In either case the artist will be working with others—clients, art directors, copywriters, account executives—to create the finished product. The Advertising Artist is usually not responsible for the creative conception of the ad—it is his or her function to supply designs that will support the concept arrived at by the art director.

In today's workplace, many Advertising Artists do much of their designing with computers. Design, color, and typographical elements are used to give the client preliminary and then more finished versions of the ad. If the Advertising Artist is working on a project for film, audiotape, or videotape, then sound and motion will be available tools as well.

The progression of an ad is usually from rough storyboard—a sort of comic-strip version of the concept—through more finished mock-ups to a complete project. Client feedback is generally solicited throughout the process, and the Advertising Artist must make changes to satisfy the wishes of the client.

Salaries

A beginning Advertising Artist might make about $20,000 a year, with entry-level salaries going as high as about $30,000 for those working for prestigious agencies in larger cities. The Advertising Artist may make as much as $55,000 after some years of experience, and some firms offer more

to talented Artists who prefer to remain in this position rather than moving up to art direction.

Employment Prospects

There is a good chance of finding an entry-level job in this field. Though there is some competition for positions, turnover is relatively high, so openings do occur. Furthermore, willingness to work for a publication such as a newspaper, or for a business that has an in-house advertising department, such as a large grocery chain or a department store, opens up additional possibilities for employment.

Advancement Prospects

It is more difficult to advance to the position of Art Director than to get that first job. Competition is stiff and jobs are few. However, many people stay in the job of Advertising Artist permanently, moving up by taking jobs with larger or more prestigious firms.

Education

Many Advertising Artists have B.A. or B.F.A. degrees in art or design, but an art school background is also acceptable for new Advertising Artists.

Experience and Skills

The best preparation for this job is working in an advertising agency or design studio as an assistant or intern. This can be done as a summer or after-school job; the important thing is to get experience doing paste-up work, color processing, illustration, and desktop publishing.

Necessary skills include computer design ability, communication skills, a good sense of color and design, and creativity.

Organizations and Associations

The Art Director's Club, the Advertising Club of New York, the Advertising Production Club of New York, The American Advertising Federation, and the Graphic Artists Guild all provide information, courses, and networking opportunities that are useful to those hoping to enter this field.

Tips for Entry

This is one of the jobs for which a well-turned-out portfolio is essential. Ask professionals in the field for guidance with your portfolio. Stay current with the latest trends in advertising and in computer design software.

ADVERTISING ART DIRECTOR

CAREER PROFILE

Duties: Manage the creation of an ad or marketing piece from its conception through the finished product

Salary Range: $30,000 to $100,000

Employment Prospects: Fair

Advancement Prospects: Fair

Prerequisites:
   Education—Bachelor's degree in art or design
   Experience—Successful work as an advertising artist
   Special Skills—Artistic ability, design sense, rendering, conceptualizing, typography, computer design, business and selling skills

CAREER LADDER

```
┌─────────────────────────────┐
│      Senior Art Director      │
└─────────────────────────────┘

┌─────────────────────────────┐
│   Advertising Art Director    │
└─────────────────────────────┘

┌─────────────────────────────┐
│      Advertising Artist       │
└─────────────────────────────┘
```

Position Description

An Advertising Art Director is responsible for the total creation of an advertisement or similar marketing piece. The Advertising Art Director may work for an advertising agency or in-house for an advertiser. The Art Director works with the agency's account executives and the client's marketing people to conceptualize the kind of advertising needed. Then he or she manages the process of assigning the project to an advertising artist, interfacing with the writer who is creating the copy, and returning to the client for feedback as the ad is developed.

The creative process includes the preparation of rough drawings and storyboards, which give the client an idea of what the finished product will be. The Art Director must be able to work with photographers and printers, or film and video artists in the case of commercials. The Art Director is responsible for all the art aspects of the finished ad.

Because the creation of advertising is a collaborative process, it is important for the Advertising Art Director to have strong managerial and people skills. He or she must have the ability to direct subordinate artists, to communicate effectively with clients, and to cooperate with account executives.

Salaries

Salaries for Advertising Art Directors are often dependent on the size and location of the agency where they work, as well as on their own experience and ability. New Art Directors working for small firms outside the advertising centers of New York, Los Angeles, and Chicago may earn $30,000 to start. Salaries increase to about $100,000 as Art Directors gain more experience and move to larger firms.

Employment Prospects

The chances of finding a job as an Advertising Art Director are fair. This is a competitive field, and there are many creative people who are interested in moving into a management position. Again, geography plays a part; smaller towns have fewer opportunities than major cities do, but the competition is also likely to be less intense outside the advertising centers. A willingness to go anywhere will improve your chances of finding an Art Director job.

Advancement Prospects

Art Directors say that it is often necessary to move out in order to move up—that is, it is not unusual to find Art Directors changing firms every couple of years as they move up the ladder. It's important to be willing to make such moves; experience in a variety of firms is thought to freshen one's work.

Education

A prospective Art Director must have a B.A. or B.F.A. degree in art or design. Some Art Directors have M.A. or M.F.A. degrees in those fields as well.

Experience and Skills

The most valuable asset for an aspiring Art Director is experience gained through summer jobs or internships with advertising agencies or design firms.

In addition, a variety of art and personal skills are important to an Art Director. He or she must have drawing and artistic ability, as well as a strong design sense. Computer art skills are a must. The prospective Art Director must be able to do renderings and must have comprehensive knowledge of typography and typesetting. Those who wish to work in electronic media must have familiarity with audio, video, and film as well. And it is important to be able to work collaboratively, to be able to negotiate with others, and to have selling skills.

Organizations and Associations

The Art Director's Club and the American Association of Advertising Agencies have helpful programs and information for people who wish to work as Advertising Art Directors (see Appendix V).

Tips for Entry

A carefully prepared portfolio is the most important tool in getting a job as an Advertising Art Director. Seek out work that will build your portfolio, get advice on your portfolio from trusted professionals, and consider enlisting a copywriter to help execute your concepts most effectively. In addition, it pays to be persistent in pursuing a job, and focusing on a particular subspecialty within advertising helps.

ILLUSTRATOR

CAREER PROFILE

Duties: Provide illustrations for magazines, ad agencies, publishers, and web sites

Salary Range: $18,000 to $65,000

Employment Prospects: Good

Advancement Prospects: Poor

Prerequisites:

Education—Bachelor's degree in fine arts or diploma from an accredited art school

Experience—Work on school publications or as an assistant in a large art department

Special Skills—Wide range of art skills, communications skills, attention to detail, deadline orientation

CAREER LADDER

```
┌─────────────────────────────────┐
│         Art Director            │
└─────────────────────────────────┘

┌─────────────────────────────────┐
│          Illustrator            │
└─────────────────────────────────┘

┌─────────────────────────────────┐
│   Design Assistant or Student   │
└─────────────────────────────────┘
```

Position Description

An Illustrator's job falls between that of a commercial artist and that of an independent artist, in terms of creative freedom and control of his or her work. Like a commercial artist, an Illustrator is given guidelines and specifications by an art director as to what the finished work should be, but the nature of the work assignments tends to leave more room for creativity to the individual artist.

Illustrators work for various types of firms, often on a freelance basis. Some of the main outlets for illustration are magazines, publishing houses, and advertising agencies.

Magazine illustration involves the creation of appropriate illustrations and designs for magazine publication. Though illustration implies a Norman Rockwell type of realistic art, today's Illustrators tend to be design-oriented, using the latest computer resources to keep the look of their work current.

Publishers use Illustrators for all kinds of projects, including book covers, technical and medical illustration for textbooks, and scholarly works. Medical illustration is particularly specialized, with just a few schools offering a tailor-made program for this field. Technical illustration covers a wider variety of subjects; a technical illustrator would be knowledgeable in such areas as science, mapmaking, biological subjects, geology, machinery, and the solar system.

Sketch artists are Illustrators who make quick sketches and renderings for advertising agency storyboards. This is not finished artwork but a kind of first draft for a print or live-action advertisement. Much sketching work is let out on a freelance basis; agencies also have in-house sketch artists.

Salaries

Salaries for Illustrators can range from $18,000 to $65,000. Naturally, those with more experience, or who work for larger firms, command the higher salaries. Freelance illustrators' incomes are determined by the amount of work they take on.

Employment Prospects

Computerized images and illustrations have made the traditional illustration market more competitive. Yet employment is fairly easy to find for a well-prepared Illustrator. There are many specialty magazines on the market today, most of which use Illustrators. The demand for Illustrators in publishing and advertising is constant, if not growing. For those who are able to work on a freelance basis, such work can be used to gain entry to an in-house position or to supplement the income from a full-time job.

Advancement Prospects

It is difficult to advance in this career. Most Illustrators view illustration as their ultimate career goal. The next step up the ladder is art direction; such jobs are few and difficult to find, and require substantial additional experience in graphics. Advertising probably provides the best opportunity for an Illustrator to work up to an art director's spot.

Education

Illustrators should hold bachelor's degrees in fine arts or should have graduated from accredited schools of art. Master's degrees are not especially important for aspiring Illustrators, though specialized schooling—such as in medical illustration—is crucial in certain areas of the field.

Experience and Skills

Work experience as a production or design assistant in a large art department is ideal for those wishing to become Illustrators. In addition, any experience working on school publications will be valuable.

Naturally, Illustrators are expected to have well-developed art skills. Familiarity with computer graphics is essential. For both freelance and in-house artists, communications skills are important in the understanding and execution of assignments. Detail orientation can be critical, especially in fields such as technical and medical illustration. Illustrators should also be able to cope with firm deadlines.

Organizations and Associations

The Society of Illustrators (see Appendix V) is the association for members of this field. The Society publishes books and mounts exhibits of Illustrators' work.

Tips for Entry

It is important for an aspiring Illustrator to have a neat, professional-looking portfolio of work to show to potential employers. College or art school programs will enable students to prepare such portfolios; the more attention and care the student devotes to portfolio preparation, the better his or her chances for a fair hearing with a potential employer.

GRAPHIC ARTIST

CAREER PROFILE

Duties: Create visual interpretation based on client's needs

Alternate Title: Graphic Designer

Salary Range: $25,000 to $75,000

Employment Prospects: Good

Advancement Prospects: Good

Prerequisites:
    Education—Bachelor's degree in art or design
    Experience—Internship or apprenticeship
    Special Skills—Computer literacy, artistic talent, photography skills, familiarity with print and type

CAREER LADDER

```
+-------------------------+
|      Art Director       |
+-------------------------+


+-------------------------+
|     Graphic Artist      |
+-------------------------+


+-------------------------+
|  Production Assistant    |
+-------------------------+
```

Position Description

The primary duty of the Graphic Artist is to take the client's ideas and translate them into visual media. Whether the client is a company working on an annual report, a college developing a brochure, or a manufacturer introducing a new product, the object is to solve communications problems cooperatively.

This means that one important requirement for a Graphic Artist is the ability to listen carefully to the client so as to understand the client's needs. Analytical skills are important, too, as the Graphic Artist may be part of the brainstorming session when the client is developing a project.

Graphic Artists may work independently, so that they are the primary client contact, or they may work for a publication, a graphic design firm, or an art department within a company. Whatever the case, maintenance of a good working relationship with the client is essential.

Graphic Artists may work on many different types of projects, using a variety of media. Familiarity with computer art and design programs is necessary, and an understanding of printing and type design is also essential.

Typically, the Graphic Artist will receive an assignment from an art director. The Graphic Artist may have further communication with the client regarding the goals of the assignment. The Graphic Artist will then work relatively independently, creating a visual presentation that combines art, photography, typography, and so on. Frequent review by the art director and client will ensure that the finished product is fully satisfactory.

Salaries

Salaries for Graphic Artists begin at about $25,000. In a design firm or large company the Graphic Artist might earn as much as $60,000, and a successful independent Graphic Artist might work up to an income of $75,000.

Employment Prospects

The employment prospects for Graphic Artists are good. This is a large field, and when times are difficult in, say, publishing, there may still be corporate jobs open to Graphic Artists. Previous internship or apprenticeship in the field can make it easier to learn about openings and get jobs.

Advancement Prospects

There is a good chance for the successful Graphic Artist in a firm to be promoted. Artistic talent, good client communications skills, and computer skills can make one valuable as a candidate for the position of art director or creative director.

Education

Most Graphic Artists have bachelor's degrees in art or design, though it is possible to get a position with a non-degree art school background and some experience.

Experience and Skills

There are many specialized skills needed by a Graphic Artist, some of which can be learned only on the job. Of course, people and communications skills are essential, but Graphic Artists must also be fully up-to-date on the latest computer graphics techniques, on matters of style in drawing and typography, and on such things as electronic media.

Organizations and Associations

Organizations such as the American Institute of Graphic Arts, the Art Directors Club and the Graphic Artists Guild (see Appendix V) can be helpful to members of this field.

Tips for Entry

A well-presented portfolio is critical in winning a position as a Graphic Artist. The job candidate should be selective, displaying only his or her best work, and it may be valuable to have a working professional in the field review the portfolio before any job interview.

WEB DESIGNER

CAREER PROFILE

Duties: Develop and design interactive web sites

Alternate Titles: Internet Designer, Web Producer, Web Developer

Salary Range: $40,000 to $100,000+

Employment Prospects: Excellent

Advancement Prospects: Excellent

Prerequisites:
Education—Graphic or Web Programming
Experience—Working knowledge of all graphic and interactive computer programs, internship at a credible design firm
Special Skills—Knowledge of and creative design sense of Quark, Photoshop, Illustrator, MS Suite, Dreamweaver

CAREER LADDER

```
┌─────────────────────────────┐
│        Art Director         │
└─────────────────────────────┘


┌─────────────────────────────┐
│        Web Designer         │
└─────────────────────────────┘


┌─────────────────────────────┐
│      Intern or Student      │
└─────────────────────────────┘
```

Position Description

A Web Designer must be able to integrate his or her knowledge of computer applications (such as Quark, Photoshop, Illustrator, MS Suite, Dreamweaver and HTML) with the requirements of an art director. The Web Designer must also use his or her expertise to translate the clients' needs into an interactive web site that is both user friendly and artistically appealing. This process begins with instructions from the art director, who will explain the client's needs and expectations for the web site. The Web Designer translates the art director's thoughts and designs into a working comprehensive, usually in the form of a sketch on paper. A meeting then takes place and ideas are refined. Then, it's time to go to the computer for an initial draft of the web site. Depending on the art director's evaluation, a new draft may be required or the final process may begin. However, the final draft is never really final—as technology and product development is constantly required.

Salaries

A beginning salary for a Web Designer is about $40,000. As the Web Designer gains knowledge and hands-on experience, he or she may be promoted to a bigger or more prestigious design firm where his or her salary can rise to $100,000+. Freelance rates range from $35–$100+ per hour.

Employment Prospects

As this book is being written, new advances in technology are creating new positions. If full-time work is not available or desired, there are numerous freelance positions available for a Web Designer. Interning at a credible design firm can also help a prospective Web Designer maximize his or her job opportunities.

Advancement Prospects

Advancing in this field is purely dependent on the prospective candidate's computer skill level, design sense, and ability to take art direction. Mastering these characteristics will ensure constant work since this field is growing rapidly.

Education

A Web Designer ideally should have a bachelor's degree in art or graphic design. However, high school graduates with intense computer and graphic training offered by various companies like the MAC Learning Center and excellent proficiency can expect employment as well.

Experience and Skills

Students can get valuable experience for this job by working on personal web sites, interactive school bulletins, and community publications. An internship or freelance job at a graphic design firm is invaluable to a career in this field. Knowledge of current computer applications, such as Quark, Photoshop, Illustrator, MS Suite, Dreamweaver, and HTML, are a must.

Organizations and Associations

Since creative inspiration is key to a Web Designer's success, he or she should constantly surf the web for new and exciting creative ideas to incorporate into his or her own designs. Designers can also look into joining organizations like the Society of Illustrators which can help offer more inspirational work ideas.

Tips for Entry

A Web Designer needs extensive computer training and knowledge of computer trends. His or her own interactive resume/portfolio will help to illustrate an understanding and design sense.

PRINTMAKER

CAREER PROFILE

Duties: Perform technical tasks involved in reproducing artwork by various processes

Alternate Title: Master Printer

Salary Range: $25,000 to $85,000

Employment Prospects: Fair

Advancement Prospects: Fair

Prerequisites:

Education—B.A. or B.F.A. degree in art required; M.F.A. in printmaking helpful

Experience—Internship

Special Skills—Proficiency in various printing processes, expertise in one or more specialty areas

CAREER LADDER

Printmaker or Master Printer

Assistant Printer

Position Description

A Printmaker works in a studio reproducing artwork for other artists or for him- or herself. There are various ways to make reproductions—silk screening, intaglio, serigraphy, lithography, etc.—and while most Printmakers are familiar with a variety of processes, it is not unusual to specialize in one or two.

This is detailed, exacting work. Depending on the process being used, one starts with an artwork and goes through various steps to create a printing plate. The plate is carefully inked, and the image is transferred to paper or another material.

A Printmaker who runs a printing studio must manage an inventory of chemicals, paper, and other materials necessary to the printing process. If there are assistants in the studio, the Printmaker must manage and teach these workers as well.

Patience and precision count in this profession. It is important, too, to be able to work well with others, whether employees or artist clients. Careful, thorough work habits are required.

Salaries

A beginning Printmaker earns about $25,000 a year. After gaining experience and more technical expertise, the Printmaker might work up to a salary of about $85,000 a year.

Employment Prospects

This is a demanding and competitive field, and positions are not easily found, but a persistent individual has a fair chance of finding a job. The economic climate has hurt the paper arts less than painting and sculpture, but there has been contraction in this area of the art world as well.

Advancement Prospects

Here, too, there is much competition, but specialized skills can help a Printmaker advance to a more responsible, better-paying job. Some well-respected Printmakers will be able to open studios of their own. And there is the chance of taking the academic route—that is, going to work at a college or art school to teach others the craft of printmaking.

Education

An aspiring Printmaker must have a B.A. or B.F.A. degree in art, and an M.F.A. in printmaking is highly desirable. It is advisable to get both depth and breadth in the various types of printmaking—that is, a good understanding of the major processes, plus a specialization in at least one process.

Experience and Skills

It is essential to apprentice with a working Printmaker. This is a field where one learns by doing, and the learning process is long and detailed. As in the formal educational setting, it is valuable to gain both broad experience and some specialized knowledge of one or two processes. It takes two to three years to learn each medium.

Other useful skills include papermaking, bookbinding, and the ability to work with others.

Organizations and Associations

The Graphic Communications International Union offers education and support for those in the printmaking field.

Tips for Entry

There are many assistant and internship positions available in print studios; be sure to get as much experience as possible with working Printmakers. College students can get jobs as technical assistants or lab assistants in print studios.

PHOTOGRAPHER

CAREER PROFILE

Duties: Work with clients to determine their preferences; take, develop, select, crop, enlarge, and sell photographs

Salary Range: $25,000 to $100,000+

Employment Prospects: Fair

Advancement Prospects: Fair

Prerequisites:
   Education—Degree from college or art school, or internship
   Experience—Work as photographer's assistant or as photographer for school publications
   Special Skills—Technical photography skills and ability to work with people

CAREER LADDER

```
┌─────────────────────────────┐
│        Photographer         │
└─────────────────────────────┘

┌─────────────────────────────┐
│   Photographer's Assistant  │
└─────────────────────────────┘
```

Position Description

Photography is a broad field with many branches, but generally speaking, the Photographer uses the specialized skills of the trade to take and process photographs.

Specialties in photography include photography for publication, in which the Photographer gets an assignment from a newspaper or other publication to take photographs of certain people, places, or events, and studio photography, in which the Photographer works with clients to photograph weddings or other occasions, or to take portraits of groups or individuals, with the client buying photographs on approval.

In addition, there is art photography, in which the Photographer takes photographs that are eventually displayed in galleries or museums and/or sold to collectors, and documentary photography, in which Photographers are hired to photograph items or areas for evidentiary purposes—for example, for a police department or an insurance company. People with photography skills may also work in photo processing labs, developing and enlarging photos.

Salaries

Many Photographers work freelance, so incomes vary quite a bit. A beginning Photographer for a newspaper, magazine, or studio might expect to make about $25,000 a year, and someone with more experience or a studio of his or her own could earn up to $100,000. Highly successful freelance and portrait photographers can make substantially more than that.

Employment Prospects

Photographers have a fair chance of finding permanent work, but the opportunity to go freelance is available to all. Success in the freelance arena depends on talent, persistence, and sales ability.

Advancement Prospects

There is only a fair opportunity to climb a well-defined career ladder—say, in the newspaper world or in a large studio. However, many people advance in this field by increasing the amount of freelance work they get or by working for more prestigious clients.

Education

While a general college degree might be nice to have, it is more important for a Photographer to be highly skilled in the techniques of the trade. This means a firm grounding in composition and lighting, film developing and enlarging, and so on. General photography courses are available at colleges and art schools; specialized coursework is given by the schools of the Professional Photographers Association and the Brooks Institute, among other places.

Experience and Skills

Again, basic and advanced photography skills are essential. In addition, sales and people skills are necessary for successful work with clients. It's important to find after-school or summer work with a photographer; people often start young in this field, as hobbyists, and those with professional experience have an advantage.

Organizations and Associations

Useful organizations for aspiring Photographers are the National Photography Association, the Professional Photographers Association, the National Photographers of America, and the American Society of Magazine Photographers.

Tips for Entry

Professionals in this field advise working on your skills constantly. Determination and persistence are valuable, and experience on school publications is important.

PRODUCTION DESIGNER

CAREER PROFILE

Duties: Supervise the overall look of a film or video

Alternate Title: Art Director

Salary Range: $25,000 to $250,000

Employment Prospects: Fair

Advancement Prospects: Fair

Prerequisites:
  Education—Bachelor's degree in art or design, or art school diploma
  Experience—Production assistant or properties work on film or video productions
  Special Skills—Drafting, creativity, business skills

CAREER LADDER

```
┌─────────────────────────────────┐
│      Production Designer         │
└─────────────────────────────────┘

┌─────────────────────────────────┐
│         Set Decorator            │
└─────────────────────────────────┘

┌─────────────────────────────────┐
│      Production Assistant        │
└─────────────────────────────────┘
```

Position Description

A film or video Production Designer is responsible for the overall look of a film or video project. As such, he or she makes countless decisions about sets, props, costumes, hair and makeup choices, lighting—in fact, the Production Designer handles all visual elements except the actors themselves.

Working closely with set decorators or assistants, the Production Designer takes instruction from the film's director about the concept for the film. It is the Production Designer's job to turn the director's ideas into visual components. This may include designing and building sets, finding existing locations for settings, locating props that will both serve the story and add to the atmosphere, coordinating the efforts of costume and lighting designers, and working with the cinematographer to perfect the appearance of the film.

Salaries

Salaries can vary widely in this field because many Production Designers are freelancers. In film and video projects it is customary for Production Designers to hire out by the week, earning a certain weekly rate. Beginning nonunion Production Designers might earn $1,000 per week, but it is unlikely that they will work fifty weeks a year. More experienced union members—particularly those who have made a name for themselves in the industry—can command as much as $5,000 per week. In addition, there are some Production Designers—

mainly those working on television series—who are hired on a longer-term basis.

Employment Prospects

It can be difficult to find work as a Production Designer, though willingness to work on small films and videos is helpful. Networking and word-of-mouth are important in finding work in this field, and aspiring Production Designers must locate in or near a production center like New York or Los Angeles.

Advancement Prospects

Advancement in this field is a matter of talent, dependability, and luck. Production Designers have to build their reputations gradually, working on increasingly prestigious projects until they become well known and sought after.

Education

There is no clear educational route for a prospective Production Designer to take, but many have college degrees in art, design or film, while a good number have art school backgrounds. Business classes will also be an asset to a future Production Designer.

Experience and Skills

The best experience for someone who wants to be a Production Designer is working on film and video projects, no matter how small. Music videos and commercials are short-term projects that nevertheless provide good background in production design. Working as a production assistant, prop assistant, or set decorator on such projects will help prepare an individual to move up into production design.

Along with general art skills, a Production Designer must be proficient in drafting, and business skills like accounting come in handy. Because this is a collaborative job, people skills and strong communications abilities are important, too.

Organizations and Associations

The American Film Institute is a useful networking organization for aspiring Production Designers.

Tips for Entry

Production Designers suggest that you get experience any way possible, even if it means volunteering your services on a project. Luck and timing play a big part in finding jobs; explore any leads you hear about and be persistent.

SET DESIGNER

CAREER PROFILE

Duties: Design scenery for stage play; supervise construction of set

Alternate Titles: Theater Designer; Stage Designer

Salary Range: $25,000 to $60,000+

Employment Prospects: Good

Advancement Prospects: Fair

Prerequisites:

Education—Bachelor's degree in art, design, or theater

Experience—Designing and building set for school or community theater

Special Skills—Drawing, painting, model-building, research skills, understanding of lighting design, ability to work collaboratively

CAREER LADDER

```
┌─────────────────────────────┐
│       Set Designer          │
└─────────────────────────────┘

┌─────────────────────────────┐
│       Scenic Artist         │
└─────────────────────────────┘
```

Position Description

A Set Designer designs and supervises the construction of sets for the theater. Working closely with a play's director—and its author, if he or she is available—the Set Designer must be familiar with a wide variety of theatrical styles and artistic media so that he or she can offer a range of alternatives to the director. Mindful of budget limits and the physical requirements of actors, the Set Designer works to produce an optimal set.

Beginning with drawings, and checking with the director throughout the design process, the Set Designer fine-tunes the design until he or she is ready to build a model of the set. The model is important because it helps the Designer communicate with the director, producer, actors, lighting and costume designers, and scene shop about the proposed design. Once the design has been approved, the Set Designer may be responsible for executing it, supervising carpenters and scenic artists in its preparation, or the set design may be turned over to a scene shop for construction. In either case, the Set Designer usually remains on call to the director and other designers to answer questions regarding the set.

Theatrical scenery is regarded as an important element in creating the atmosphere of a play, and sometimes the Set Designer must undertake research to learn about the look of another time or place. It is then his or her job to re-create or reinterpret that look to serve the play and the director's concept.

Salaries

A beginning salary for a Set Designer is about $25,000. As the Set Designer gains experience, he or she may be able to move to larger or more prestigious theaters, where the salary level can rise to about $60,000. For those at the top of the profession, the design fees for Broadway plays can add up to an even greater income.

Employment Prospects

Despite arts funding cutbacks, there are many entry-level design jobs available at theaters all over the country, especially for those willing to work long hours for low pay. Regional theater is less competitive than New York, though there are far more jobs in New York than elsewhere.

Advancement Prospects

It is somewhat more difficult to advance in this field than to get that first job. The normal upward path is through increasingly larger and more prestigious theaters, and the competition for jobs intensifies significantly on the way.

Education

The most specifically tailored education for a Set Designer is a master of fine arts degree in theater. However, people with bachelor's degrees in art, design, or theater can get work as Set Designers if they have experience working for school and community theaters.

Experience and Skills

The most important experience for a Set Designer is work in designing and building sets. Fortunately, there are ample unpaid opportunities to do this in high school, college, and community theater groups.

Set Designers need to have good personal and communication skills because of the collaborative nature of the work. In addition, they need to be familiar with many different art media because of the variety of techniques used to create sets. Drawing, model-building, and carpentry skills are important, and a thorough knowledge of research techniques is essential.

Tips for Entry

It pays to work tirelessly in community and summer stock theaters. Get to know the designers there and learn from them. You can network your way into more responsible jobs.

BOOK DESIGNER

CAREER PROFILE

Duties: Prepare book manuscript for printing, including typographic design, photo design, art, and layout

Salary Range: $22,000 to $39,000

Employment Prospects: Fair

Advancement Prospects: Poor

Prerequisites:

    Education—Bachelor's degree in art or design, or art school diploma

    Experience—Internship or apprenticeship with publisher or design firm

    Special Skills—Design sense, thorough knowledge of typography, illustration and computer applications, familiarity with photography, understanding of the special requirements of book design and print media

CAREER LADDER

```
┌─────────────────────────────────┐
│   Senior Book Designer or       │
│   Art Director                  │
└─────────────────────────────────┘

┌─────────────────────────────────┐
│   Book Designer                 │
└─────────────────────────────────┘

┌─────────────────────────────────┐
│   Design Assistant              │
└─────────────────────────────────┘
```

Position Description

A Book Designer is responsible for taking an edited book manuscript through the design process so it can be typeset and reproduced in a chosen style. Thus the Book Designer must design every aspect of the book interior, including the use of illustrations and/or photographs in the text, the specifications of what style and size of type to use for chapter or section headings, captions, footnotes, and so on, and the look of the book's cover.

The Book Designer may work for a publisher, for a book packager, or independently. In any case, he or she must interface with both the employer and the author to understand the book's concept and its intended audience. At the other end of the process, the Designer must communicate his or her design decisions to the typesetter, compositor, or printer so that the design can be executed properly. Hence, it is important for the Book Designer to have a full understanding of printing processes and capabilities.

Among the design elements available to the Book Designer are photographs, illustrations, tables, and graphs. The Book Designer, along with editor and author, makes decisions about where and how to use these elements, so a familiarity with them is important.

Salaries

Book Designers start at a salary of about $22,000, and salary levels can rise to about $39,000, especially in bigger cities and at larger publishing houses. Independent Book Designers can make more based on the amount of work they are able to obtain and their own skill.

Employment Prospects

An aspiring Book Designer has a fair chance of finding a job in the field. Though publishing in general has not been particularly strong in recent years, there are still opportunities for newcomers, especially those with a strong computer design background and knowledge of layout applications.

Advancement Prospects

Book Designers can move up within a publishing firm by becoming senior Book Designers or art directors. Those who want to remain Book Designers can work on increasingly more complex and challenging projects. Similarly, a Book Designer who wishes to go freelance can work independently, hiring out to book packagers and publishers on a project-by-project basis.

Education

Book Designers usually have bachelor's degrees in art or design, but art school graduates can succeed in this field, too. A strong liberal arts background is useful, and thorough training in computer graphic design is invaluable.

Experience and Skills

Students can get valuable experience for this job by working on such publications as school newspapers and yearbooks. An internship or summer job at a publishing house, magazine, or newspaper is excellent preparation for a Book Designer. Special skills needed include a thorough understanding of typography, creativity, and design ability, and familiarity with photography, illustration, and computerized design programs.

Organizations and Associations

Book Designers should look into such organizations as the American Institute of Graphic Arts and Book Publishers for career guidance and professional support.

Tips for Entry

A Book Designer needs strong art training and a carefully chosen and presented portfolio. Ask a professional in the field to critique your portfolio to make sure it shows your abilities to best advantage.

ARCHITECT

Duties: Design building or renovation projects, prepare construction documents, choose materials, oversee construction

Salary Range: $25,000 to $100,000

Employment Prospects: Excellent

Advancement Prospects: Excellent

Prerequisites:

Education—Degree in architecture from an accredited school (either four years undergraduate plus two years graduate, or a five-year combined program)

Experience—Internship with an architectural firm

Special Skills—Artistic ability, mathematical ability, people skills, computer aided design and drafting skills, problem solving

```
+-----------------------------+
|   Senior Architect or       |
|   Independent Architect     |
+-----------------------------+

+-----------------------------+
|        Architect            |
+-----------------------------+

+-----------------------------+
|        Draftsman            |
+-----------------------------+
```

Position Description

An Architect is a person licensed to design and oversee the construction of a residential, commercial, or institutional building, addition, or renovation project. Using the skills gained from a five- or six-year university education in architecture, the Architect first consults with clients to learn their needs. Returning to the client for approval at every stage, the Architect prepares a schematic design showing what the project will look like, along with a feasibility study that takes into account such matters as land use and budgets. The design development process is more complex, moving to materials choices and design details. Then the Architect prepares design documents such as blueprints, which will be used by construction contractors and reviewed by municipal boards for code compliance. Finally most Architects become involved with the administration of the construction process, overseeing the work and interfacing with the developer or general contractor as well as the client.

In addition, Architects who work independently or who have their own firms must manage the business needs of the firm and work on marketing and business development. Some Architects actually function as developers, putting their own capital into building projects they design and making profits from the eventual leasing or selling of the building. Architects are often trained in urban planning and interior design, and prepare development feasibility studies as well. There are also opportunities for the general creative problem solving abilities of an architect in many diverse fields such as industrial product design, interior design, web page design, graphic arts, and set design (TV and theater).

Salaries

Because the construction industry is enjoying a boom market, architecture jobs are relatively plentiful and salaries are relatively high. An entry-level Architect might make $25,000 to $30,000, with salaries rising to $100,000 for more experienced Architects. It should be noted that the architectural field changes rapidly and in tandem with the regular market and economic conditions. Job security is low.

Employment Prospects

The current economy has drastically increased the number of jobs for architects, after development across the country emerged in the late 90s from a decade-long slump. Employment prospects are excellent with architecture firms, and there is work for independent Architects in such areas as home additions and renovations. An additional area of employment for Architects is with government bodies, which need Architects to write architectural standards for building and review permit applications.

Advancement Prospects
Because the economy is booming, advancement prospects are excellent for Architects.

Education
All potential Architects who intend to take the professional exams and become licensed Architects must attend an accredited school of architecture—either two years of graduate work following an undergraduate degree or a five-year combined program, plus three years of internship type work experience—before being eligible to write the eight-section National Council of Architectural Registration Boards (NCARB) architecture exams. Each state has different internship requirements. The Intern Development Program (IDP) oversees work requirements; NCARB handles licensing and examination requirements.

Experience and Skills
Aspiring Architects need good math skills, artistic ability, and strong people skills. An understanding of sculpture, drawing, and painting is helpful. Computer skills and proficiency in programs such as CADD (Computer Aided Design and Drafting) and Autocad are essential. It is extremely helpful to have experience working for an architecture or construction firm—summer or after-school work as early as during high school is advantageous, no matter how low level the job.

Organizations and Associations
The American Institute of Architects (AIA) is one of a number of professional architecture organizations mandated to unite, represent, promote, enhance, and improve the profession and practice of architecture.

Tips for Entry
It is important to get a feel for the profession by getting your foot in the door and finding a job with an architect as early as possible. Networking is essential in order to find openings.

INTERIOR DESIGNER

CAREER PROFILE

Duties: Create designs for rooms and other interior spaces and oversee their execution

Alternate Title: Interior Decorator

Salary Range: $24,000 to $100,000+

Employment Prospects: Good

Advancement Prospects: Good

Prerequisites:
  Education—Bachelor's degree in interior design
  Experience—Internship with design firm or with interior design department of a furniture sales organization
  Special Skills—Drawing and drafting skills, knowledge of architecture, good design and color sense, selling skills, people skills

CAREER LADDER

```
┌─────────────────────────────────┐
│   Senior Interior Designer or    │
│  Independent Interior Designer   │
└─────────────────────────────────┘

┌─────────────────────────────────┐
│       Interior Designer          │
└─────────────────────────────────┘

┌─────────────────────────────────┐
│       Design Assistant           │
└─────────────────────────────────┘
```

Position Description

An Interior Designer works with a client to plan and execute a design for an interior space, be it a living room, a hotel lobby, or an office. Working with such items as fabrics, paint, wallpaper, lighting, furnishings, floor coverings, and accessories, the Interior Designer creates plans for a space that will serve the client's needs.

The two major branches of interior design are residential and commercial (or contract) design. In residential design, the Interior Designer works closely with the person who hires him or her to design an apartment or house interior. If major renovations are planned, the Interior Designer may also work with an architect on the project. In addition, craftspeople such as painters, tilers, cabinetmakers, and upholsterers may take direction from the Interior Designer. In residential design, the Designer uses listening and communications skills to understand the client's wishes and to help choose design solutions.

In commercial or contract design the Interior Designer works with architects, developers, and perhaps clients who will be occupying a particular space. Again, listening and communications skills are essential to understanding client needs. The Designer will be responsible for lighting, floor coverings, wall finishes, fabrics furnishings, and accessories, but in contract design, space planning is an important element of the Designer's job as well.

It is worth noting that many Interior Designers get a foothold in the field by working in furniture stores, home improvement centers, and the furniture departments of large department stores. Such stores hire Designers to provide services, often free of charge, to store customers. Designers in these settings may offer help in color and furniture choices, floor planning, and choosing contractors.

Salaries

There is a wide range of salaries paid to Interior Designers. Many people work freelance in this field, so their incomes depend on the amount of time they devote to their work. Beginning full-time Interior Designers might expect to make about $24,000, with the ability to earn upwards of $40,000 as they advance in an interior design firm. But successful Designers who work independently can earn a great deal more than that—$100,000 or more.

Employment Prospects

Most Interior Designers feel that current employment prospects are good. Contributing to the growth in this field is the proliferation of home offices due to Internet accessibility, increased attention to ergonomic design needs, and a healthy economy which boosts spending in this area. Also, government regulations regarding building codes have opened up a large area in compliance—that is, understanding and implementing changes for handicapped access and geriatric needs.

Advancement Prospects

The prospects are good for Interior Designers to advance in the field particularly in commercial design. There are more jobs in large cities, which have large merchandise marts as well as more office and hotel work.

Education

A bachelor's degree in interior design is essential for those who wish to go the professional design route, though there is still room for art school graduates and art or design majors with college degrees to find work in the residential sector.

Experience and Skills

The best possible experience for the aspiring Interior Designer is to work as an assistant at a design firm or for an independent Interior Designer. Even low-level clerical work is valuable. Skills needed include strong interpersonal and communications ability, drafting and drawing skills, excellent color and design sense, and business and sales skills.

Organizations and Associations

The key organizations in this field are the American Society of Interior Designers (ASID) and the International Society of Interior Designers (ISID).

Tips for Entry

It is important for aspiring Interior Designers to be up on current design trends, so careful reading of trade magazines like *Architectural Digest* is important. Also, the student chapters of the organizations listed above can be very helpful in providing job leads and seminars.

PACKAGING DESIGNER

CAREER PROFILE

Duties: Design packaging materials and artwork for consumer goods

Salary Range: $25,000 to $100,000

Employment Prospects: Good

Advancement Prospects: Fair

Prerequisites:
    Education—B.F.A. in design
    Experience—Work in a graphic design studio or package design firm
    Special Skills—Knowledge of drawing, rendering, typography; excellent computer design skills

CAREER LADDER

```
┌─────────────────────────────┐
│      Design Director        │
└─────────────────────────────┘

┌─────────────────────────────┐
│     Packaging Designer      │
└─────────────────────────────┘

┌─────────────────────────────┐
│      Design Assistant       │
└─────────────────────────────┘
```

Position Description

A Packaging Designer works on the line between graphic design and industrial design. Creating packaging for various products involves both engineering concerns, such as the type of materials needed to keep food fresh or to protect fragile contents, and artistic concerns, such as creating eye-catching graphics and easily recognizable logos.

In this world, the art-oriented Packaging Designer (as opposed to the one with an engineering background) works on the shape, color and message of an item's package. This may include such decisions as whether to package a bottle in a box or to print the advertising and consumer information on the bottle itself; size and shape of the type for all the written material on the package; design and color choices for any artwork on the package.

In general, package art attempts to attract the eye of the consumer and to establish an idea of what the package contains. Thus, cookies intended for kids might be packaged in a bright-colored box with cartoon pictures, while biscuits for adult teatime might be packaged in a pastel-colored box covered with sophisticated script and realistic photos of the product inside.

The Packaging Designer must also work with many new government-mandated labeling requirements for consumer goods. Regulations may specify a certain size of type as well as the specific information that must be used to identify contents.

Salaries

A new Packaging Designer might expect to make about $25,000 per year. Those who have several years experience in the field may make up to $100,000 per year at a package design firm or a consumer goods company.

Employment Prospects

Mainly because of new government regulations, this is a growing field. Designers who wish to work in packaging have a good chance of finding an entry-level job.

Advancement Prospects

While it may have previously been difficult to advance in packaging design the prospects are more positive these days since packaging has become more of a specific skill. A Packaging Designer may look for advancement by moving between in-house packaging departments and specialized packaging design firms.

Education

Because of the need to interface with the technical side of the packaging business, it is necessary to have a bachelor's degree in design to enter this field. Some packaging designers come from university programs that have subspecialties in packaging design.

Experience and Skills

Design experience is needed by aspiring Packaging Designers. This can be acquired through work in a graphic design studio or by an internship in a packaging design department.

Packaging Designers must have strong computer-aided design skills as well as a strong sense of color and design. Creativity is important, and abilities in drawing, rendering, and typography are essential.

Organizations and Associations

People trying to enter this field should contact the Packaging Design Council and the Art Directors Club for professional courses, networking opportunities, and job search support.

Tips for Entry

It is important to be current on trends in the field. Spend time looking at packages in supermarkets and drugstores—get a feel for what works and what doesn't as well as for what is eye-catching or popular.

CLOTHING DESIGNER

CAREER PROFILE

Duties: Create clothing designs and prepare them for manufacture

Alternate Title: Fashion Designer

Salary Range: $24,000 to $100,000+

Employment Prospects: Good

Advancement Prospects: Fair

Prerequisites:

Education—Bachelor's degree in design apparel or fashion, or art school background in fashion; business courses helpful

Experience—Work as an assistant to a designer

Special Skills—Creativity, initiative, fashion sense, business and marketing skills

CAREER LADDER

```
┌─────────────────────────────┐
│   Senior Designer or        │
│   Independent Designer       │
└─────────────────────────────┘

┌─────────────────────────────┐
│   Clothing Designer          │
└─────────────────────────────┘

┌─────────────────────────────┐
│   Studio Assistant or        │
│   Assistant Designer         │
└─────────────────────────────┘
```

Position Description

A Clothing Designer creates designs for apparel that will be manufactured and sold. Taking inspiration from current fashion as well as from art, nature, history, the human form, and ideas about color and images, the Clothing Designer makes drawings that are turned into prototypes of the apparel. Working with pattern makers, the Designer breaks down the design into pieces that can be cut and sewn.

All aesthetic decisions regarding the clothing are made by the Clothing Designer, including color, pattern, and texture of the fabric, fastenings such as buttons, zippers, and hooks, and finishings such as thread, seams, and linings.

The Clothing Designer must have a thorough understanding of the target customer for the clothing. Price and style of the finished garment must be attractive for the kind of customer the Designer has in mind. If the design requires a complex manufacturing process or expensive materials, the garment will cost more to produce and must bring a higher price when sold. By the same token, the Designer must be aware of the manufacturer's skill level; if the garment is produced in a shop that is not skillful enough to do a quality job, there will be defects, resulting in returns and customer dissatisfaction.

Salaries

Because this is a popular and competitive field, starting salaries may be as low as $24,000, but a talented Designer can work up to a salary of $100,000 or more. Of course, those working for larger and more prestigious clothing manufacturers will receive the higher salaries.

Employment Prospects

This is an area in which there are always entry-level jobs. Though one would probably not be a full-fledged Designer right away, there is always a demand for studio assistants and assistant designers, especially those willing to work hard for low pay. Even secretarial work in a design firm may lead to a Designer position.

Advancement Prospects

It is more difficult to advance in this field because of the competitiveness noted above. Many people are vying for senior Designer positions. However, it is possible to advance by becoming an independent Designer, either by selling finished designs directly to clothing manufacturers or by becoming a manufacturer oneself. Such a Designer would hire workers or workshops to produce the clothing, and then he or she would handle the marketing of the goods to retailers.

Education

In order to get a job as a Clothing Designer you will need a bachelor's degree in design or fashion design, or an art school diploma in fashion design. Some coursework in business and marketing would be especially helpful as well.

Experience and Skills

The best possible experience for a prospective Clothing Designer is to work as an assistant to a successful Designer. Even gofer work in a design firm will be helpful for getting your foot in the door. Specific skills required include design and sewing skills, drawing ability, fashion sense, initiative, and a good understanding of what will sell to a particular group of customers.

Organizations and Associations

The American Craft Council (ACC) is a useful organization for those interested in clothing design, and the National Association of Fashion and Accessory Designers (NAFAD) is targeted to assist African-American Clothing Designers.

Tips for Entry

As in many art-related careers, your portfolio is critically important in getting a job. Working Clothing Designers suggest that prospective Designers stay focused on a particular design area. Successful candidates are those who believe in themselves and who are persistent.

TEXTILE DESIGNER

CAREER PROFILE

Duties: Produce or reproduce patterns for printing on textiles

Alternate Title: Textile Artist

Salary Range: $22,000 to $150,000

Employment Prospects: Poor

Advancement Prospects: Poor

Prerequisites:
　　Education—B.F.A. degree in textile design
　　Experience—Service work with a Textile Designer
　　Special Skills—Drawing, painting; good eye for color and design

CAREER LADDER

```
┌─────────────────────────┐
│     Design Director      │
└─────────────────────────┘

┌─────────────────────────┐
│     Textile Designer     │
└─────────────────────────┘

┌─────────────────────────┐
│      Service Worker      │
└─────────────────────────┘
```

Position Description

Textile Designers create or re-create patterns for printing on fabric. Working with their knowledge of fabrics, printing processes, and design needs, these artists use paint and computers to lay out and repeatedly trace patterns to create a printing medium.

The Textile Designer is responsible for selecting the color combinations for the design—perhaps several different variations for a single design. Mathematical design skills are important, as the Designer must measure the patterns and make them fit the fabric correctly.

The Textile Designer may use any of a variety of sources for inspiration. Artworks, historical patterns, and patterns in nature may be used for ideas.

Textile Designers currently in the industry advise newcomers that this is a laborious field, with many hours spent alone sitting at the drawing board.

Salaries

Current economic conditions make this a difficult field; consequently, starting salaries are low. Beginning Textile Designers may make $22,000 to $25,000. Salary growth is achieved by upward movement in a firm or by winning more and more freelance work; a design director at a major firm can make as much as $150,000.

Employment Prospects

It is not easy to find work as a Textile Designer. Though entry-level jobs in textile design service work may be available,

opportunities to work as a full-fledged Textile Designer are relatively rare.

Advancement Prospects

It is also difficult to advance to the position of design director, as the field is very competitive. Alternatively, some Textile Designers choose to work freelance and sell or license their work to manufacturers or retail stores.

Education

Again, the competitive nature of this field makes it imperative for the aspiring Textile Designer to get a thorough education in the basics, making a bachelor of fine arts degree in textile design necessary.

Experience and Skills

The prospective Textile Designer should first find a job doing service work for a Textile Designer. This includes changing colors for an existing pattern, tracing patterns for a layout, and correcting pattern flaws.

Special skills needed include creativity, talent in drawing and painting, and good color and design sense. Computer literacy is also necessary.

Organizations and Associations

The Graphic Artists Guild has a textile division that is helpful to people in this field, especially for networking.

Tips for Entry

New York City is the center for this profession. If you can't find work with a design firm or manufacturer, look for a job with a textile converter. As an alternative, a newcomer to the field can look for an agent who will help him or her get free-lance work for a fee.

JEWELRY DESIGNER

CAREER PROFILE

Duties: Design jewelry pieces, either to make yourself or to have made by a manufacturer

Salary Range: $20,000 to $75,000+

Employment Prospects: Fair

Advancement Prospects: Fair

Prerequisites:

Education—Bachelor's degree in art, design, or jewelry
Experience—Internship
Special Skills—Artistic ability, metalwork skills, business skills, understanding of jewelry construction

CAREER LADDER

```
┌─────────────────────────────┐
│   Senior Designer or         │
│   Independent Designer       │
└─────────────────────────────┘

┌─────────────────────────────┐
│   Jewelry Designer           │
└─────────────────────────────┘

┌─────────────────────────────┐
│   Apprentice                 │
└─────────────────────────────┘
```

Position Description

The job of a Jewelry Designer is to come up with ideas for jewelry pieces, render them on paper, and make (or have someone else make) the finished pieces. This may include finding sources for materials used to make the jewelry, finding workers who can execute the designs, and supervising the manufacturing. Alternatively, the designer who works within a jewelry manufacturing company may be responsible only for the design concept and the illustration of the design itself. And freelance Jewelry Designers earn a living by selling finished designs to various manufacturers.

Jewelry Designers get their ideas from a variety of places, including fashion magazines, nature, artworks, and the human body. The particular artistic contribution of the designer is to translate these ideas into a piece of jewelry that will be attractive to potential buyers. Sometimes a customer brings an idea to the Jewelry Designer, who then designs a piece that combines the client's specifications with what the designer knows about jewelry construction; in that case, the designer's job is to meet the client's needs as closely as possible.

Salaries

A beginning Jewelry Designer might expect to make $20,000 working for a jewelry manufacturer, but it is possible to work up to a salary of around $75,000 or more. The income of a Jewelry Designer who works independently, though, can vary depending on time commitment, skill, and success.

Employment Prospects

For those willing to go the independent route, making jewelry and selling at craft shows has been a good way to progress in this field. Getting work with a manufacturer is tied to the economic climate since jewelry is a luxury item and in difficult times, sales slack off. Currently, the market is strong.

Advancement Prospects

The competitive nature of the business has resulted in fair advancement prospects for the Jewelry Designer. Some designers have found that the only way up is out—that is, to become an independent designer and manufacturer, selling to stores or at craft shows.

Education

A Jewelry Designer typically has a bachelor's degree in art, design, or jewelry. Some Jewelry Designers, however, are educated at art schools or in specialized craft programs. Coursework in metalsmithing, illustration, and sculpture are useful, and business classes are important for those who plan to work on their own.

Experience and Skills

An internship with a jewelry manufacturer or independent jeweler is extremely useful, and any business or sales experience can be helpful—even working as a salesperson in a jewelry store. Necessary skills include various art skills, such as drafting, illustration, knowledge of color, perspective, and sculpture, rendering and metalwork.

Organizations and Associations

People interested in becoming Jewelry Designers might want to contact the American Craft Council (ACC), the Jewelers Board of Trade (JBT), and the Goldsmiths of America for career guidance.

Tips for Entry

For those who wish to work as Jewelry Designers in manufacturing companies, it's a good idea to be focused on the kind of work you'd like to do and to be persistent in contacting potential employers. For aspiring designers who like to work on their own, it is important to create distinctive style for your work and to get out and show it—in craft shows, to store buyers, even selling it on the street.

CONSERVATOR

CAREER PROFILE

Duties: Prepare, clean, reconstruct, retouch, and document artwork

Alternate Title: Restorer

Salary Range: $28,000 to $45,000

Employment Prospects: Good

Advancement Prospects: Good

Prerequisites:
    Education—Master's degree in art history or art conservation; specialized training in restoration
    Experience—Internship in restoration
    Special Skills—Drawing and painting, science background, an artistic eye

CAREER LADDER

```
┌─────────────────────────────┐
│     Senior Conservator      │
└─────────────────────────────┘

┌─────────────────────────────┐
│         Conservator         │
└─────────────────────────────┘

┌─────────────────────────────┐
│    Assistant Conservator    │
└─────────────────────────────┘
```

Position Description

A Conservator is responsible for the treatment of artwork—repairing damage, preserving quality, and documenting the status of the work. This involves preparatory steps, such as uncrating and photographing the work, followed by cleaning, retouching, structural repair, and/or other operations.

Major museums employ Conservators, as do commercial operations that provide conservation and restoration services to the public.

Conservation and restoration is a specialized field, and it takes considerable training to prepare for this career. The Conservator must be educated and have practical training in fine arts and art history, and in addition must have a considerable mastery of physics and chemistry in order to understand and work with art materials.

Salaries

Salaries for art conservators range from $28,000 to $45,000 per year.

Employment Prospects

Employment prospects for Conservators are good. This is a field that is growing as collectors become increasingly aware of the need to preserve and care for the artwork they own. In addition, there are areas, such as photo conservation, that are wide open for those interested in pursuing a career in restoration.

Advancement Prospects

Conservators can expect to advance to supervisory positions in this career fairly readily. Again, the expansion within the field will continue to open up new positions as time goes on. As the Conservator gains experience, he or she may move up to supervise other conservators or to manage a department of conservation for an institute or a business.

Education

The educational requirements for this career are extensive and specific. The aspiring Conservator should work for a bachelor's degree in art history and a master's degree in art history or art conservation. In addition, there are specialized training schools that offer programs in restoration and conservation; such training is a must. Electives should be used to gain a full knowledge of physics and chemistry, up to the level of organic chemistry, in order to understand the science of art materials.

Experience and Skills

The art conservation training programs offer the student the kind of apprenticeship necessary for this special field. Any kind of experience working with or for a Conservator will be equally valuable.

The aspiring Conservator should have drawing and painting skills, as well as an artistic eye to see into and beyond the surface of the artwork he or she seeks to restore.

Organizations and Associations

The professional organization for Conservators and restorers is the American Institute for Conservation of Historic and Artistic Works (AICHAW) (see Appendix V).

Tips for Entry

Focusing on the growing areas of this field, such as photograph restoration or lithograph restoration, may provide the widest possible opportunity for finding employment.

MUSEUMS

CURATORIAL ASSISTANT

CAREER PROFILE

Duties: Provide secretarial and research support to curators

Alternate Title: Curatorial Secretary

Salary Range: $12,000 to $20,000

Employment Prospects: Fair

Advancement Prospects: Fair to good

Prerequisites:

    Education—Undergraduate degree in art history
    Experience—Familiarity with museums and secretarial skills helpful
    Special Skills—Research ability, resourcefulness, and good organizational abilities

CAREER LADDER

```
┌─────────────────────────────┐
│      Assistant Curator      │
└─────────────────────────────┘

┌─────────────────────────────┐
│     Curatorial Assistant     │
└─────────────────────────────┘

┌─────────────────────────────┐
│     College or Internship    │
└─────────────────────────────┘
```

Position Description

Curatorial departments generate a great deal of paperwork, including general correspondence, the compilation of accurate lists of art objects to be included in a temporary exhibition, or the preparation of loan agreement forms which are used when borrowing or lending works of art. Most curatorial departments regularly publish informational brochures, catalogues, and other publications which must be typed and proofread. Record-keeping is especially important when working with art objects in transit. Curatorial Assistants provide secretarial, clerical, and research support for curators in all of these areas. Usually, people who take these jobs are interested in pursuing a career in museums and bring with them a background in art history. This is a good "foot in the door" position.

Museums follow standard procedures to keep track of objects in their collections or works they will borrow for a temporary exhibition. Curatorial Assistants must learn these conventional methods and make sure they are followed in all of the correspondence, contracts, and manuscripts generated in their department. Since most curatorial departments are understaffed, the Curatorial Assistant often becomes a jack-of-all-trades who may write letters for a curator one day and spend the next in the library researching the history of a particular painting or sculpture.

In a large museum Curatorial Assistants may be hired to work exclusively on a special project, like a major temporary exhibition. In addition to managing correspondence and basic research, the Curatorial Assistant may have important organi-

zational duties. For instance, in a juried exhibition to which artists submit slides, the Curatorial Assistant might log in all submissions, transfer the slides to projectors for viewing, and notify artists of the curator's decisions.

A Curatorial Assistant must work quickly but accurately. Mistakes can be embarrassing to the museum or detrimental to an artist, so attention to detail and the ability to meet deadlines are important attributes.

In addition a Curatorial Assistant may:

- research the location of photographs to be used in publications
- take minutes in curatorial meetings
- process bills and requests for payment in the curatorial department
- engage the museum photographer or a freelance photographer to document exhibitions

Salaries

Salaries for Curatorial Assistants tend to be quite low, ranging from $12,000 to $20,000, though starting salary can be higher in larger establishments. Another factor is the size of the museum, since larger museums offer more opportunity.

Employment Prospects

The Curatorial Assistant is an entry-level job in the curatorial department and is therefore desirable in spite of its considerable secretarial and clerical duties. Although it is often difficult to get these positions, turnover is higher than in other curatorial jobs, creating more frequent openings. The applicant should have both a good general knowledge of art history and excellent secretarial skills.

Advancement Prospects

Without going back to school for a graduate degree it is difficult to advance from Curatorial Assistant to assistant curator. Chances are better for Curatorial Assistants who have worked on special projects and proven their insight and effectiveness in this context. However, Curatorial Assistants are certainly in a good position to learn the rudiments of museum work and to absorb a good deal of art history from the curators they work for.

Education

An undergraduate degree in art history or a related field is required, along with secretarial training. Proficiency with a computer is necessary.

Experience and Skills

Curatorial Assistants must have good judgment, be efficient and highly organized people. They must have excellent secretarial skills, including typing, filing, and the ability to write basic correspondence. In addition to these practical skills, they must have a good basic knowledge of, or sensitivity to, art objects they are working with, and a disposition that can withstand pressure.

ASSISTANT CURATOR

CAREER PROFILE

Duties: Assume responsibility for one cluster of curatorial duties within a curatorial department, for instance the management of a subcollection

Salary Range: $18,000 to $35,000

Employment Prospects: Poor to fair

Advancement Prospects: Good

Prerequisites:

Education—Undergraduate degree, and preferably an advanced degree in art history

Experience—Background in curatorial work

Special Skills—Outstanding knowledge of art history; writing skills; familiarity with collection management and the organization of special exhibitions

CAREER LADDER

```
┌─────────────────────────────┐
│     Associate Curator       │
└─────────────────────────────┘

┌─────────────────────────────┐
│     Assistant Curator       │
└─────────────────────────────┘

┌─────────────────────────────┐
│    Curatorial Assistant     │
└─────────────────────────────┘
```

Position Description

Although Assistant Curators are the most junior curators in a museum, they often have considerable responsibility. Like associate curators, they may be assigned to long-term projects or assume responsibility for a special subcollection. Since there are, typically, few full curators in a museum, and only a slightly larger number of associate curators, all of whom tend to be stable in their positions, Assistant Curators may be given greater and greater responsibility in the course of their tenure at a museum but not receive a change in title.

In addition to special projects like the organization of a temporary exhibition, Assistant Curators are usually given specific research or administration-oriented duties by a senior curator. For instance, in preparation for a temporary exhibition an Assistant Curator might be asked to research the location of particular works of art, compile bibliographies on exhibiting artists, or describe specific objects to be used as catalogue entries in a publication accompanying the exhibition. Assistant Curators might take responsibility for ongoing duties, like visiting local artists to critique their work or handling general correspondence within the department.

An Assistant Curator who works closely with a particular collection may handle all administrative details relating to loan requests. Any museum with a collection receives requests from outside museums to borrow works of art for temporary exhibition. In a large museum, or one with a particularly important collection, these requests can be frequent and time-consuming. An Assistant Curator would consult with the conservator about the fitness of the work to travel, as well as with senior curators who have jurisdiction over the collection. Once a decision has been made the Assistant Curator would handle all correspondence with the outside organization, dealing with conditions of the loan or the reasons for its denial.

In a small museum, Assistant Curators' responsibilities might include secretarial support for other curators and additional clerical or organizational duties. Although many Assistant Curators are able to organize exhibitions and write about art, their jobs tend to be task-oriented, but may be related to the overall planning issues of the curatorial department.

In addition an Assistant Curator may:

- compile and coordinate the production of scholarly catalogues
- give gallery talks for the general public
- act as a liaison with the public relations officer

Salaries

Although Assistant Curators' salaries range from $18,000 to $30,000, they may be as high as $35,000 in a major museum.

Employment Prospects

As with all curatorial positions, it is very difficult to get a job as an Assistant Curator in a large museum. Although in a small museum the job may be an entry-level position, this does not reduce the competition, since there are many more interested applicants than there are opportunities. It is easier to find a curatorial job in a smaller institution, but even in such museums the candidate must have distinguished him- or herself academically or with work in the field. In a large museum, Assistant Curatorships with significant responsibility are extremely difficult to get.

Advancement Prospects

Once one has entered curatorial work, chances are usually good that further opportunities will present themselves. However, it is often difficult to jump from Assistant to Associate Curator, not only because there are fewer positions as one climbs the ladder, but also because an Assistant Curatorship may not call for the creative work with which to distinguish oneself.

Education

Although an undergraduate degree in art history may be sufficient in some museums, a graduate degree in the field is necessary for an Assistant Curatorship in a large or prestigious museum.

Experience and Skills

An Assistant Curator must have an excellent grasp of art history, particularly of a specialized field relevant to the museum. He or she must have superior writing, research, and public speaking skills. In a large institution it is also necessary for the Assistant Curator to be aware of the workings of a museum, including the procedure for processing loan requests and the organization of temporary exhibitions. More than senior curators, it is important that an Assistant Curator has excellent organizational skills. Computer skills are extremely helpful.

ASSOCIATE CURATOR

CAREER PROFILE

Duties: Assume responsibility for several clusters of curatorial duties within a curatorial department

Salary Range: $18,000 to $59,000

Employment Prospects: Poor to fair

Advancement Prospects: Good

Prerequisites:

Education—An undergraduate and advanced degree in art history

Experience—Considerable curatorial background, including experience in organizing exhibitions and managing collections

Special Skills—Excellent knowledge of a specialized area of art history, excellent writing skills

CAREER LADDER

```
┌─────────────────────────────┐
│          Curator            │
└─────────────────────────────┘

┌─────────────────────────────┐
│      Associate Curator      │
└─────────────────────────────┘

┌─────────────────────────────┐
│      Assistant Curator      │
└─────────────────────────────┘
```

Position Description

The Associate Curator works in conjunction with the curator in managing a museum's collections and organizing temporary exhibitions. Although the Associate Curator has less administrative responsibility than the chief curator or curator, he or she has significant authority in developing the museum's artistic program. Although the structures of curatorial departments vary from institution to institution, it is typical for Associate Curators to deal with a broad area of the museum's program, and with the various curatorial duties which relate to that area. For instance, in a Department of Prints and Drawings, an Associate Curator might be responsible for all activities relating to drawings, including the acquisition of works as well as the organization of temporary exhibitions. A department may be structured so that an Associate Curator supervises all temporary exhibitions within it; in some museums, an Associate Curator is responsible for all research related to works in the collection.

Regardless of what the Associate Curator's specific responsibilities are, the job is usually structured so that he or she spends the preponderance of the time planning and implementing a limited number of projects from start to finish. For instance, in a large museum with an active Department of Painting and Sculpture, an Associate Curator may spend two or three years working intensively on a single major exhibition, researching works of art relevant to a theme, undertaking correspondence with potential lenders of art, preparing a catalogue, and communicating the goals and themes of the exhibition to other members of the staff, such as the Director of Education, the designer, the public relations officer, and the grants officer. The Associate Curator may be responsible for supervising the growth, maintenance, and interpretation of a particular aspect of the collection. For instance, within the area of ancient art, he or she might be responsible for Egyptian artifacts.

In addition to responsibilities related to his or her own projects, Associate Curators may share some of the curator's administrative responsibilities. He or she may supervise an assistant curator or have a fund-raising responsibility related to specific exhibitions or collections. In many museums, certain exhibitions or programs are developed collaboratively among a group of Associate Curators.

In addition the Associate Curator may:

- manage an administrative area of curatorial activity, like the request of loans from the permanent collection
- consult with the chief curator and curator in long-range planning for the department
- contribute articles to museum publications

Salaries

The salary for Associate Curators ranges from $18,000 to $59,000, but tend to start in the $20,000 to $25,000 range.

Employment Prospects

As with all curatorial positions, it is very difficult to get a job as an Associate Curator. It is possible to enter this position right after receiving an advanced degree in art history, but chances are better if the candidate has had three to five years of curatorial experience.

Advancement Prospects

In most museums Associate Curator is a mid-level or senior position, with a lot of room to prove him- or herself through publications, the building of collections and the organization of exhibitions. Prospects are therefore good that an Associate Curator will advance to the position of curator and eventually chief curator. In most institutions, and especially in larger, prestigious museums, curators hold their positions for many years, so the prospects are often better for advancement if one looks outside of one's present institution.

Education

An undergraduate degree in art history or a related field is required, and usually an advanced degree in art history is necessary.

Experience and Skills

The Associate Curator must be able to manage a project well from start to finish. This involves excellent planning skills, the ability to communicate a project's goals, and to research funding, as well as an excellent knowledge of art history and superior writing and communication skills. The Associate Curator must be aware of the procedural and legal aspects of museum collections, as well as the methods utilized in researching and seeking art objects for a temporary exhibition. He or she must be able to stay abreast of new art-historical attitudes and insights into his or her field, and combine intellectual flexibility and curiosity with administrative skills.

CURATOR

CAREER PROFILE

Duties: Supervision of activity and personnel in a major set of curatorial programs, or of a curatorial department

Salary Range: $30,000 to $80,000+

Employment Prospects: Poor to fair

Advancement Prospects: Good

Prerequisites:
    Education—Undergraduate and advanced degrees in art history
    Experience—Extensive curatorial background, distinguished contribution to his or her field of art history
    Special Skills—Excellent writing skills, creativity in art-historical point of view, and excellent ability to interpret works of art

CAREER LADDER

```
+-------------------------------+
|         Chief Curator         |
+-------------------------------+

+-------------------------------+
|            Curator            |
+-------------------------------+

+-------------------------------+
|       Associate Curator       |
+-------------------------------+
```

Position Description

Under the supervision of the chief curator are a group of Curators who are responsible for a major constellation of activities or departments of the museum—e.g., the department of antiquities or of twentieth century painting and sculpture. Each Curator has administrative duties related to his or her area of specialization, and has primary responsibility for exhibitions, research, publications, acquisitions, and donor contracts within this area. The Curator may also supervise other associate and assistant curators on his or her curatorial team. In a small museum the positions of Curator and chief curator may be combined, and there may be greater flexibility in the division of responsibility within a curatorial department.

The Curator of a collection in a museum has two broad objectives: to build a comprehensive collection of high quality within his or her area and to interpret this collection through publications and special exhibitions. Curators must spend a good deal of their time researching and acquiring objects for the collection. This means attending international auctions as well as cultivating relationships with major private collectors, in the hope that they will eventually leave their collections to the museum. Building a fine museum collection requires a mastery of the art history for the period of the collection as well as the subtle ability to represent the depth and richness of a historical period or an artist through a limited number of objects. Every Curator

has a different amount of acquisition funds available to him or her, and each must deal with the relative scarcity of art objects, but all must be able to work within these limitations to create a collection of quality and historical importance.

Not only must the Curator put together museum collections, but he or she must also interpret them for the public. This includes the installation of the collection in the museum's galleries in such a way as to indicate a historical progression; the publication of catalogues which describe the significance of particular objects in the collection; or the organization of special exhibitions which explore in depth an aspect of the collection. Often, the temporary exhibition of a private collector's works is a means of attracting a gift from that collection in the future.

When organizing a temporary exhibition the Curator must develop the exhibition's theme and compile a list of artists to be included. He or she, with the help of associate and assistant curators, must then research the availability of objects and request to borrow them from other institutions, individuals, or galleries. Most temporary exhibitions are accompanied by interpretive catalogues written or edited by the Curator. The Curator is normally responsible for writing or editing didactics (wall texts) and other educational materials related to the exhibitions. The Curator may be needed to supply factual, descriptive information about the exhibition to the museum's press office as well as make themselves available for interviews or questions from the press if responsible for an exhibit. When outside institutions make requests to borrow objects in the museum's collection, the Curator, in conjunction with junior members of the staff, the registrar, and the conservator, determines whether the loan should be made.

Although most Curators spend the preponderance of their time working with art, they also share responsibility with the department of development for raising money for their programs, and have the administrative responsibility for managing budgets and personnel relevant to their activity.

In addition a Curator may:

- lecture to the public on the museum's collections
- participate in training of docents or other educational personnel within the museum (more so in a smaller institution)
- contribute articles to scholarly art journals on objects in the museum's collection
- provide advice for private collectors associated with the museum
- authenticate objects within his or her area of specialization

Salaries
Curators average a salary between $30,000 and $40,000, though the average is higher in larger museums and may be as high as $80,000.

Employment Prospects
Positions as Curator are extremely difficult to get and require proven expertise in an area of specialization as well as an impressive record of publications and exhibitions. The Curator in many museums is as much a scholar as an admin-istrator, so the necessary qualifications for the job are often as rigorous as those for a college professor.

Advancement Prospects
Advancement prospects for the Curator are good. He or she may advance to the position of chief curator and eventually director if performance has been impressive.

Education
The Curator should have an undergraduate degree in art history and a graduate degree in his or her area of specialization. As with the chief curator, a graduate degree is not always absolutely necessary, but it is a great advantage.

Experience and Skills
The Curator must have expertise in his or her area of specialization as well as excellent writing, research, and public speaking skills. He or she must be familiar with the conservation principles of art objects, as well as know the current market, collecting ethics, and customs regulations in the area of specialization. Good Curators have a special affinity for, and sensitivity to, art objects which is hard to describe or quantify. Curators should have a sense of how to relate objects to be displayed in order to convey relationships and qualities in a cogent and logical manner. In addition the Curator must be an efficient administrator and be able to research and request funds from private and public sources. Since most Curators work closely with private collectors, they must have a skillful and subtle facility for social interaction.

CHIEF CURATOR

CAREER PROFILE

Duties: Supervise artistic direction and administration of all curatorial departments

Salary Range: $35,000 to $80,000+

Employment Prospects: Poor to fair

Advancement Prospects: Good

Prerequisites:
   Education—Undergraduate and advanced degree in art history
   Experience—Extensive curatorial background and administrative skills
   Special Skills—Excellent scholarly and creative grasp of art history; administrative, planning, and leadership ability

CAREER LADDER

```
┌─────────────────────────────┐
│         Director            │
└─────────────────────────────┘

┌─────────────────────────────┐
│       Chief Curator         │
└─────────────────────────────┘

┌─────────────────────────────┐
│          Curator            │
└─────────────────────────────┘
```

Position Description

The Chief Curator is one of the key positions in a museum. He or she has administrative responsibility for curatorial affairs and, in cooperation with the director, outlines the museum's curatorial policy. The Chief Curator supervises the creation and growth of collections as well as the museum's development of temporary exhibitions. This job includes considerable fund-raising and contact with benefactors, as well as responsibility for developing a budget for the curatorial department and supervision of its staff. In addition to these administrative responsibilities, the Chief Curator also organizes exhibitions and acquires and interprets objects in his or her area of specialization.

Curators are responsible for both the acquisition and care of museum collections and the organization of temporary exhibitions. In some institutions these different duties are shared equally by a group of curators; in others, curators specialize in temporary exhibitions while their colleagues are entirely concerned with the care of a particular segment of the collection. The Chief Curator must structure this activity in a way appropriate to the areas of interest of the institution. He or she develops an exhibition policy which responds to the needs of the community, the strengths of the museum and its staff, and activity in the field at large.

The Chief Curator and the director are the primary spokespeople to the community for the museum's collections and exhibitions. They must communicate the goals and activities of the curatorial departments to potential funders in the public and private sectors as well as to volunteer groups which help to fund the museum. The Chief Curator seeks and maintains contacts with collectors and benefactors in the community with the hope that they will contribute money or works of art to the institution.

Although the Chief Curator may not be directly involved in the daily work of maintaining a collection or organizing exhibitions, he or she is intimately involved with all major artistic decisions made by members of the department. Especially in large museums with encyclopedic collections ranging from ancient objects to contemporary art, the Chief Curator must balance the activities of the various departments and work toward an integrated program. The Chief Curator also communicates curatorial needs and directions to the director of finance, the director of development, the curator for education, and often the public relations officer.

In addition the Chief Curator may:

- supervise museum publications
- develop a fund-raising strategy for the curatorial department

Salaries

Chief Curators average salaries between $35,000 and $80,000. Salaries are directly related to the size of a museum and can be as high as $80,000 in a major institution with a great deal of curatorial activity.

Employment Prospects

The position of Chief Curator is one of the most highly sought-after jobs in museum work, and competition is extremely stiff. At all but the smallest museums, an applicant must have built a significant reputation in the field before he or she is able to reach this position.

Advancement Prospects

As in all curatorial work, one's record of exhibitions and publications is a primary test of ability. With a good reputation as a curator, as well as proven effectiveness as an administrator, prospects are good for a Chief Curator to advance to the position of director at his or her own institution or another museum.

Education

In virtually every case an undergraduate degree in art history or a related field and a graduate degree in art history, with a concentration in one of the areas of interest of the museum, are necessary. It is often possible, especially in institutions which collect and exhibit only contemporary art, to attain the position of Chief Curator without a graduate degree, but in this case an impressive record of publications and exhibitions is necessary.

Experience and Skills

Not only must the Chief Curator have demonstrated a high level of ability in interpreting works of art, organizing exhibitions, and building collections, but he or she must also be an effective administrator, able to manage a large budget and raise funds in the community. An excellent grasp of art history and superior writing and communications skills are necessary, as well as a flair for diplomacy. Excellent public relations skills, sensitivity and diplomacy in interpersonal dealings, and marketing expertise are all factors that must support professional (and academic) expertise, the two most essential qualifications for a Chief Curator. The Chief Curator must be adept at planning and be able to take into account issues of marketing and development when designing exhibition policy. The ability to manage a staff is necessary, as well as a proficiency in working with department heads of other areas of the museum.

PUBLIC RELATIONS ASSISTANT

CAREER PROFILE

Duties: Manage the clerical activity of the public relations department and assist in preparing press materials

Salary Range: $20,000–$25,000

Employment Prospects: Fair to good

Advancement Prospects: Fair to good

Prerequisites:
Education—Undergraduate degree in public relations, journalism, or the liberal arts
Experience—Excellent secretarial skills
Special Skills—Knowledge of art history, familiarity with the structures and methods of servicing the press

CAREER LADDER

```
┌─────────────────────────────────┐
│     Public Relations Officer     │
└─────────────────────────────────┘

┌─────────────────────────────────┐
│    Public Relations Assistant    │
└─────────────────────────────────┘

┌─────────────────────────────────┐
│            College               │
└─────────────────────────────────┘
```

Position Description

A great deal of information is processed and circulated by the museum's public relations department. The Public Relations Assistant is responsible for maintaining efficient systems for disseminating this information to the press and the general public. Although responsibilities include a good deal of clerical and organizational work, like typing and copying press releases, supervising mailings, and maintaining a file of press clippings, the Public Relations Assistant is usually given ample opportunity to develop his or her writing skills and to work directly with members of the press.

The public relations department provides several different types of information, ranging from brief listings or copy for short public service announcements on radio and television to detailed program descriptions that are many pages long. For each of these types of press releases, and for different media outlets like daily and weekly newspapers, magazines, radio, and television, there are specific deadlines for information. The Public Relations Assistant must maintain an accurate schedule of deadlines so that releases are sent out on time and to the proper people. He or she supervises bulk mailings of this material and answers telephone inquiries from members of the press.

When a magazine or television station decides to do a story on an exhibition or program, they usually require materials like photographs, slides, and background reading. Members of the press often like to speak to curators or artists. In advance of a program or exhibition the Public Relations Assistant works with the curatorial department

and the public relations officer to identify, obtain, and reproduce black and white photographs and photocopied articles that will be made available for the press. During the course of the program he or she will provide further supplementary materials to the press when necessary.

One of the most important resources the public relations department maintains is a file or scrapbook of clippings. The Public Relations Assistant is responsible for finding and compiling this material, or gathering it from a clipping service.

In addition the Public Relations Assistant may:

- assist in writing and editing the museum's newsletter
- write short releases or public service announcements
- coordinate invitations and refreshments for press conferences
- update press lists

Salaries

Depending upon the size of the public relations department and the writing responsibilities of the Public Relations Assistant, he or she can make between $15,000 and $20,000 and $25,000.

Employment Prospects

Positions as Public Relations Assistant are entry-level jobs and provide a good overall introduction to the mechanics of press relations as well as the structure of the museum. Competition is tough, but it is generally less difficult than getting an entry-level position in a curatorial department. This position is more commonly found in larger museums. In smaller institutions, the Public Affairs Coordinator may take on these responsibilities, and/or interns and volunteers help out.

Advancement Prospects

Since publicizing a museum requires a sensitivity to art and a knowledge of the specialized art press, as well as competence in the basic procedures of press relations, Public Relations Assistants who learn the field by participating in it have a good chance to move up to the job of public relations officer. It is also possible that the Public Relations Assistant may be promoted to other administrative posts within the museum in fund-raising or financial management, or to an entry-level job in the curatorial department.

Education

Although a special degree in public relations, journalism or communications is not necessary, it would be helpful. Secretarial programs and proficiency on the computer are valu-able training for this job. Coursework in art history and a demonstrated skill at writing are crucial.

Experience and Skills

The Public Relations Assistant must be levelheaded and very well organized. He or she must be able to coordinate as many as 30 press releases at a time and cheerfully explain programs and seek out supplementary information for members of the press. A good writer will go far in this job, as the public relations officer learns that he or she can delegate press release writing to the Assistant. Fast and accurate typing and research skills are a must.

It is important to be proactive and resourceful, and to have the ability to brainstorm and add creative input.

Organizations and Associations

The Public Relations Society of America (see Appendix V) serves public relations professionals in all types of organizations.

PUBLIC RELATIONS OFFICER

CAREER PROFILE

Duties: Communicating the goals and programs of the museum to the print and electronic press

Alternate Title: Director of Public Relations, Public Affairs Coordinator

Salary Range: $24,000 to $45,000

Employment Prospects: Poor to fair

Advancement Prospects: Fair to good

Prerequisites:

Education—Undergraduate degree in public relations, journalism, or communications

Experience—Background in press relations, knowledge of the procedures of promotion and advertising

Special Skills—Excellent writing skills, interpersonal ability, and knowledge of art history

CAREER LADDER

```
┌─────────────────────────────┐
│     Director of Finance     │
└─────────────────────────────┘

┌─────────────────────────────┐
│  Public Relations Officer   │
└─────────────────────────────┘

┌─────────────────────────────┐
│ Public Relations Assistant  │
└─────────────────────────────┘
```

Position Description

Attendance is directly related to a museum's image and its effectiveness in communicating its exhibitions and other programs to a broad public. The Public Relations Officer is responsible for developing a positive profile for the museum and building strong relationships with all forms of media. The Public Relations Officer provides the press with a variety of news releases and listings describing museum programs and exhibitions. Since a good press release often makes the difference between an exhibition that is reviewed and one that is ignored, the Public Relations Officer must be able to write concise, arresting summaries of a variety of museum programs.

Most museums publish a newsletter to make their members, patrons, and the general public aware of upcoming events. In addition to schedules and exhibition descriptions the newsletter often includes general institutional news, special articles, or even art-historical essays. The Public Relations Officer has editorial responsibility for this publication. He or she must work closely with all departments to collect information about upcoming programs and write about them. Since the newsletter is typically considered an important benefit for museum members, the Public Relations Officer often works closely with the membership officer to develop its format and content. In

many museums the responsibilities of the Public Relations Officer include publishing an annual report, as well as all in-house publications.

As the primary liaison between museum staff and the general public, the Public Relations Officer must interpret complex artistic concepts in terms that a general audience can appreciate. As in every aspect of public relations work, those entrusted with publicizing a museum do much of their work informally by getting to know, and regularly speaking with, members of the press.

In addition to promoting the museum through the media, the Public Affairs Coordinator is responsible for developing and implementing a total marketing plan. For specific exhibits, the Public Affairs Coordinator must market to targeted audiences who have a special interest in the exhibits' subject matter through marketing strategies, advertising (in-house or with an agency), public relations, and promotions.

While larger institutions will have more staff members to divide the responsibilities of the public relations/public affairs department, most museums have one main Public Relations position. The person holding this position will therefore be responsible for a large variety of tasks which cover all of the institution's needs in association with the public.

In addition the Public Relations Officer may:

- organize press conferences for special events
- engage and work with an outside public relations, marketing firm, or advertising agency
- help develop income-producing activities like catalogue distribution or bookstore management
- participate in institutional strategic planning process
- manage the museum's web site
- fulfill all photography needs and maintain all photo files of past exhibits and promotional shots
- group tour promotion
- recruit intern(s) or volunteers to assist with projects

Salaries

Public Relations Officers typically earn between $24,000 and $30,000, although salaries can be as high as $45,000 in a large museum in a major city. If the Public Relations Officer works primarily with national press and is involved in forging an overall marketing strategy for the museum, salaries tend to be higher.

Employment Prospects

Since working in museum public relations is attractive to writers interested in art, competition is often stiff. Writing skills and press connections provide an advantage, as does familiarity with several of the areas in which the museum has programs. In a small museum this position can be entry level.

Advancement Prospects

Since the Public Relations Officer is usually the senior member of a small department, there is little room for growth within this area. However, his or her job responsibilities include a significant amount of marketing or strategic planning, so the Public Relations Officer might advance to fund-raising as development officer. The museum is a good training ground for publicizing a broad range of activities, and many museum Public Relations Officers advance to related jobs outside of the arts.

Education

An undergraduate degree in public relations, journalism, or communications and coursework in art history are basic training for a Public Relations Officer. Any special courses in public speaking, writing, editorial work, or marketing are advantageous. Since the Public Relations Officer supervises regular mailings of press information, strong organizational and clerical skills come in handy.

Experience and Skills

It is essential that the Public Relations Officer write well and quickly. Experience as a journalist is invaluable, as is previous work in public relations. Since responsibilities include interviewing the curatorial staff for information, knowledge of art history and an ability to sensitively encapsulate ideas are important. Deadlines are a constant reality for the Public Relations Officer, so the ability to handle pressure and react calmly is a great advantage. Since the Public Relations Officer is an important representative of the museum, he or she must speak well and skillfully initiate and maintain relationships with press people.

Organizations and Associations

The professional association for public relations officers is the Public Relations Society of America (see Appendix V) and the International Association of Business Communicators.

REGISTRAR

CAREER PROFILE

Duties: Supervise cataloguing and maintenance of museum collections

Salary Range: $20,000 to $50,000

Employment Prospects: Poor to fair

Advancement Prospects: Fair to good

Prerequisites:
Education—Undergraduate degree in art history and training in handling artworks
Experience—Knowledge of registrarial and conservation procedures
Special Skills—Good interpersonal and administrative skills, knowledge of the technical procedures of creating and maintaining artworks

CAREER LADDER

```
┌─────────────────────────────────┐
│   Director or Chief Curator      │
└─────────────────────────────────┘

┌─────────────────────────────────┐
│           Registrar             │
└─────────────────────────────────┘

┌─────────────────────────────────┐
│       Assistant Registrar       │
└─────────────────────────────────┘
```

Position Description

The Registrar works directly with the museum's collections: He or she maintains orderly files on each work, supervises packing and shipping of incoming and outgoing loans and, with the conservator, works to ensure the artwork's proper storage and maintenance. Perhaps no one in the museum knows its collections as intimately as the Registrar, who must combine a knowledge of art history with administrative skills.

When an object enters the museum's collection it is documented by a card or file which includes the artist's full name, the exact title of the work, the materials used to make it, how it was purchased or who gave it to the museum. Along with this basic information, the Registrar typically records the provenance of the object—where it was made, who owned it, and any special historical significance. A complete list of the exhibitions in which the artwork has been included as well as a summary of its condition while in the museum's collection supplement each object's file. The Registrar is also responsible for deaccessioning procedures (when works are removed from the collection).

When the museum organizes a special exhibition which includes art borrowed from other institutions or individuals, or when objects from the museum's collections are requested for exhibition elsewhere, the Registrar is responsible for proper packing and shipping of the artwork. This includes making arrangements for the fabrication of crates, working with fine art shippers to schedule pickups and deliveries, and preparing paperwork to document transfer of the art object. When international shipping is necessary the Registrar must handle the customs proceedings or work with a customs agent.

Often works of art are given to a museum with special stipulations or on extended loan. The Registrar must be aware of the laws concerning gifts to museums as well as those pertaining to copyrights and the right to photographically reproduce a work. The Registrar works closely with the museum's insurance agent to develop a policy which will adequately protect the collection. He or she prepares insurance claims for damaged objects. The Registrar also oversees the storage facilities for works of art in the museum, and keeps track of the location of each particular work.

The Registrar works closely with the curatorial staff to arrange shipping for temporary exhibitions and to provide information on the characteristics, history, and condition of objects in the collection. Along with the conservator, the Registrar is always consulted to determine the fitness of a particular artwork to travel.

In addition the Registrar may:

- prepare a catalogue of the museum's collection
- conduct research on specific objects in the collection
- assist the curatorial staff in organizing exhibitions drawn from the museum's collections

- participate in workshops on conservation techniques, and work with curators to assess and develop proper storage methods for the care and preservation of the collections
- continually survey the physical condition of the collections in terms of security, temperature, and humidity control while on exhibition or in storage
- manage the museum's photographic and slide collections (with the administrative assistant) responding to purchase and publications requests, overseeing forms, fees, cataloguing, and storage
- data entry of object information into computer collections management program

Salaries

Depending on the size of the collections in his or her care, the Registrar's salary averages between $20,000 and $35,000. In a large museum a Registrar can make as much as $50,000.

Employment Prospects

The Registrar is entrusted with the care of the museum's collection, so it is unlikely that anyone without a good deal of experience in museum registration or a curatorial field would be hired. In an arts organization without a collection Registrars are often hired to oversee the shipping and handling of art. This kind of position is easier to get with minimal experience.

Advancement Prospects

The prospects for advancement depend on the Registrar's ambitions. In many smaller museums, the Registrar is also a part-time curator, and this kind of split job may lead to an entirely curatorial position. In a large museum, registrarial work is complex and satisfying. Once one has learned the field, the chances for advancement to better jobs in other museums are good.

Education

The Registrar should have a degree in art history, and particularly in the area of the museum's specialization, or some degree in the liberal arts. Coursework in library science or museum administration is valuable, as is an advanced degree or some training in conservation techniques and principles.

Experience and Skills

There is an accepted universal process for recording information about works of art which the Registrar should know well, or at least be familiar with. Previous experience in a registrarial position is invaluable, as is a knowledge of conservation and proper storage procedures. Since a large part of the Registrar's work is administrative, he or she should be aware of the records management and data processing systems, as well as the insurance requirements for the storage and transportation of art. The Registrar must work with professionals ranging from fine arts shippers to lawyers to curators. Excellent communications skills and a high level of organization are a great advantage.

CONSERVATOR

CAREER PROFILE

Duties: Ensure the physical safety of art objects and repair them when necessary

Salary Range: $30,000 to $60,000

Employment Prospects: Fair to good

Advancement Prospects: Good

Prerequisites:

Education—Graduate training in conservation, undergraduate degree in art history, chemistry, or fine arts

Experience—Background in the technology of art materials and conservation techniques

Special Skills—Sensitivity to art objects, good personal artistic ability

CAREER LADDER

```
┌─────────────────────────────┐
│   Chief Conservator or      │
│   Head of Department        │
└─────────────────────────────┘

┌─────────────────────────────┐
│      Conservator            │
└─────────────────────────────┘

┌─────────────────────────────┐
│   Assistant Conservator     │
└─────────────────────────────┘

┌─────────────────────────────┐
│   Associate Conservator     │
└─────────────────────────────┘
```

Position Description

The purpose of a collecting museum is not just to purchase and exhibit works of art, but also to ensure that they are properly stored and maintained. The Conservator works closely with the registrar to prevent the deterioration of artworks, and he or she treats them when damage occurs. Conservators are as much scientists as museum professionals; they must be rigorously trained in the technology and materials originally used to make the works of art or decorative objects collected by a museum, and also trained in the chemical and physical processes of their deterioration.

The Conservator sees that objects are fumigated, kept at proper levels of temperature and humidity, and protected from air pollutants or exposure to damaging light intensities and wavelengths. Depending upon what kind of objects are involved—and in a museum they could range from a delicate watercolor to an Egyptian mummy—different procedures are necessary for protection. Often a conservation department in a major museum includes specialists in several different types of objects.

In order to keep track of the condition of the museum's collections the Conservator writes reports on specific objects. Whenever a request is made from an outside institution to borrow a work from the museum's collection, the Conservator is asked to examine that object and make a recommendation on its fitness to travel. The decision of the Conservator is crucial to the museum's ability to lend works. In some cases, the Conservator will specify conditions under which the object may be exhibited—for example, special levels of light or protective cases.

The conservation field has changed dramatically in the course of the 20th century. New technologies, materials, and a redefined philosophy have all contributed to the realization that a Conservator is the one responsible for the care and protection of the integrity of the object entrusted to her/him. It is crucial that the Conservator keep his or her knowledge current by belonging to a professional conservation organization which expects adherence to a code of ethics.

In addition the Conservator may:

- treat or report on objects owned by private collectors or other museums
- work closely with the curatorial staff to inform them of proper conservation procedures
- enlist the opinion of outside conservation specialists

Salaries

The average salary range for Conservators is $30,000 to $40,000. If the Conservator supervises a large department of conservation scientists, or his or her expertise is highly specialized, salaries can be as high as $60,000.

Employment Prospects

Conservation is a small field but requires extensive training and experience as well as an artistic affinity to the objects one will work on. Once the proper training is received, chances are good for employment.

During the last year of conservator school or thereafter, aspiring Conservators should complete an internship in the field. An internship bulletin is put out every month from the American Museum Association. It is a good idea to reference AVISO for internship opportunities. Good initial positions for Conservators starting their careers include six-month to one-year openings at foundations that take on yearly projects like the Crest Foundation or the Mellon Foundation.

Advancement Prospects

A good Conservator is crucial to the maintenance of the museum's collection. Once one has demonstrated his or her competence, prospects for advancement are good.

Education

It is necessary for Conservators to have graduate-level training, in a conservation program of two or more years, in the theory, principles, and practice of conservation, including a year's training in the principles of general material conservation, and a minimum of one year's training or internship in a special field. Undergraduate training should include courses in cultural or art history, scientific studies such as chemistry, physics, or biology, studio arts, and manual skills.

Experience and Skills

Most positions require at least two years of postgraduate on-the-job experience. In addition to good scientific, artistic and technical skills, the Conservator must have good writing skills and the ability to work well with the registrar and curators. Since the Conservator must maintain a laboratory, he or she must have administrative skills as well.

Organizations and Associations

The professional organization for Conservators is the American Institute for Conservation of Historic and Artistic Works (see Appendix V).

EDUCATOR

CAREER PROFILE

Duties: Teach museum-sponsored classes for schoolchildren or adults

Alternate Titles: Instructor; Lecturer

Salary Range: $18,000 to $25,000

Employment Prospects: Good

Advancement Prospects: Good

Prerequisites:

Education—Undergraduate degree in education or art history

Experience—Background in teaching art history and studio art

Special Skills—Creative grasp of art history, rapport with children

CAREER LADDER

```
┌─────────────────────────────────┐
│       Head of Education          │
└─────────────────────────────────┘

┌─────────────────────────────────┐
│          Educator                │
└─────────────────────────────────┘

┌─────────────────────────────────┐
│  College or Graduate Training    │
└─────────────────────────────────┘
```

Position Description

Educators conduct the museum's education programs. There may be one or several teachers within the education department, or in a small museum the head of education may do most of the teaching him- or herself. The Educator is supervised by the head of education and, although it is not the Educator's responsibility to originate curricula for seminars or other education programs, he or she usually has a good deal of impact on programs during the process of planning and development.

Museum Educators typically work primarily with children. Three types of programs are most common: studio art classes, single visits to the museum by groups of schoolchildren, and multi-session seminars for a small number of students. In many communities a museum is an important adjunct to the school system, providing special programs in the arts. The Educator exposes participants in studio art classes to a range of artistic media, some as complex as etching or lithography, while using the collections of the museum to demonstrate these processes to the students. In the one-time visit programs and multi-session seminars, curriculum is usually well-defined by the head of education and must be followed by the Educator. These programs usually combine studio exercises with art-historical lectures and open discussion as a means of helping children understand and articulate the meaning of a work of art, or an art-historical period. A single visit to the museum may include

all of these elements, which are developed more thoroughly in multi-session seminars.

Education programs depend on cooperation between museum staff and the school system's teachers and administrators. In some programs the museum's Educators work directly in the schools as well as in their own institutions. It is important that the museum staff win the trust of school officials and work with them closely to develop and implement programs.

In addition the Educator may:

- assist the head of education in fund-raising for outreach programs
- organize and implement teacher workshops to let schools know about the museum's programs

Salaries

A full-time Educator averages a salary between $18,000 and $25,000. In a small museum it is likely that the salary will be at the low end of this range. Educators may also be hired by museums on a part-time basis.

Employment Prospects

Although training in teaching is necessary, this position can be an entry-level job in a museum. Prospects are fair if the candidate combines proper training with flexibility and an excellent knowledge of the areas of interest covered by the museum. It is often easier to start by getting part-time teaching positions.

Advancement Prospects

Educators often move on to positions with more responsibility, like the head of education, but many continue teaching throughout their careers.

Education

Educators should have either an undergraduate degree in art history or fine arts with teaching experience or courses in education, or an undergraduate degree in education with a concentration in art history is necessary. A teaching certificate or graduate degree in museum education teaching or art history is desirable.

Experience and Skills

Since teaching in a museum context may be more unconventional than within a school, it is necessary for the Educator to combine excellent teaching skills with creativity and flexibility about his or her profession. In addition, the Educator must be able to work closely with colleagues in the school system and be adept at navigating the bureaucratic systems of public schools. An excellent knowledge of art history is necessary, as is a love for working with children.

DOCENT COORDINATOR

CAREER PROFILE

Duties: Train and schedule volunteer lecturers, or docents

Salary Range: $25,000 to $30,000

Employment Prospects: Fair

Advancement Prospects: Fair

Prerequisites:

    Education—Undergraduate degree in art history or related field

    Experience—Background in teaching and good organizational skills

    Special Skills—Creativity, diplomacy, good public speaking skills

CAREER LADDER

```
┌─────────────────────────────────┐
│      Head of Education or        │
│   Head of Public Programming     │
└─────────────────────────────────┘

┌─────────────────────────────────┐
│       Docent Coordinator         │
└─────────────────────────────────┘

┌─────────────────────────────────┐
│    Docent, Teacher, or Intern    │
└─────────────────────────────────┘
```

Position Description

In a large museum with an active education program or a high volume of visiting adult groups, special volunteers called docents are used as museum lecturers. The Docent Coordinator, who is directly supervised by the head of education, is responsible for training docents and scheduling their activities. In some cases the Docent Coordinator is also a museum lecturer who, under supervision of the head of public programming, leads gallery talks and even gives courses or workshops for the public. Depending upon the size of the museum's docent program, this position may be part time or it may be included in the responsibilities of the head of education.

The docent gives introductory lectures in the museum's galleries covering aspects of its permanent collection or temporary exhibitions. These presentations vary in structure depending on the audience—whether of schoolchildren or an adult group. In most museums docents are given specialized training if they are interested in working with children. The Docent Coordinator is responsible for designing and implementing initial docent training, and providing a series of updates as they are required for temporary exhibitions or other changes in the museum's program. The Docent Coordinator also schedules group visits and provides docents for them. In some cases docents may offer informal tours weekly or daily in the galleries which are open to museum visitors.

Once or twice a year the Docent Coordinator offers a multi-session training seminar for new docents. This course provides art-historical background appropriate to the museum's areas of interest as well as insights into either public speaking strategies appropriate for adult groups or developmental educational theories for children. In most museums, docents are trained to lecture about specific aspects of the permanent collection so that they will gain experience in a particular area and refine their skills. After this initial training session, the Docent Coordinator regularly updates his or her volunteers through meetings where art-historical materials and lectures are offered. Often, special educational events, like visits to other museums, are organized for docent groups. Whenever a temporary exhibition opens, the Docent Coordinator provides a special series of seminars to prepare docents to lead tours through it.

An effective, enthusiastic team of docents is an important educational resource for the museum. The Docent Coordinator must recruit and cultivate dedicated volunteers who will help interpret the museum's collections and programs.

In addition the Docent Coordinator may:

- administer other education programs
- provide secretarial or clerical support for the head of education
- offer special courses or seminars for the general public

Salaries

A full-time Docent Coordinator averages a salary between $25,000 and $30,000. In a small museum it is likely that the salary will be at the low end of this range. Docent Coordinators may also be hired part time.

Employment Prospects

The Docent Coordinator may be an entry-level position, sometimes offered to an exceptional docent or intern. However, since a good knowledge of art history, plus research skills and teaching strategies, is necessary, the candidate must have appropriate informal and formal training. It may also be possible to begin working part time as a Docent Coordinator, leading to other jobs within the education department.

Advancement Prospects

Advancement prospects for the Docent Coordinator are only fair, since his or her activity is confined within a relatively narrow scope. Nevertheless, the position provides a good introduction to both outreach education and public programming, and an excellent performance may lead to the position of head of public programming or head of education.

Education

An undergraduate degree in art history is necessary, and coursework in teaching or museum education is invaluable. A graduate degree in art history or education is also helpful.

Experience and Skills

The Docent Coordinator must combine an excellent knowledge of art history with research and organizational skills. Although the curriculum for docent training is developed in conjunction with the head of education, the Docent Coordinator is in charge of the extensive administrative duties involved with scheduling meetings and matching visiting groups with docents. In addition, it is extremely important that the Docent Coordinator enjoy working with people and be able to communicate his or her enthusiasm effectively. When working with volunteers it is necessary to convey a sense of appreciation for their work and of their value to the institution. An ability to nourish the volunteer is as essential to this job as art-historical knowledge and administrative efficiency.

CURATOR OF EDUCATION

CAREER PROFILE

Duties: Supervise the design and implementation of all education programs

Alternate Titles: Director of Education

Salary Range: $25,000 to $65,000+

Employment Prospects: Poor to fair

Advancement Prospects: Good

Prerequisites:
Education—Undergraduate and advanced degrees in art history, education, or museum studies
Background—Extensive experience in museum outreach and public programming; administrative experience
Special Skills—Ability to assess educational needs and design appropriate programs; excellent knowledge of art history

CAREER LADDER

```
┌─────────────────────────────────┐
│           Director              │
└─────────────────────────────────┘

┌─────────────────────────────────┐
│      Curator of Education       │
└─────────────────────────────────┘

┌─────────────────────────────────┐
│  Head of Public Programming or  │
│      Head of Education          │
└─────────────────────────────────┘
```

Position Description

The Curator of Education develops, implements, administers, and evaluates the museum's education programs. As head of one of the museum's major departments, the Curator of Education supervises as many as 30 employees in a large museum. Museum education encompasses interpretive materials in the galleries, lectures, courses, classes, and workshops, as well as outreach to schoolchildren and other special populations like the elderly or the handicapped. The Curator of Education sets a policy for the museum's educational activity and works with his or her staff to fund and implement programs.

Educational activity in a museum is closely related to the institution's collections and exhibition policies. The Curator of Education works closely with the director and curators to develop specific programs like didactic brochures and special orientation areas featuring interactive computer programs, web sites, and videotapes, as well as lectures and courses that will help museum visitors understand the history and meaning of the exhibited art objects. Once this policy is set, the head of public programming carries it out in concert with the Curator of Education.

As he or she assists the head of public programming in creating a policy for programming, the Curator of Education also works with the head of education. He or she takes responsibility for some of the administrative work of creating liaisons with school department officials and education specialists. As the administrative head of the education department, the Curator of Education must work closely with federal and state funding agencies to procure funding for outreach and public programs.

The Curator of Education is the primary spokesperson within the museum and in the community for the educational activities of the institution. He or she must develop a budget for the department, attract funding, and evaluate performance of the various programs to the director and trustees of the institution. It is also important for the Curator of Education to stay abreast of new developments in museum education through participation in professional organizations, and to stay aware of the evolving exhibition policies of the museum in order to set proper educational policies to interpret them.

In addition the Curator of Education may:

- organize and implement education programs in addition to planning and administering them
- organize special didactic exhibitions
- edit an educational newsletter or publication for museum members or the general public

Salaries

Curators of Education make an average salary between $25,000 and $45,000. Salaries are closely related to the size of the department and the degree of administrative responsibility.

Employment Prospects

The Curator of Education is one of the most sought-after jobs in a museum and competition is extremely strong. Applicants need a combination of an impressive educational background and extensive experience in museum education or curatorial work. Since this position is a desirable one, with a great deal of responsibility, turnover is minimal, making prospects even more difficult.

Advancement Prospects

The Curator of Education is the head of a department, so advancement within the education area is not possible. However, the Curator of Education may be able to advance to the position of director, depending upon the objectives and policies of the institution. It is also possible to advance to the position of Curator of Education at a larger museum.

Education

An advanced degree in education or in an area of the museum's specialization or in museum studies is typically necessary, as well as an undergraduate degree in art history or education. Teacher training and coursework in writing and public speaking are helpful.

Experience and Skills

The Curator of Education must have a good knowledge of art history as well as a knowledge of museum education techniques and resources. He or she must be aware of the objectives, curricula, and operation of school systems and other educational institutions. Since there is a good deal of public interaction built into this job, the Curator of Education must have excellent speaking and writing skills as well as strong enthusiasm for the objectives and programs of the museum. The Curator of Education must be adept at research and be aware of the formal means of evaluating educational programs. Since this is a position which requires the design of museum policy, the Curator of Education must have a wide knowledge of his or her field, as well as the ability and vision to set a direction and organize a staff.

HEAD OF EDUCATION

CAREER PROFILE

Duties: Design and supervise museum outreach programs for children, the elderly, the handicapped, or other underserved populations

Salary Range: $25,000 to $40,000

Employment Prospects: Poor to fair

Advancement Prospects: Good

Prerequisites:

    Education—Undergraduate degree in art history and graduate degree in education, museum studies, or museum education

    Experience—Background in teaching art and designing curricula

    Special Skills—Administrative ability, creativity, knowledge of current educational theories

CAREER LADDER

```
┌─────────────────────────────────┐
│      Curator of Education        │
└─────────────────────────────────┘

┌─────────────────────────────────┐
│      Head of Education or        │
│    Head of School Programs       │
└─────────────────────────────────┘

┌─────────────────────────────────┐
│           Educator               │
└─────────────────────────────────┘
```

Position Description

Outreach is one of the primary areas of educational activity in a museum. Through its outreach programs an institution actively recruits special populations, like schoolchildren, the elderly, or the handicapped, by designing special educational programs for them. The Head of Education works with the curator of education to develop an outreach policy, and then he or she designs and implements individual programs.

In most museums the primary outreach audience is schoolchildren. Museums may provide many different types of program, from a single, highly structured visit to the museum to multiple-session seminars which involve a small number of students in an extended art experience. Most inner-city art museums make special efforts to serve minority students within their area. In developing programs with local school systems, the Head of Education must be sensitive to the needs of collaborating schools and be able to tailor the museum's education programs to their goals. Often the success or failure of outreach education depends on the ability of the person in this position to gain the trust of the teachers and school system administrators, as well as the public funding necessary to implement programs. The Head of Education represents the museum in the educational world and must be adept at communicating its outreach goals and offerings.

In order to design effective programs, the Head of Education must be aware of developmental theories for the age groups of children served by the museum, as well as knowing the standard museum educational models. Using this knowledge, he or she is able to develop a specific curriculum for schoolchildren, relating works in the museum's permanent collection or in temporary exhibitions to subjects they learn in school. The Head of Education either teaches these programs personally or trains and supervises a group of teachers or docents who do. Museum education ranges from very conservative lecture-oriented programs to experimental methods of teaching which involve open discussion and creative exercises.

Although children are the museum's primary outreach audience, many institutions broaden their activity by using art either as a tool for students who need remedial help or as a therapeutic experience for the handicapped. Many museums even have programs for the blind. The Head of Education may also organize visits to the museum by community groups, nursing home residents, or any other population interested in an interpretive experience within the museum.

In addition the Head of Education may:

- attend workshops or conferences on educational theory
- perform significant fund-raising for outreach education programs, especially to public funding agencies
- organize special workshops for teachers to communicate the programs of the museum

Salaries

Although salaries can be as low as $22,000, they average between $25,000 and $35,000 and can be $40,000 or more at larger museums.

Employment Prospects

As in all museum education positions, competition is tough for Head of Education. It is unlikely for an applicant to be hired without extensive teaching experience and/or a graduate degree in education with a specialization in museum studies. Proven ability to build curricula is also necessary. Even with these qualifications, there are only a limited number of jobs available and many people interested in them.

Advancement Prospects

Prospects are good for a Head of Education to become the curator of education. Outreach education is a fundamental community service performed by the museum which gives this position a good deal of visibility and prestige. The possibilities of getting a position in a larger museum with greater outreach activity are also good.

Education

The Head of Education should have an undergraduate degree in art history or a related field, and a graduate level degree in education or museum studies, as well as specific training in teaching.

Experience and Skills

The Head of Education must have an excellent knowledge of the educational principles and models appropriate to the populations served by the museum, as well as teaching experience and expertise. It is fundamental that he or she be adept at negotiating with school administrators and teachers as well as the public funding agencies which typically make outreach programs possible. Excellent verbal and written skills are a great benefit. In order to stay abreast of new educational developments, the Head of Education must have research skills and memberships in educational associations. As with any teaching-related position, this job requires an empathy for and enthusiasm about the populations served.

EDITOR

CAREER PROFILE

Duties: Coordinate the production and editing of museum publications

Alternate Titles: Head of Publications, Publication Coordinator

Salary Range: $22,000 to $55,000+

Employment Prospects: Poor to fair

Advancement Prospects: Fair

Prerequisites:

Education—Undergraduate degree in English or journalism

Experience—Knowledge of editorial procedures and publication production

Special Skills—Excellent writing skills and technical knowledge of grammar

CAREER LADDER

```
┌─────────────────────────────────────┐
│              Editor                  │
└─────────────────────────────────────┘

┌─────────────────────────────────────┐
│   Assistant Editor in Museums or     │
│         Other Publishing             │
└─────────────────────────────────────┘

┌─────────────────────────────────────┐
│              College                 │
└─────────────────────────────────────┘
```

Position Description

Museums produce a great deal of written material, and in a large institution there is usually an Editor responsible for supervising the creation of printed matter. In some cases the Editor is concerned only with scholarly and educational publications, leaving promotional and membership-related publishing to those departments. In other cases the Editor handles everything written that is prepared by the museum.

The Editor reads, corrects, rewrites, or revises the material under his or her supervision to ensure that it is presented clearly, in precise language and proper grammatical form. This requires a close working relationship with the director, curators, the public relations officer, and other museum professionals who generate publications. After editorial suggestions are made, the Editor is also responsible for proofreading copy and choosing a printing house.

The Editor works closely with the museum designer or a freelancer if there is no full-time designer to adapt the institution's overall graphic image to each specific project. The Editor might also be responsible for carrying out the search for photographic material to illustrate a publication, or may be asked to commission the museum photographer or freelancer to make photographs for a publication. The Editor must manage copyright procedures for museum publications and also apply for Library of Congress catalogue listings. If a publication involves an outside author, the Editor may act as liaison with him or her.

More and more frequently major museums are publishing their catalogues in conjunction with a university or art press. The Editor must attempt to create this sort of partnership and carry through on it. He or she may also be involved with distributing museum publications, especially catalogues of the important exhibitions, by publishing a promotional newsletter with listings of available books.

In addition the Editor may:

• prepare public relations releases about upcoming publications
• write a great deal of copy for the museum, from promotional texts to essays in art history
• advise the Curator of Education on lecture programs
• edit a journal published by the museum

Salaries

Editors make on the average between $22,000 and $35,000 and some earn upwards of $55,000.

Employment Prospects

Both editorial and museum work are highly desirable individually, so their combination can be even more competitive. A prospective Editor needs to have not only an expert grasp of grammar, but also a considerable knowledge of art history. Not every museum has a separate publications department, which makes available opportunities even fewer.

Advancement Prospects

Unless the Editor has curatorial ambitions, there are not many places he or she can move within the museum. Managing a large publications department, however, can prepare the Editor for a better job in publishing, either in a university setting or with a company that specializes in art publications. The Editor might also obtain a job as a magazine or journal editor on an art publication.

Education

The Editor should have a degree in either English or journalism, with significant coursework in the area of the museum's specialization, or a degree in art history, with demonstrated technical language skills.

Experience and Skills

Although editorial work requires an expert knowledge of grammar, an excellent grasp of stylistic form, and the ability to use language precisely, a good Editor must have more than this technical knowledge. He or she must have the ability to understand the intention of the author and, when necessary, rephrase his or her words so they read more precisely. This usually requires an excellent knowledge of the field under consideration as well as superior writing skills. The Editor must be able to proofread accurately, be thoroughly aware of copyright law, and be familiar with the publishing industry, preferably with experience at an outside press. Experience in distributing special-interest books is valuable.

HEAD OF PUBLIC PROGRAMMING

CAREER PROFILE

Duties: Organize and administer museum lectures, symposia, workshops, and gallery talks

Salary Range: $20,000 to $40,000

Employment Prospects: Poor to fair

Advancement Prospects: Good

Prerequisites:
   Education—Undergraduate degree in art history; graduate degree is a benefit
   Experience—Background in research and administration; very good academic knowledge of the field
   Special Skills—Good ability to get along with people, excellent organizational skills and speaking style

CAREER LADDER

```
┌─────────────────────────────────┐
│      Curator of Education        │
└─────────────────────────────────┘

┌─────────────────────────────────┐
│   Head of Public Programming     │
└─────────────────────────────────┘

┌─────────────────────────────────┐
│      Lecturer or College or      │
│        Graduate Training         │
└─────────────────────────────────┘
```

Position Description

The Head of Public Programming plans, organizes, and implements the museum's lectures, symposia, workshops, gallery talks, and other academic events. In most museums lectures interpret and enrich the institution's permanent collection, or temporary exhibitions, so the Head of Public Programming must monitor curatorial planning and stay abreast of the issues relevant to the museum's areas of interest, and the academic experts working in those areas. In smaller museums, a curator may have responsibility for public programs.

Most museums program several types of lecture events, meant to appeal to a variety of audiences. Typically, gallery talks by curators, artists, or art historians are frequently available for museum visitors. Special lectures by experts are organized for audiences interested in issues of art history and criticism; and academic symposia may be presented for a highly trained audience of art historians and curators. Courses and workshops in areas relevant to the museum's collections are offered to people interested in learning more about art. The Head of Public Programming must be adept at identifying these different audiences and tailoring programs to their interests. He or she must also be able to find appropriate speakers for each context.

After designing a policy for public programming in cooperation with the curator for education and the curatorial staff, the Head of Public Programming is responsible for implementing his or her events. After initial research to identify potential speakers, the Head of Public Programming contacts them to negotiate fees and conditions of the lecture or event. He or she is responsible for preparing promotional materials, arranging for the use of audiovisual equipment, and entertaining visiting lecturers.

The Head of Public Programming is one of the most academic positions within a museum. He or she must keep up with the latest developments in the museum's fields of interest, and maintain a network of contacts among art historians, artists, and critics.

In addition the Head of Public Programming may:

* document lecture events through written transcripts or videotapes
* teach or lecture in gallery talks and courses
* supervise museum docents if there is no docent coordinator
* design interpretive materials for museum galleries, like brochures, interactive computer programs, web sites, or videotapes

Salaries

Although salaries can be as low as $18,000, they average between $20,000 and $30,000 and can be as high as $40,000.

Employment Prospects

The Head of Public Programming is one of the most desirable positions in the museum; it combines a significant involvement in art history and contact with experts in the field. Competition is very stiff. Applicants must have extensive knowledge of the museum's areas of interest as well as academic or critical contacts. Excellent writing skills and previously published works are helpful.

Advancement Prospects

The Head of Public Programming has good prospects for becoming the curator of education. It is also possible, depending upon his or her interests and the structure of the museum, for the Head of Public Programming to enter the curatorial area. Lecture programs can be an innovative aspect of the museum's activities, so it is possible to distinguish oneself in this field.

Education

An undergraduate degree in art history or a related field is necessary, and an advanced degree in a similar area of museum studies or museum education is an advantage—in some museums, a requirement.

Experience/Skills

The Head of Public Programming must be adept at all kinds of research, both academic and informal. He or she must be able to grasp concepts perceptively and quickly. Since the Head of Public Programming works closely with experts in many fields related to the museum's work, strong communications skills are necessary. This position also requires excellent writing skills and the ability to work efficiently and quickly. Since the Head of Public Programming handles the administrative details of organizing lectures, paying lecturers, assisting with publicizing their talks, and providing special audiovisual aids, he or she must be an effective administrator.

EXHIBIT DESIGNER

CAREER PROFILE

Duties: Design installations of permanent museum galleries and temporary exhibitions

Salary Range: $25,000 to $35,000+

Employment Prospects: Fair to good

Advancement Prospects: Fair to good

Prerequisites:
    Education—Degree in graphic or industrial design, or environmental architecture
    Experience—Background in exhibit design
    Special Skills—Sensitivity to art; excellent knowledge of graphic design styles and techniques

CAREER LADDER

```
┌─────────────────────────────────────────┐
│   Chief Curator or Director of Finance    │
└─────────────────────────────────────────┘

┌─────────────────────────────────────────┐
│            Exhibit Designer               │
└─────────────────────────────────────────┘

┌─────────────────────────────────────────┐
│      College or Assistant Designer        │
└─────────────────────────────────────────┘
```

Position Description

Museums interpret works of art in many different ways. One of the most direct is through gallery installations which either establish connections between related artworks or create a chronological or historical context on written wall labels or in other types of documentation. Although in small and even medium-size museums curators typically design exhibitions, most large museums employ an Exhibit Designer whose job it is to translate curatorial and educational ideas into gallery installations.

Especially when a museum is planning a large temporary exhibition, or an installation of objects from the permanent collection, the Exhibit Designer must work closely with curators to translate their concept to the galleries. After consultations, the Exhibit Designer creates preliminary plans, renderings, and scale models, showing the configuration of walls to be built in the gallery space, placement of works, and any special pedestals, cabinets, or cases that need to be fabricated for the exhibition. The Exhibit Designer decides on the color to be used on gallery walls and works with the graphic designer to create signs for the exhibition.

Not only must the Exhibit Designer have a highly refined understanding of art objects and how they interact with one another in terms of color and scale, but he or she must also be aware of the principles of conservation and preservation of artworks so that they may be installed with proper light and safety precautions. The Exhibit Designer works closely with the preparator and his or her crew to fabricate special

exhibition cabinets, cases, pedestals, or display tables; a knowledge of and experience with the techniques of exhibit production is thus necessary.

The Exhibit Designer supervises the installation of the exhibition or permanent installation and designs proper lighting once artworks are in place. Lighting art objects correctly is a special skill in which the Exhibit Designer must be expert. He or she may also be involved with designing special educational presentations, like an orientation room or didactic gallery space.

In addition the Exhibit Designer may:

- act as graphic designer for the museum
- personally fabricate special exhibition materials like cabinets and display cases
- manage the budget for gallery installations

Salaries

An Exhibit Designer makes an average salary between $25,000 and $35,000, but may make as much as $60,000 in a large museum.

Employment Prospects

Only medium- and large-sized museums employ full-time Exhibit Designers, so positions are limited and usually require considerable experience. With an appropriate degree and a portfolio of relevant design, work prospects are fair.

Advancement Prospects

Since the Exhibit Designer must synthesize many skills—a sensitivity to art history, a practical knowledge of design, and an awareness of fabrication techniques—a good one has excellent chances to advance to a better job in a different museum or to launch a freelance career.

Education

A degree or certificate in graphic design, industrial design, commercial arts, or architecture and interior design is necessary. Coursework in studio arts, typography, and theater design is beneficial.

Experience and Skills

The Exhibit Designer must be able to take a concept from the curator of an exhibition or permanent installation and translate it into a coherent, appealing presentation. This requires an excellent grasp of art concepts and the ability to make refined aesthetic judgments, as well as excellent communications skills and the ability to compromise. The Exhibit Designer must know how to make renderings and scale models as well as how to fabricate actual exhibition furnishings like cabinets and pedestals. He or she needs a working knowledge of conservation principles and a familiarity with lighting design. Since the Exhibit Designer often supervises the preparator and his or her crew and manages the budget for an installation, he or she must have good administrative skills.

GRAPHIC DESIGNER

CAREER PROFILE

Duties: Design printed materials and museum signs

Salary Range: $22,000 to $35,000+

Employment Prospects: Fair

Advancement Prospects: Fair

Prerequisites:
  Education—Undergraduate degree in graphic arts
  Experience—Background in designing a range of publications
  Special Skills—Knowledge of art history; creativity

CAREER LADDER

```
┌─────────────────────────────────┐
│       Director of Finance       │
└─────────────────────────────────┘

┌─────────────────────────────────┐
│        Graphic Designer         │
└─────────────────────────────────┘

┌─────────────────────────────────┐
│   College or Assistant Designer │
└─────────────────────────────────┘
```

Position Description

Museums publish in several formats. Invitations to openings and special events, newsletters, calendars, didactic brochures, and exhibition catalogues are all important marketing and educational tools. In a large- or medium-size museum with a good deal of publishing activity, an in-house Designer helps to manage design and printing and works to create a unified graphic image for the museum.

In most museums several different departments prepare written materials for museum members, visitors, and the general public. It is important that the Graphic Designer balance the objectives of each publication with the need to establish a coherent graphic image for the institution. This is a primary public relations and marketing strategy which enhances the museum's visibility in the community. The Graphic Designer may work with the director and other high-level management of the museum to develop general design principles which are followed in all of the museum's printed materials.

To develop an appropriate design, the Graphic Designer works on each printed piece with the person in charge of the project. This usually involves a preliminary presentation of ideas followed by more developed mock-ups of the piece submitted for final approval. In a complex project like a newsletter or exhibition catalogue, the preliminary development of a design may take several weeks. The Graphic Designer then negotiates with printers and supervises the reproduction and printing of the piece. He or she must create a schedule for the production of all museum publications and be sure that deadlines are met. The Graphic Designer

usually supervises the museum photographer, who contributes photographs to the publications.

With curators and the exhibition designer, the Graphic Designer conceives all printed materials accompanying an exhibition, like didactic wall labels, object labels, and special graphics for title walls. Often, large museums advertise their major exhibitions with banners on the front of the building or at other sites throughout the city. The Graphic Designer is responsible for creating these materials.

In addition, the Graphic Designer may:

- design print advertisements for the museum
- assist in designing exhibitions if there is no exhibit designer
- work with outside advertising agencies on special promotional campaigns for the museum
- design museum stationery and other office materials

Salaries

A museum Graphic Designer will average a salary between $22,000 and $35,000 and may make as much as $60,000 in a large museum with a busy publications program. Even museums without a full-time Graphic Designer need design services. Freelance fees can range from $40 to $150 per hour.

Employment Prospects

Since the business of museums is art, it takes a special designer to create an appropriate graphic image for this kind of institution. Experience with a wide variety of publications is a great benefit, as is a sensitivity to art. Since many designers find museum work attractive, competition is tough.

Advancement Prospects

If there is only one Graphic Designer in a museum, there is little chance of advancement. However, doing design work for an arts organization is a good way to gain freelance jobs elsewhere, or advance to a job with more responsibility in another museum.

Education

An undergraduate or graduate degree in graphic design is absolutely necessary. A liberal arts degree or coursework in art history is invaluable.

Experience and Skills

Excellent design skills and a knowledge of every aspect of the production process of printed materials is essential. Supplementary art classes or art history are useful. Since this job includes a good deal of organizational responsibility and interaction with museum staff as well as outside vendors, the Graphic Designer must have excellent communications skills. As in all areas of graphic design the ability to understand a client's intention and articulate his or her visual ideas is of the utmost importance.

LIBRARIAN

CAREER PROFILE

Duties: Manage the museum's library of books and slides

Salary Range: $22,000 to $45,000+

Employment Prospects: Fair

Advancement Prospects: Fair

Prerequisites:
    Education—Advanced degree in library science, undergraduate degree in art history or related field
    Experience—Background in library work, knowledge of art history
    Special Skills—Excellent research skills, knowledge of foreign languages

CAREER LADDER

```
┌─────────────────────────────────────┐
│   Director or Chief Curator or       │
│       Director of Finance            │
└─────────────────────────────────────┘

┌─────────────────────────────────────┐
│            Librarian                 │
└─────────────────────────────────────┘

┌─────────────────────────────────────┐
│   College or Assistant Librarian     │
└─────────────────────────────────────┘
```

Position Description

Many large museums maintain their own library as an in-house resource for the curators and the education staff as well as for visiting museum professionals, scholars, and members of the general public. The Librarian administers the museum library, manages the acquisition and cataloguing of books, periodicals, and manuscripts, and performs a variety of services related to written or visual materials for the museum staff.

The Librarian must keep abreast of the materials published in the museum's areas of concentration. Often the library includes not only books and magazines but also visual resources like slides, black-and-white photographs, and videotapes, which may be used by members of the education staff to illustrate lectures, or by curators as aids in organizing exhibitions. Often the Librarian is asked by members of curatorial departments to conduct background research for a particular exhibition or special project. In some cases the Librarian is also the curator of a museum's graphics or illustrated book collection.

A museum's archives are usually catalogued and preserved in its library. Materials like exhibition files, correspondence, transcripts of lectures, and museum publications form an important resource for art historians as well as the museum staff. The Librarian controls access to this information and also develops copyright and reproduction policy for archival material. He or she may be called upon to answer the inquiries of scholars or art critics into the museum's history.

The Librarian may also work closely with the registrar to catalogue the institution's collections. He or she can assist staff members who edit museum publications by verifying facts or helping with copyediting and proofreading.

In addition the Librarian may:

- publish articles interpreting the museum's archives or publish actual documents
- advise the public relations staff about museum history on the occasion of special anniversaries or celebrations
- assist curators in organizing special exhibitions or in preparing didactic materials for them

Salaries

On the average, museum Librarians make between $22,000 and $45,000, but salaries can reach $65,000.

Employment Prospects

Generally only large museums maintain their own libraries, so opportunities are limited. Moreover, it is necessary that the Librarian have considerable knowledge of art history as well as training in library sciences. Even with appropriate education competition is tough.

Advancement Prospects

As in many areas of museum work, once one has broken into an area, prospects for advancement are fair. There may be only one Librarian in a museum, so movement up the ladder may mean a job in a large museum or another art library. It is also possible that the Librarian may move into a curatorial or registrarial position, depending upon his or her ambitions and skills.

Education

An advanced degree in library science is necessary and an undergraduate degree in art history is highly desirable. Coursework in computer systems and in writing or English is helpful.

Experience and Skills

The Librarian must have excellent research skills, including the ability to provide bibliographic support and familiarity with computerized information services. Knowledge of a foreign language is a great asset. He or she must be completely versed in the aspects of librarianship: acquisitions, cataloguing, reference, and administration. A broad knowledge of art history is invaluable, as is the ability to handle detail skillfully.

Organizations and Associations

The professional association for librarians is the American Library Association (see Appendix V).

PHOTOGRAPHER

CAREER PROFILE

Duties: Photograph art objects and museum installations

Salary Range: $22,000 to $35,000

Employment Prospects: Poor to fair

Prerequisites:
Education—Technical training in studio photography
Experience—Background in photographing works of art
Special Skills—Sensitivity to art objects; knowledge of lighting; versatility

CAREER LADDER

```
┌─────────────────────────────┐
│      Registrar or           │
│    Director of Finance      │
└─────────────────────────────┘

┌─────────────────────────────┐
│        Photographer         │
└─────────────────────────────┘

┌─────────────────────────────┐
│      College or             │
│   Assistant Photographer    │
└─────────────────────────────┘
```

Position Description

Most large museums maintain a staff Photographer who produces documentary photographs of the museum's collection and installation photographs of its exhibitions. It is extraordinarily difficult to photograph art in such a way that the color, scale, and presence of an object is conveyed in a single picture, so the Photographer must be sensitive to the original works and expert in lighting and other technical aspects of photography.

Every work of art a museum owns must be photographed for the registrar's records; in some cases, several pictures of a single object are required to communicate its essence. If an object is damaged, the Photographer must photograph the damaged area of the work for insurance purposes. Museum Photographers usually document temporary exhibitions by taking slides of gallery installations. In a contemporary museum he or she may also provide pictures of empty galleries for artists who will make a site-specific installation.

In addition to these ongoing tasks, the Photographer is regularly called upon to work on special projects. In some instances, he or she may research or rephotograph old pictures to be used as explanatory material in an exhibition. The Photographer plays an important role in museum publications by preparing illustrations for exhibition catalogues, newsletters, and promotional literature. The Photographer may also be called upon to produce educational slide shows for the public or document events at the museum, like members' openings, benefit parties, or special lectures.

The Photographer works closely with the museum's designer and public relations officer to maintain a visual record of what has happened at the museum. Usually he or she is responsible for maintaining the photographic files of programs and events sponsored by the institution. The Photographer must also run the museum's darkroom, including maintenance and purchase of equipment and materials.

In addition the Photographer may:

• assist in designing museum publications
• assist curators in obtaining photographs and conducting photographic research
• assist in developing newspaper or magazine advertisements for the museum

Salaries

Many museum Photographers, especially those who work for small institutions, are employed on a freelance basis, making from $150 to $375 per day. Although this may sound lucrative, the museum may need a photographer's services only a few days every month. Staff photographers employed full time make between $22,000 and $35,000, depending upon the extent of their responsibilities.

Employment Prospects

Generally only large museums with significant collections or a very active publications program employ a full-time Photographer. Since the pay scale for a museum Photographer is relatively low, it is possible to get a museum job on moderate experience. Some past work with art objects is essential.

Advancement Prospects

Unless the Photographer has a good deal of art-historical knowledge, or another type of skill attractive to the museum, it is unlikely that he or she will be able to advance within the organization. However, once a Photographer has worked for an institution it is easier to get freelance work from artists, galleries, or other museums. For someone interested in the arts, a job as a museum photographer is a good first step toward a freelance career. If the Photographer has design skills he or she may advance to the position of museum designer.

Education

Although a college degree in photography or liberal arts is attractive, a high school diploma and certified technical training in photography, with an emphasis on studio photography and the use of large-format equipment, is sufficient. Apprenticeship training may be acceptable or desirable.

Experience and Skills

Some experience in commercial photography and processing as well as studio experience is necessary. Since the Photographer often works on several projects at once, good organizational and administrative skills will come in handy. Familiarity with art history and experience handling art objects are invaluable to a museum Photographer. Since he or she often works under tight deadlines, it is important for the Photographer to be efficient, tactful, and coolheaded. Knowing how to manage a darkroom is also a necessary skill.

PREPARATOR

CAREER PROFILE

Duties: Install temporary and permanent installations

Alternate Title: Installation Manager

Salary Range: $22,000 to $40,000+

Employment Prospects: Fair

Advancement Prospects: Fair

Prerequisites:
Education—Undergraduate degree preferred; training in carpentry
Experience—Background in handling and installing art; excellent carpentry skills
Special Skills—Problem-solving ability, good interpersonal skills

CAREER LADDER

```
┌─────────────────────────────────┐
│  Registrar or Chief Curator or   │
│      Director of Finance         │
└─────────────────────────────────┘

┌─────────────────────────────────┐
│           Preparator             │
└─────────────────────────────────┘

┌─────────────────────────────────┐
│      Exhibition Technician       │
└─────────────────────────────────┘
```

Position Description

The Preparator is responsible for physically installing works of art in permanent installations or temporary exhibitions as well as constructing any cabinetry, pedestals, or temporary walls necessary. He or she works closely with the exhibition designer, conservator, and registrar to ensure the safe arrival of works of art in the galleries and their proper installation. When objects in the museum's collection travel (for a temporary exhibition elsewhere) the Preparator is usually responsible for building crates to protect them during transport.

In preparation for an installation in the galleries, the Preparator receives instructions or detailed plans from the museum's exhibition designer or, in a smaller museum, the curator responsible. He or she orders paint, lumber, hardware, and other materials necessary for the installation and begins any construction that can be done in advance. Once works of art begin to arrive the Preparator transports them to the galleries or to museum storage until installation occurs. He or she is also responsible for preparing objects for exhibition. For instance, if a portfolio of photographs arrives, the Preparator will prepare mats for them and then frame them, or exhibit them under a piece of Plexiglas or glass.

No matter how well planned an installation is, it is always a hectic time when instructions from the designer and curator must be realized under a strict deadline. The Preparator works with a crew which he or she hires, usually part time, and must be adept at assigning tasks to them so that the many details associated with a museum installation are carried out efficiently. In addition to hanging paintings, installing sculptures, or framing photographs, the Preparator is often responsible for fabricating didactic materials like object labels or documentary photographs.

The Preparator must work in concert with the registrar to log incoming and outgoing objects and assess their condition. When an institution has no conservator, the Preparator will usually have some knowledge of conservation techniques. Even when there is someone in this position, the Preparator can assist in restoring or treating art objects. The Preparator supervises, stocks, and maintains the budget for the museum workshop and should have excellent carpentry skills.

In addition the Preparator may:

• assist the registrar in arranging transportation for art objects
• assist in building maintenance, especially carpentry
• participate in the planning stages of an installation in order to help curators design installations
• work directly with an artist to prepare an exhibition of his or her work

Salaries

The Preparator makes between $22,000 and $40,000 and can make a higher salary in a major museum.

Employment Prospects

Employment prospects are fair. It is necessary that a Preparator have experience in handling art objects and excellent carpentry skills. One way of improving one's chances for this position is to work on the installation crew in order to learn the necessary skills. In larger museums the Preparator and his or her crew are union workers, so jobs are a bit harder to get.

Advancement Prospects

A Preparator who develops skills as a conservator or registrar may have the opportunity to advance to one of these positions.

Education

Training in carpentry is necessary. Coursework in art history, art conservation, museum management, or graphic design is helpful.

Experience and Skills

In addition to excellent knowledge of carpentry, the Preparator should have versatile problem-solving skills. He or she must be well acquainted with the hardware associated with installing works of art as well as the various techniques available. A professional knowledge of painting and framing is desirable. The Preparator must manage a crew effectively, so the ability to work efficiently and divide responsibility is imperative, as is the capacity to work well with other museum professionals. Some knowledge of budget management is desirable.

MEMBERSHIP OFFICER

CAREER PROFILE

Duties: Recruit and record museum members, plan special events for them

Alternate Titles: Director of Membership, Membership Secretary

Salary Range: $19,000 to $45,000+

Employment Prospects: Fair to good

Advancement Prospects: Fair

Prerequisites:

Education—Undergraduate degree in business, marketing, or related field

Experience—Background in marketing, managing special events

Special Skills—Good organizational skills, excellent interpersonal abilities

CAREER LADDER

```
+-----------------------------------+
|      Director of Development      |
+-----------------------------------+

+-----------------------------------+
|        Membership Officer         |
+-----------------------------------+

+-----------------------------------+
|  Department Assistant or College  |
+-----------------------------------+
```

Position Description

A museum's membership is one of its basic sources of support. For a yearly fee, members receive information about exhibitions and programs, discounts on special activities, and free admission to the galleries. The Membership Officer is responsible for recruiting members and managing the planning and promotion of special members' events and educational programs, such as classes, films, workshops, on-line activities, lectures, and openings.

Usually the Membership Officer reports to the director of development and is considered part of the fund-raising staff. However, in most museums, he or she works closely with the curator for education to provide educational as well as social experiences for museum members. In order to recruit new supporters, most museums print an informational brochure edited and written by the Membership Officer which describes the institution's areas of activity and special programs. This form of promotion is supplemented by direct-mail campaigns aimed at groups likely to join the museum. The Membership Officer must stay abreast of current marketing techniques and design effective ongoing promotions. He or she may also develop and deliver slide presentations about the museum to interested community groups.

The Membership Officer also coordinates special auxiliary or volunteer committees of the museum. He or she works with these groups to plan special events like lectures or benefit parties which contribute to the fund-raising effort of the institution. In many museums the Membership Officer is a position which requires a good deal of socializing with high-level museum supporters.

The administrative tasks involved with maintaining lists of members and potential members, direct-mail campaigns, mailings of newsletters and other information to members, maintaining a web site for members, as well as sending renewal letters when memberships lapse, are among the responsibilities of the Membership Officer. More and more frequently, museums are using sophisticated computer systems to maintain contact with their membership.

In addition the Membership Officer may:

- design and maintain a members' lounge in the museum
- assist the public relations officer in editing the museum's newsletter or web site
- advise on marketing campaigns which may take place in other areas of the museum

Salaries

In some museums the Membership Officer is a low-level administrative position whose responsibilities are primarily clerical. Salaries in that case are as low as $19,000 and may rise to $25,000. When the Membership Officer has more substantive development responsibilities, salaries can be much higher.

Employment Prospects

Especially in a small museum, the Membership Officer can be an entry-level position with few requirements for special skills. Since the job is often one with high turnover, positions open up for people who are interested in the arts and who have a good head for detail. As museums focus more on earned income potential, Membership Officers will need more formal training in marketing and competition will increase.

Advancement Prospects

The Membership Officer has a fair chance of advancement within the museum. If he or she runs a successful recruitment campaign, attracts high-level donors to the museum, and maintains a healthy membership in general, then the Membership Officer has a chance to advance to director of development. However, if responsibilities are primarily clerical, the potential for advancement is minimal.

Education

An undergraduate degree in business, public relations, marketing, public administration, or liberal arts is appropriate for this position. Coursework in art history is preferred, and secretarial skills and proficiency on a computer are necessary.

Experience and Skills

It is important that the Membership Officer have a broad familiarity with nonprofit fund-raising. Knowledge of marketing techniques and the potential for using computers in a museum context is helpful. Since the Membership Officer is a liaison with the public, he or she should be comfortable both talking on the phone and explaining the programs and policies of the museum to groups. Writing skills and a knowledge of art history are critical.

GRANTS OFFICER

CAREER PROFILE

Duties: Process grant applications to government agencies, foundations, and corporations

Alternate Titles: Development Associate, Assistant Director of Development

Salary Range: $22,000 to $35,000

Employment Prospects: Fair

Advancement Prospects: Good

Prerequisites:
  Education—Undergraduate degree in arts administration or liberal arts
  Experience—Background in grant writing and fundraising
  Special Skills—Excellent writing and organizational ability

CAREER LADDER

```
┌─────────────────────────────────┐
│      Director of Development     │
└─────────────────────────────────┘

┌─────────────────────────────────┐
│          Grants Officer          │
└─────────────────────────────────┘

┌─────────────────────────────────┐
│     Department Assistant or      │
│             College              │
└─────────────────────────────────┘
```

Position Description

The Grants Officer is responsible for processing grant applications to government agencies, foundations, and corporations. He or she also assists with or writes applications and maintains a reference library of potential funding sources, their guidelines and deadlines. Since most granting agencies require absolute compliance with their guidelines, the Grants Officer must be highly organized and attentive to detail. Responsibilities include typing, filing, and other clerical duties related to grant applications.

In addition to program descriptions, government grants require a project budget, general financial information on the museum, and materials to illustrate the artistic content of the proposal, like slides, reviews, videotapes, or records. The Grants Officer is responsible for gleaning the appropriate information from both the financial and curatorial staff. He or she must be able to coordinate a complex variety of information from several sources while under pressure to maintain deadlines. This requires tact, patience, and organizational skills.

With the guidance of the director of development, to whom the Grants Officer reports, he or she must analyze potential funding sources to determine which of the museum's programs, if any, might be funded by them.

This means obtaining and reading government funding agency guidelines, foundation annual reports and fundraising newsletters to learn more about potential donors, and then following up on this information through telephone interviews with potential funders. Although grant project descriptions are typically written by the curatorial or other staff member who has conceived the project, the Grants Officer edits these proposals and tailors them to the priorities of a particular granting agency. Often several different proposals to different funders may be submitted for a single project.

Most granting agencies require the museum to submit a report describing how the grant was spent. The Grants Officer must keep these records up to date and complete. He or she must also monitor requests for payment from the granting agency once the grant has been received.

In addition the Grants Officer may:

- participate in informational meetings held by funding agencies
- assist the director of development in running special fundraising campaigns
- provide secretarial support for the director of development

Salaries

Depending upon experience and responsibility, the Grants Officer makes between $22,000 and $35,000.

Employment Prospects

The Grants Officer can be an entry-level position in the museum which combines exposure to all departments of the organization with good administrative experience. Prospects are best in a small museum where the Grants Officer is a crucial member of the fund-raising team.

Advancement Prospects

Advancement prospects for the Grants Officer are quite good, especially since the position is a key liaison among the development, financial, and curatorial departments. Inevitably, activity will go beyond the processing of grants into other aspects of fund-raising, preparing the Grants Officer to become a director of development. As in all fund-raising jobs, success is measured by dollars earned, so a person in this position who creatively matches programs with appropriate funding sources will be greatly valued. Often the Grants Officer in a museum can advance to a position in a government or corporate funding agency.

Education

A degree in arts administration is desirable but not essential for this position. Coursework in art history, especially in the areas covered by the museum, is important, as are excellent writing skills. Secretarial training and proficiency on a word processor are valuable qualifications.

Experience and Skills

Familiarity with the procedures of government grants or in foundation administration is invaluable for a Grants Officer. He or she must be skilled in analyzing complex instructions and guidelines and in answering questions precisely. It is absolutely necessary that the Grants Officer be sensitive to the artistic goals and programs of the museum and be able to articulate them concisely and persuasively. Organizational skills are crucial in this job, which often calls upon the Grants Officer to process several different grants at once. He or she must be able to develop systems for processing information quickly and accurately in order to meet deadlines, and must also maintain files of the museum's fund-raising activity. A basic knowledge of accounting and the budget-making process is necessary.

DIRECTOR OF DEVELOPMENT

CAREER PROFILE

Duties: Plan and implement the museum's fund-raising strategy

Alternate Titles: Development Officer, Assistant Director for Fund-raising

Salary Range: $30,000 to $95,000

Employment Prospects: Fair

Advancement Prospects: Fair to good

Prerequisites:

Education—Undergraduate degree in business, arts administration, or marketing

Experience—Extensive background in all areas of fund-raising

Special Skills—Excellent social skills, good writing ability and knowledge of art history

CAREER LADDER

```
┌─────────────────────────────────┐
│            Director             │
└─────────────────────────────────┘

┌─────────────────────────────────┐
│     Director of Development     │
└─────────────────────────────────┘

┌─────────────────────────────────┐
│         Grants Officer          │
└─────────────────────────────────┘
```

Position Description

As in all nonprofit organizations, fund-raising is crucial to a museum's financial health. The Director of Development, who is in charge of raising money from government, private, and corporate sources, designs and implements fund-raising strategy. This job involves a great deal of pressure since, no matter how well-planned or intelligent his or her efforts are, the Director of Development cannot be sure they will meet with success. Regardless of the hit-or-miss quality of the job, development professionals are primarily evaluated on their performance, and an organization depends on their bringing in a certain percentage of the annual budget's funding.

In most museums the Director of Development supervises a grants officer, who prepares proposals to government agencies, foundations, and corporations, and a membership officer, who works with auxiliary support groups and the general museum membership. While much of the day-to-day business of fund-raising is handled by these members of the department, the Director of Development is often out on the road meeting with the administrators of corporations and foundations and high-level individual supporters of the museum. It is more often through direct lobbying rather than letters and written proposals that the museum wins new benefactors. The Director of Development must blend a knowledge of museum programs with a persuasive, appealing social presentation.

In addition to this ongoing activity, the Director of Development plans and launches special fund-raising projects, like membership drives, endowment or building appeals, and special benefits. To implement a fund-raising campaign the Director of Development works with key members of the museum's board of trustees to set goals and a strategy for appealing to donors.

Directors of Development must be creative, hardworking professionals. They must understand the sometimes unreasonable demands made on them from within the museum's staff to raise money, and must compete with other arts organizations for limited private and public funds.

In addition, the Director of Development may:

- supervise earned income or marketing efforts
- assist in developing the annual budget
- prepare the museum's annual report
- coordinate activities of the board of trustees

Salaries

Since Directors of Development raise money, they are usually among the best-paid museum professionals. Although a

Director of Development can make as little as $30,000 in a small museum, most make more, depending on the size of the organization. Some Directors of Development make as much as $95,000.

Employment Prospects

Because of the pressure involved as well as the ever-present possibility that a Director of Development will not raise his or her portion of the operating budget, there is a reasonable amount of turnover in fund-raising positions. However, fund-raising, which includes a great deal of socializing and contact with the wealthy, is for many a glamorous and appealing job. So even though opportunities may open up frequently, competition is tough. Since fund-raising is both crucial to museum operations and difficult to guarantee, a professional with a proven track record has a great advantage.

Advancement Prospects

Since the Director of Development is the head of a department, his or her primary path of advancement within the museum is to director of finance, if this is a superior position, or director. It is unlikely, however, that one could advance to the position of director without considerable expertise in the artistic areas of the museum. A fund-raising professional with a proven track record has a very good chance of moving into a position with more responsibility at another museum or arts organization.

Education

A degree in business, arts administration, public relations, or marketing is preferred, although a background in art history is also suitable. Coursework in writing and public speaking will come in handy.

Experience and Skills

The Director of Development must know how and where to look for funds. This means an awareness of corporate, government, and foundation sources which are appropriate to his or her organization, as well as the research skills to find new potential benefactors. Fund-raising professionals must be skilled in creating a network of colleagues and potential funders. Although the ability to adapt to virtually any social situation is a crucial skill, the Director of Development must also be able to understand and communicate the programs and goals of the museum, both verbally and in written form. On a practical level, he or she must be able to organize, implement, and supervise an effective fund-raising campaign, know how government and foundation grants are processed and evaluated, and be aware of the legal circumstances and tax benefits of individual giving.

DIRECTOR OF FINANCE

CAREER PROFILE

Duties: Responsibility for the museum's financial and personnel management policies and accounting procedures

Alternate Titles: Business Manager, Administrator

Salary Range: $30,000 to $85,000

Employment Prospects: Fair to good

Advancement Prospects: Fair

Prerequisites:

Education—Undergraduate degree in business or museum management; advanced degree preferred

Experience—Background in accounting, budget making and management, personnel management

Special Skills—Creativity in financial management, sensitivity to the special financial issues related to nonprofit organizations

CAREER LADDER

```
┌─────────────────────────────┐
│          Director           │
└─────────────────────────────┘

┌─────────────────────────────┐
│     Director of Finance     │
└─────────────────────────────┘

┌─────────────────────────────┐
│       Accountant or         │
│     Personnel Manager       │
└─────────────────────────────┘
```

Position Description

The Director of Finance is responsible for the museum's financial management. He or she typically develops an annual budget, supervises personnel and operation of the physical plant, handles legal issues, and maintains accounting procedures. Although the Director of Finance reports to the director, the position is often the top administrative post in a museum.

Since most museums receive a significant part of their income from foundations and public grants, the Director of Finance must be familiar with fund accounting and grants administration. Typically he or she works closely with the curatorial or development staff to prepare funding requests, and therefore must be aware of exhibition planning and collection management. Often the Director of Finance is also involved in maximizing the museum's earned income through store sales, food services, or direct-mail marketing.

In a large museum the Director of Finance can supervise hundreds of employees; even in a small institution, he or she must design and implement personnel policies, including salary guidelines, job descriptions, and benefit packages. The Director of Finance must oversee the maintenance and improvement of the museum building, including developing a plan for gallery guards and security as well as an insurance policy to cover collections, exhibited art, and the physical plant.

Managing the finances of a museum is a creative job which inevitably requires flexibility and a talent for compromise. The annual budget is an important planning tool for all departments and its preparation requires sensitivity to artistic as well as financial priorities. Most nonprofit organizations have at least occasional cash flow difficulties, and the Director of Finance must establish procedures to accommodate unpredictable situations.

In addition the Director of Finance may:

- hire and fire administrative personnel
- participate in planning and fund-raising for an endowment
- plan and automate office procedures including computer and telephone systems

Salaries

The Director of Finance is typically one of the best-paid employees in a museum. In a large institution, he or she can make as much as $85,000, although a small museum may pay as little as $30,000. Since Directors of Finance have skills that are transferable outside of the nonprofit world, their salaries must be competitive with analogous posts in business.

Employment Prospects

Museums desperately need creative financial managers who are willing to take on the challenges the nonprofit world presents. With training in business and a strong interest in working in the arts, prospects are good. It is easier to begin in a smaller institution where responsibilities might include fundraising and clerical work as well as financial planning. Organizational skills and a knowledge of accounting are crucial.

Advancement Prospects

The Director of Finance is in charge of one aspect of the museum's activity, so there is nowhere to advance within his or her department. It is possible to go on to the position of director, but this is unlikely unless the Director of Finance has considerable knowledge of art history and curatorial work. Chances are very good for a Director of Finance to advance to a better position in another museum or arts funding agency.

Education

An undergraduate degree in business or museum management is necessary, and an advanced degree in these fields is an advantage.

Experience and Skills

Since the budget is an important planning and administrative tool for the museum, the Director of Finance must be able to synthesize a complex set of needs and programs, drawing on many members of the museum's staff. He or she must be exceptionally creative in the approach to financial management and an adept manager of personnel. Although knowledge of accounting procedures is of primary importance, a sensitivity to art history and to the larger mission of the museum is invaluable.

DIRECTOR

CAREER PROFILE

Duties: Provide artistic, fund-raising, and financial direction for the museum, and represent its programs to the institution's board of trustees and the public

Alternate Title: Executive Director

Salary Range: $60,000 to $180,000

Employment Prospects: Poor

Advancement Prospects: Good

Prerequisites:

Education—Undergraduate and advanced degrees in art history

Experience—Extensive work experience in museums and demonstrated curatorial and fund-raising ability

Special Skills—Leadership ability; excellent planning skills, speaking skills, and interpersonal skills

CAREER LADDER

```
┌─────────────────────────┐
│        Director         │
└─────────────────────────┘

┌─────────────────────────┐
│      Chief Curator      │
└─────────────────────────┘

┌─────────────────────────┐
│         Curator         │
└─────────────────────────┘
```

Position Description

The Director of a museum gives conceptual form to its programs and collections. In doing so, he or she mediates between the governing body of the institution, or board of trustees, and the staff which implements programs. The Director must be adept at guiding museum trustees in their policymaking by representing his or her own attitudes and those of the staff. He or she must also be capable of leading museum employees to develop programs which meet the goals of the board of trustees in the areas of curatorial work, fund-raising, and financial management.

Depending on the size of the museum, and the structure of its financial department, the Director plays an important role in maintaining financial stability. This usually means a good deal of fund-raising within the community. With the director of development, the Director courts corporations, individuals, and government agencies to ensure required funding. As the most visible representative of the museum, the Director must be able to convey the goals of his or her organization to the community and the media. This includes a good deal of social activity as well as conversations with the press and, depending upon the size of the museum and its stature, local and regional government officials.

The Director usually has a distinguished expertise in one of the areas of specialization of the museum. In addition to his or her financial and policy responsibilities, the Director helps negotiate major curatorial projects, like international exchanges, the acquisition of major works of art, or gifts from important art collectors. He or she may also undertake the organization of exhibitions or other curatorial projects.

The balance of these broad responsibilities varies significantly from museum to museum, depending upon how the staff is structured and the interests of the Director. In some cases, he or she may leave daily operations and program issues largely in the hands of his or her staff in order to pursue major long-range goals for the museum, such as the expansion of the building or the creation of new areas of specialization.

As the leader of the museum, the Director must supervise all personnel issues, including hiring, firing, creating new positions, and structuring benefit plans for employees. Administrative duties are compounded by the necessity of keeping up to date with the plans and projects of key staff members and dealing with personnel-related issues of morale and employee incentives. Especially in a small museum, the success of the organization rests largely on the creativity, strength, and administrative know-how of the Director.

In addition the Director may:

- write an annual report for the museum
- take on honorary or advisory positions related to the museum's work in the community
- act as chief curator, especially in a small museum

Salaries

The average salary for a museum Director ranges from $60,000 to $80,000. As with most museum positions, however, salary is proportional to the size of the institution and can be as high as $180,000.

Employment Prospects

The position of Director is probably the most competitive post to attain in an extremely competitive field. Not only must a potential Director have distinguished him- or herself in an area of specialization covered by the museum, but he or she must also demonstrate an excellent track record for financial management and fund-raising. In most museums it is desirable for the Director to have charismatic appeal as well, and to have demonstrated effective policy making. The choice of a Director for a particular institution largely depends on the long-range goals of that institution. For instance, if the museum is planning an expanded building, then it is likely that a Director will be hired who has already ushered a museum through such a phase of expansion. In a small museum, a distinguished record as a chief curator may qualify a potential Director, but in many cases Directors are chosen from those who have already held the position in a similar institution.

Advancement Prospects

Once one has become a Director chances are reasonably good that he or she can gain a more prestigious directorship elsewhere. As with all museum work, however, a good repu-
tation is crucial to advancement, and the Director must be distinguished in the areas of curatorial work, fund-raising, and financial management. It is also possible that a museum Director might enter a related field as the Director of a state funding agency or another organization that sets policy in the arts.

Education

In virtually every case it is necessary for the Director to have an advanced degree in an area of the museum's specialization. Coursework in museum management and administration issues is desirable. Training in writing and communications is particularly helpful.

Experience and Skills

The museum Director must combine a persuasive, charismatic personality with excellent knowledge of art history in his or her field and superior management and financial abilities. This is a rare combination, so it is especially important that the Director knows his or her strengths and be able to structure a staff which takes full advantage of them and compensates for his or her weaknesses. The Director must have specialized knowledge of at least one area of the museum's collections, or in the management of a particular type of museum. He or she must have the ability to implement the policy established by the museum's governing body, and must encourage active participation—both financial and conceptual—from the board of trustees. He or she must be able to communicate long-range policy to the staff as well as to the community. A good working knowledge of both the budget-making process and the particular fiscal characteristics of nonprofit organizations is absolutely necessary, as is familiarity with the legal aspects of museum operation and with current and prospective legislation affecting museums.

ART GALLERIES

PREPARATOR

CAREER PROFILE

Duties: Prepare gallery for new shows; install exhibitions

Salary Range: $20,000 to $40,000

Employment Prospects: Fair

Advancement Prospects: Fair

Prerequisites:
  Education—Bachelor's degree preferred; carpentry training
  Experience—Art-handling experience required
  Special Skills—Carpentry; problem-solving skills

CAREER LADDER

```
+---------------------------+
|         Registrar         |
+---------------------------+

+---------------------------+
|         Preparator        |
+---------------------------+

+---------------------------+
|          Intern           |
+---------------------------+
```

Position Description

The Preparator is responsible for readying the gallery for new exhibitions and installing the artwork for those exhibitions. The Preparator may be called upon to construct walls or pedestals, alter lighting, paint, and crate and uncrate artwork.

It is important for the Preparator to know how to handle and light art properly. The safe unpacking, display, and repacking of artwork is done under the care of the Preparator.

The exhibit design is usually undertaken by the gallery owner or director; the Preparator carries out his/her instructions, sometimes with the help of a crew of temporary workers. Long hours must be logged before an opening, often requiring extensive travel time. The Preparator should be well organized and able to work under deadline pressure.

Salaries

The Preparator can earn from $20,000 to $40,000 a year, depending on his or her skills and on the gallery's size and location.

Employment Prospects

Chances for employment as a Preparator are fair. Competition is somewhat less intense for this position than for other gallery jobs because of the special skills required.

Advancement Prospects

The Preparator has a fair chance of advancing if he or she can gain some experience as a registrar. This would most commonly be done by making a lateral move into the registrar's position in a gallery.

Education

Preparators usually have bachelor's degrees, along with some kind of apprenticeship with a carpenter.

Experience and Skills

Previous gallery or museum experience is necessary to gain skill in the proper handling of artwork. Carpentry is the most important skill for a Preparator. He or she should also be a good problem solver and an organized person and have a good eye for art.

Organizations and Associations

Gallery employees may wish to join one of the many art dealers' associations (see Appendix V).

Tips for Entry

Those interested in becoming Preparators should look for part-time or volunteer work on installation crews in museums or art galleries.

ARCHIVIST

CAREER PROFILE

Duties: Prepare artist biographies; assemble bibliographies; handle curator relations; maintain photographic files of artwork

Alternate Title: Researcher

Salary Range: $18,000 to $35,000

Employment Prospects: Fair

Advancement Prospects: Fair

Prerequisites:
Education—Bachelor's degree required; art history background preferred; a master's degree is helpful
Experience—Previous work in a gallery or museum
Special Skills—Research and writing skills; organizational skills

CAREER LADDER

```
┌─────────────────────────────────┐
│           Registrar             │
└─────────────────────────────────┘

┌─────────────────────────────────┐
│           Archivist             │
└─────────────────────────────────┘

┌─────────────────────────────────┐
│   Receptionist or Student or    │
│             Intern              │
└─────────────────────────────────┘
```

Position Description

The Archivist handles many of the documentation functions of the gallery. He or she must research and keep files on the provenance of the gallery's artwork and must prepare biographies of the artists represented. The Archivist also works up bibliographies relating to works in the gallery. He or she maintains photo documentation files of the artwork.

The Archivist usually takes care of the gallery's relations with museum curators, who may request loans of artwork in the gallery's possession. In addition, the Archivist helps to prepare catalogues for gallery exhibitions.

In smaller galleries the Archivist's functions may be handled by the registrar.

Salaries

Compensation for Archivists ranges from $18,000 to $35,000 per year, depending on gallery size and location.

Employment Prospects

The chances of finding a job as an Archivist are fair. There are relatively few such positions available, but the job turnover rate is reasonably rapid.

Advancement Prospects

The Archivist has a fair chance of being promoted to another position within a gallery. Generally speaking, the Archivist can expect to spend some time working as a registrar before moving up to the job of gallery director.

Education

The Archivist must have a bachelor's degree, preferably with a major in art or art history, or a master's degree, which can be helpful.

Experience and Skills

Previous experience in an art gallery or museum is required of the prospective Archivist. The Archivist must have strong research and writing abilities. In addition, he or she should have excellent organizational skills for the recordkeeping aspects of the job.

Organizations and Associations

Archivists might wish to join one of the art dealers' organizations listed in Appendix V.

BUSINESS MANAGER

CAREER PROFILE

Duties: Handle bookkeeping, payroll, payables and receivables; order supplies

Alternate Title: Office Manager

Salary Range: $18,000 to $50,000

Employment Prospects: Fair

Advancement Prospects: Fair

Prerequisites:
Education—Bachelor's degree; accounting and business courses required
Experience—Bookkeeping
Special Skills—Detail orientation; organizational skills

CAREER LADDER

```
┌─────────────────────────────┐
│      Gallery Director        │
└─────────────────────────────┘

┌─────────────────────────────┐
│      Business Manager        │
└─────────────────────────────┘

┌─────────────────────────────┐
│    Registrar or Accountant   │
└─────────────────────────────┘
```

Position Description

The Business Manager of an art gallery is responsible for the smooth running of the gallery's accounts. He or she handles the bookkeeping, including payroll, accounts receivable, and accounts payable. The Business Manager usually does the purchasing of supplies, setting up a purchase order system.

Though the Business Manager has little direct involvement with customers and artists, he or she may assist clients on the telephone. The position offers good preparation for an individual who hopes eventually to become a gallery owner.

Salaries

The Business Manager can expect to make between $18,000 and $50,000, depending on the size and geographic location of the gallery and on his or her own level of expertise.

Employment Prospects

An individual with some gallery experience and some business background has a fair chance of finding a job as a Business Manager.

Advancement Prospects

Chances for advancement are fair. The Business Manager may find a position as a gallery director if he or she has a good deal of experience. Alternatively, the Manager could move into a registrar or archivist position in order to gain additional experience.

Education

The Business Manager should have a bachelor's degree with some background in both art and business. Any accounting coursework will be especially useful.

Experience and Skills

Bookkeeping experience is required of an aspiring Business Manager. Because the Business Manager is responsible for the business aspects of the gallery, he or she should be a well-organized, detail-oriented person.

Organizations and Associations

Gallery employees may wish to join one of the art dealers' organizations listed in Appendix V.

REGISTRAR

CAREER PROFILE	CAREER LADDER

Duties: Recordkeeping; tracking of artwork; appraising condition of pieces; complete familiarity with collection

Salary Range: $18,000 to $45,000

Employment Prospects: Fair

Advancement Prospects: Good

Prerequisites:
  Education—Bachelor's degree required; art history major preferred
  Experience—Previous gallery or museum work
  Special Skills—Administrative and organizational ability; strong computer skills are a must

```
┌─────────────────────────┐
│     Gallery Director     │
└─────────────────────────┘

┌─────────────────────────┐
│        Registrar         │
└─────────────────────────┘

┌─────────────────────────┐
│         Archivist        │
└─────────────────────────┘
```

Position Description

The Registrar is responsible for the tracking and maintenance of all artwork held by the gallery. This includes extensive recordkeeping relating to the works, their condition, and their history; tracking of the exact location of works as they move between warehouse and gallery and out on loan for exhibition; proper packing, transportation, and unpacking of works; and insurance of such pieces.

In addition, the Registrar may be involved in assisting customers, handling unsolicited materials from artists who wish to work with the gallery, or such archivist duties as catalogue preparation and research on specific pieces.

The Registrar must be completely familiar with all the gallery's holdings. The position of Registrar is a pivotal one within the gallery, as most higher positions are available only to persons who have strong Registrar experience.

Salaries

The Registrar can expect to make between $18,000 and $45,000 a year. Naturally, the higher salaries go to experienced Registrars in major art galleries.

Employment Prospects

The chances of finding a job as a Registrar are fair. Because Registrar experience is vital to people interested in both gallery and museum careers, the competition can be intense.

Advancement Prospects

An experienced Registrar has a good chance of advancing in his or her career. Having gained valuable Registrar experience, he or she becomes qualified for the position of gallery director or of Registrar at a larger gallery.

Education

A bachelor's degree, preferably in art history, is required by most galleries.

Experience and Skills

The aspiring Registrar should have some previous experience working in a museum or art gallery. It is important for the Registrar to have excellent administration skills. The Registrar oversees a large number of files that must be kept current and well organized.

Organizations and Associations

Gallery employees might wish to join one of the art dealers' organizations listed in Appendix V.

Tips for Entry

Because previous experience is so important for a Registrar, the job candidate should consider part-time or volunteer work at a gallery or museum. Secretarial or work-crew experience will be a plus on the resume, and the contacts made can be valuable.

GALLERY DIRECTOR

CAREER PROFILE

Duties: Manage gallery; assist customers; make sales; handle publicity; help plan shows

Salary Range: $30,000 to $80,000+

Employment Prospects: Fair

Advancement Prospects: Poor

Prerequisites:

Education—Bachelor's degree required; art background preferred; master's degree is helpful

Experience—Previous work as a registrar

Special Skills—Interpersonal skills; sales ability; art knowledge

CAREER LADDER

```
┌─────────────────────────────┐
│        Gallery Owner        │
└─────────────────────────────┘

┌─────────────────────────────┐
│       Gallery Director      │
└─────────────────────────────┘

┌─────────────────────────────┐
│          Registrar          │
└─────────────────────────────┘
```

Position Description

The Gallery Director is hired by the gallery owner to handle the day-to-day operations of the gallery. The owner determines the direction of the gallery, choosing artists and setting the themes for shows; the Director carries out the owner's wishes in preparing and presenting the shows.

The Director works with customers, assisting them and making sales. He or she must be familiar with the artwork inventory of the gallery and knowledgeable about the artists represented.

The Director usually handles publicity, mainly in the form of press releases regarding the openings of new exhibitions. He or she also manages the other employees of the gallery and deals with the gallery's artists in the owner's absence.

Because the preparation of a show can be hectic, the Director often works evenings and weekends.

Salaries

Salaries for Gallery Directors vary widely according to gallery size, geographic location and an individual's experience. The range of salaries is roughly from $30,000 to $80,000 per year.

Employment Prospects

Chances for employment as a Gallery Director are fair. Major cities have many galleries, and an individual with solid gallery experience should be able to find a Director's job.

Advancement Prospects

There is little opportunity to advance from the position of Gallery Director unless one has the capital to open a gallery of his or her own.

Education

Most Gallery Directors have bachelor's degrees. The usual majors are art and art history, but requirements are generally not strict; any liberal arts background is acceptable.

Experience and Skills

A Gallery Director should have several years of experience in gallery work, particularly as a registrar. Sales ability is important to a Director. He or she should also have strong interpersonal skills in order to deal effectively with customers, employees, and artists.

Organizations and Associations

Gallery employees might join any of the gallery associations (see Appendix V).

EDUCATION

ART TEACHER

CAREER PROFILE

Duties: Instruct students in studio art techniques; grade student artwork; advise students

Alternate Title: Studio Art Instructor

Salary Range: $18,000 to $45,000

Employment Prospects: Fair

Advancement Prospects: Poor

Prerequisites:

Education—Bachelor of fine arts degree usually required; master of fine arts degree preferred; teaching certificate may be required

Experience—Work as an artist

Special Skills—Teaching ability; communications ability

CAREER LADDER

```
┌─────────────────────────────────┐
│  Art Department Chairperson or   │
│      Art School Director         │
└─────────────────────────────────┘

┌─────────────────────────────────┐
│          Art Teacher             │
└─────────────────────────────────┘

┌─────────────────────────────────┐
│        Student or Artist         │
└─────────────────────────────────┘
```

Position Description

An Art Teacher instructs students in various art skills. Art Teachers work on many levels—in elementary and secondary schools, in colleges and art schools, in adult and community education programs, and with private students. Art Teachers may also specialize in terms of the media they teach. For instance, an elementary school Art Teacher is likely to help students work in painting, drawing, and clay modeling, but an art school instructor will probably specialize in oil painting or metal sculpture or pastels.

Clearly, the environments in which Art Teachers work vary widely, and the prospective Teacher should do some thinking about the kind of environment he or she prefers. Elementary and secondary school Art Teachers work with young people, helping them to enjoy art, while looking for early signs of talent. Such Teachers must have college degrees and teaching certification, including several education courses and student teaching experience.

College art instructors work with more advanced students. Generally, such instructors will have earned master of fine arts degrees. They tend to specialize in one medium, and they instruct students in art theory and practice. As college instructors, they may move up and become assistant, associate, and full professors.

Art school Teachers may not have any particular educational background, but they will have experience in working as artists. In a community art school, the Teachers may be local

art hobbyists, but in a studio art conservatory the Teachers would be accomplished and recognized in their fields.

Of course, an important part of teaching art students is the evaluation and constructive criticism of their work. The Teacher is there to help the student to improve his or her skills and to advise the student regarding future work. In addition, the Art Teacher may be involved with curriculum planning for the art department.

Salaries

Because the positions themselves vary greatly, there is a wide range of salaries—from $18,000 to $45,000 per year. Part-time Teachers would earn proportionally less. The highest salaries are offered on the college and professional art school level.

Employment Prospects

It is somewhat difficult to find a position as an Art Teacher since competition is fierce. Many art graduates look to teaching as a way to supplement the income from their own artwork, or as a way to make a living until they can afford to become full-time artists.

Advancement Prospects

Advancement in this career is difficult to achieve. There is great competition for promotion on the college level. In other areas of art teaching, the only avenue for advancement is to move up to administration, and there are only a few administrative positions available.

Education

As noted above, educational requirements vary according to the type of school in which one wishes to teach, with colleges requiring master's degrees, elementary and high schools requiring bachelor's degrees and teaching certificates, and other schools basing their requirements upon experience.

Art Teachers should be able to communicate well with their students and to criticize their work in a helpful and constructive way. Of course, they should also have strong art skills of their own.

Organizations and Associations

The major organization for Art Teachers is the National Art Education Association (NAEA) (see Appendix V).

Tips for Entry

Those seeking to enter this field might gain experience by teaching art to children at a camp or in an after-school program, either in a paid position or as a volunteer.

ART SCHOOL DIRECTOR

CAREER PROFILE

Duties: Managing business aspects of school; teaching art; hiring, marketing, scheduling

Alternate Title: Art School Dean

Salary Range: $25,000 to $75,000+

Employment Prospects: Poor

Advancement Prospects: Poor

Prerequisites:
  Education—Bachelor's degree in art or art education; master's degree helpful
  Experience—Teaching art in public or private school
  Special Skills—Art skills, teaching skills, business acumen, ability to deal with the public

CAREER LADDER

```
┌─────────────────────────────┐
│    Art School Director      │
└─────────────────────────────┘

┌─────────────────────────────┐
│        Art Teacher          │
└─────────────────────────────┘

┌─────────────────────────────┐
│     Student or Artist       │
└─────────────────────────────┘
```

Position Description

An Art School Director manages—and, often, owns—a private art school. Such a school is generally small and geared to providing enrichment to school-age youngsters. It may also cater to senior citizens and others pursuing art as a hobby, but only a few such schools offer professional-level training to people who are planning careers as artists.

The School Director is responsible for the day-to-day operations of the school, including both its business and instructional affairs. The Director must arrange for classroom space, teaching personnel, and materials to work with. The Director recruits students through advertising, personal contacts, open houses, and the like. He or she must see to general office functions, such as bookkeeping and correspondence, and handle class scheduling.

The Director is assumed to be knowledgeable about art education, and he or she will supervise and perhaps train the school's teachers. The Director may teach classes as well.

Many Art School Directors own their schools, so they are entrepreneurs who may see this as their ultimate goal. Others are employed as directors, and they may go on to larger schools, to careers as working artists, or to become owners of their own art schools.

Salaries

An Art School Director may make from $25,000 per year in a small school to $75,000 or more in a larger school. A self-employed owner/director may make even more if his or her school is especially profitable.

Employment Prospects

The opportunities to become an Art School Director are poor unless one has the capital to start one's own school. There are many art educators who are qualified to handle the educational aspects of the position, but a business background will greatly enhance an art teacher's qualifications for this job.

Advancement Prospects

Advancement from this position is unlikely. Only rarely will an Art School Director move up to head a larger or more prestigious school. An owner/director may consider greater profitability to be a kind of advancement.

Education

Most Art School Directors have at least bachelor's degrees in art education. Many have master's degrees in art education, and a number of practical business courses would be extremely helpful.

Experience and Skills

The Director should have several years of experience as an art teacher. Any experience in business and in dealing with the public will be useful. Demonstrated success as a working artist may help the Director to attract students to the school.

In addition to art and teaching skills, the Art School Director should have some sales and marketing ability, managerial skills, and good communication skills (in order to recruit students for the school).

Organizations and Associations

An Art School Director may be a member of the National Art Education Association (NAEA) (see Appendix V).

Tips for Entry

The candidate for this job should be articulate. Public relations is an important aspect of the position; introverts will find it difficult to succeed.

ART HISTORY INSTRUCTOR

CAREER PROFILE

Duties: Teach art history on the college level; advise students; work on curriculum; research and write on art history

Alternate Titles: Art History Teacher, Art History Professor

Salary Range: $25,000 to $75,000

Employment Prospects: Poor

Advancement Prospects: Poor

Prerequisites:
Education—Master's degree in art history required; doctorate preferred
Experience—Teaching
Special Skills—Research and writing skills; communications skills

CAREER LADDER

```
┌──────────────────────────────────────┐
│   Art History Department Chairperson  │
└──────────────────────────────────────┘

┌──────────────────────────────────────┐
│        Art History Instructor         │
└──────────────────────────────────────┘

┌──────────────────────────────────────┐
│               Student                 │
└──────────────────────────────────────┘
```

Position Description

An Art History Instructor educates college students on art history. A beginning Instructor may give a survey course covering a wide portion of the history of art; as the Instructor gains experience, he or she is more likely to give more specialized courses on particular periods, movements, artists, or media.

The Art History Instructor may be hired strictly on a courses-taught basis, being paid by the credit (this is often the case in community colleges), or may be hired onto a "tenure track," with the hope of progressing to assistant, associate, and, finally, full professor of art history. Tenure track Instructors must devote considerable time to independent research and writing in art history, as the publication of articles and books is important to their career advancement.

All Art History Instructors spend time preparing lectures, grading papers, advising students, and performing whatever paperwork the university requires of them.

Salaries

Art History Instructors generally make $25,000 to $75,000 per year, with the higher salaries going to the more experienced Instructors. Part-time teaching work may be available for those interested in the field; such work is usually compensated by a flat fee per course or credit taught.

Employment Prospects

It is difficult to find a position as an Art History Instructor. There are more graduates in this field than there are positions available, so the competition for jobs is keen.

Advancement Prospects

Advancement opportunities are very limited in this field. In a community college, an experienced and accomplished Instructor may move up to become chairperson of the art history department, but in a university the Instructors must produce publications of high quality—as well as perform their normal classroom duties—in order to achieve promotion.

Education

Art History Instructors must have master's degrees in their field, and the doctoral degree is required for most positions.

Experience and Skills

Teaching experience, usually gained while a graduate student, is required for this position. The Instructor should have excellent communications and teaching skills. Research and writing ability are important to those hoping to advance in their careers.

Organizations and Associations

The National Art Education Association (NAEA) is the organization for this profession (see Appendix V).

Tips for Entry

In order to find a teaching job, the graduate student should work to make contacts with art history professors at many colleges. Publication of articles in art history will help the graduate student to become known in the field.

ART THERAPIST

CAREER PROFILE

Duties: Diagnose and treat clients using art therapy techniques

Salary Range: $25,000 to $60,000

Employment Prospects: Fair

Advancement Prospects: Poor

Prerequisites:

Education—Completion of curriculum required by The American Art Therapy Association (AATA); master's degree required

Experience—Internship as part of educational program

Special Skills—Sensitivity, communications skills, art skills

CAREER LADDER

```
┌─────────────────────────┐
│       Supervisor        │
└─────────────────────────┘

┌─────────────────────────┐
│      Art Therapist      │
└─────────────────────────┘

┌─────────────────────────┐
│         Student         │
└─────────────────────────┘
```

Position Description

Art therapy is a helping profession in which psychological and creative arts skills are used to diagnose and treat emotional problems or to foster self-awareness and personal growth. Art Therapists are trained to work with people in such settings as nursing homes, hospitals, schools, guidance centers, and private practices.

Art Therapists are trained in both art and psychotherapy, and any of a variety of psychological approaches may be applied to art therapy. But the underlying principle of art therapy is that there are emotional benefits available through the use of art media to express and communicate feelings.

An Art Therapist may work alone in a private practice or may function in an institutional setting, but increasingly Art Therapists are found working as members of therapeutic teams. Such teams may include psychologists, psychiatrists, nurses, occupational therapists, social workers, and others who work together to help clients or patients. Clients may be treated individually or in groups.

Salaries

Salaries for Art Therapists range from about $25,000 per year to about $60,000 per year. Those who work in larger institutions and those who have more experience are likely to receive higher pay. Art Therapists with doctoral degrees or those in private practice have an earning potential of $75 to $90 per hour.

Employment Prospects

Art Therapy is a relatively new and growing field, and there is an increasing number of positions available, especially for a graduate who can creatively develop new opportunities for the specialty. Thus a well-prepared Art Therapist has a fair chance of finding a position.

Advancement Prospects

Opportunities for advancement in the field of art therapy are limited. In larger institutions, an Art Therapist might be promoted to supervise other Art Therapists or a therapy team, but such positions are difficult to find. In general, the Therapist would continue to practice in that position.

Education

Training for art therapy is specialized and is offered at relatively few colleges, although as the field grows, more and more schools have been including this program in their curricula (see Appendix I). Undergraduate preparation at a college with a program accredited by the American Art Therapy Association is a must, and a master's degree is required for employment in the field.

Art therapy education includes study in the fine arts and the behavioral and social sciences. Specialized art therapy training includes study of the history, theory, and practice of art therapy.

Experience and Skills

Art therapy students receive practical experience as part of their training, but any additional paid or volunteer work with children, older adults, or emotionally troubled people will be beneficial.

An Art Therapist should have a compassionate nature and should be sensitive to others. Certainly a caring and understanding personality is needed in order to function well in this field. Art skills and creative ability are important, as is a positive, helpful attitude.

Organizations and Associations

The American Art Therapy Association (AATA) is the main organization for Art Therapists (see Appendix V). It is also possible that Art Therapists working in hospital or school settings might join an employees' union on site.

Tips for Entry

Any work with people—paid or volunteer—will be beneficial to those wishing to enter this field. All types of art experience—classes, independent work, museum-going—are helpful, too.

FUNDING AGENCIES
FOR THE ARTS

ADMINISTRATIVE ASSISTANT

CAREER PROFILE

Duties: Provide administrative support for a department or senior personnel

Alternate Title: Secretary

Salary Range: $15,000 to $32,000

Employment Prospects: Fair to good

Advancement Prospects: Poor to fair

Prerequisites:
Education—Secretarial school or undergraduate degree in the arts or a related field
Experience—Background in secretarial skills and administration
Special Skills—Excellent typing, word processing, filing, and other clerical abilities; excellent organizational skills

CAREER LADDER

```
┌─────────────────────────────────┐
│   Assistant Program Specialist   │
└─────────────────────────────────┘

┌─────────────────────────────────┐
│     Administrative Assistant     │
└─────────────────────────────────┘

┌─────────────────────────────────┐
│        Intern or College         │
└─────────────────────────────────┘
```

Position Description

The Administrative Assistant is responsible to one person or department, and provides overall administrative support. In a program area he or she would set up all panel meetings, coordinate all written and verbal contact, and follow up with panelists and update files and payments to them. Responsibilities might also include computerizing a regularly updated panelist contact file that would contain relevant data about panelists' work, credibility in particular disciplines or art organizational talents, and other pertinent information.

An Administrative Assistant in the budget and management area of the agency would provide advanced technical and business support; maintain administrative procedures in the department or agencywide; and suggest improvements in these procedures. He or she might be involved in processing routine requests for funds from granted artists or organizations, and assist in answering questions from the agency's constituency about financial policy.

Regardless of what area the Administrative Assistant serves in, he or she has extensive clerical and secretarial duties. There is a great deal of paperwork involved in government agencies, and the Administrative Assistant must be able to perform it efficiently and well. In the case of an Administrative Assistant in a program area, checking applications from outside artists or organizations for completeness is an important duty.

Although Administrative Assistants are primarily support staff, funding agencies, like most arts-related organizations, are often understaffed and someone in this position may be asked to take on some of the duties of the program specialist or assistant program specialist.

In addition the Administrative Assistant may:

- type all correspondence for a person or department
- coordinate the production of designed materials or information
- manage bulk mailings to the agency's constituency

Salaries

Salaries range from $15,000 to $32,000 depending on the size of the funding agency and the extent of responsibilities.

Employment Prospects

The Administrative Assistant is an entry-level position, so prospects are reasonably good that someone with basic secretarial or accounting training and with a demonstrated interest in the arts could obtain this position.

Advancement Prospects

Since this position is primarily secretarial, chances are not too good for advancement. If the funding agency is small, or very busy, and the Administrative Assistant is able to take on duties related to the conception and running of a program or other department, chances are better to advance.

Education

Secretarial school or basic training in accounting are necessary. But the applicant is also usually required to have a degree in the arts or a related field.

Experience and Skills

The Administrative Assistant must have excellent research, clerical, and accounting skills. He or she must be proficient in using a computer either for word processing or to create financial spreadsheets. The person who fills this job must be very organized, able to communicate well on the telephone, and have adequate writing skills. Since Administrative Assistants often have to balance duties given to them by several members of a department, they must have a good sense of humor and be able to work under pressure.

ASSISTANT PROGRAM SPECIALIST

CAREER PROFILE

Duties: Assist program specialist in administration and management of an agency program

Salary Range: $17,000 to $35,000

Employment Prospects: Fair

Advancement Prospects: Good

Prerequisites:
   Education—Undergraduate degree in the arts or humanities or in arts administration
   Experience—Background in administration and management, preferably in the arts
   Special Skills—Good organizational skills, attention to detail

CAREER LADDER

```
┌─────────────────────────────────────┐
│         Program Specialist          │
└─────────────────────────────────────┘

┌─────────────────────────────────────┐
│    Assistant Program Specialist     │
└─────────────────────────────────────┘

┌─────────────────────────────────────┐
│     Administrative Assistant or     │
│              College                │
└─────────────────────────────────────┘
```

Position Description

The Assistant Program Specialist is primarily responsible for the day-to-day administration of a granting program. Under the supervision of the program specialist, he or she manages communications with constituents of the program, reviews applications from the field to be sure the applicants are eligible for the particular program, monitors budgets for grants which are given, and generally assists the program specialist with all of his or her duties.

In order to make artists and art institutions aware of their programs, funding agencies publish their guidelines, complete with instructions and application forms. Not only does the Assistant Program Specialist assist in the preparation of these materials, but he or she must also ensure their effective distribution. This involves maintaining an accurate and comprehensive mailing list, and making periodic bulk mailings. Like the program specialist, the Assistant Program Specialist regularly speaks on the phone with constituents to discuss their plans and whether they are competitive for funding.

Most funding agencies require very specific sorts of written material and documentation with a grant application. When applications arrive, the Assistant Program Specialist must review them to be sure that all of this material is included. If elements are missing, he or she must call the applicant and request supplementary material. Once a grant is given, the funded organization—a museum, for instance—must request the funds with special forms, often including extensive documentation of money spent. The

Assistant Program Specialist must maintain this system effectively and be sure that all requests for grant money are legitimate.

In a large program—for instance, the Museum Program at the National Endowment for the Arts—an Assistant Program Specialist may have primary responsibility for a subsection of the program, like special exhibitions or catalogues.

In addition, the Assistant Program Specialist may:

- undertake research for the program specialist in order to find expert panelists in the field
- make travel or entertainment arrangements for expert panelists
- write and distribute press releases on the agency's funding program

Salaries

Salaries range between $17,000 to $35,000, and may be more in a large funding agency.

Employment Prospects

The Assistant Program Specialist could be an entry-level position for someone with education in the arts and good administrative skills. However, as with most positions in the arts, competition can be very difficult. In a situation where the Assistant Program Specialist has significant individual responsibility, experience in the arts is essential.

Advancement Prospects

The prospects are good that an Assistant Program Specialist will advance to the position of program specialist after a number of years in the job. Chances are better if he or she has taken primary responsibility for one subarea of the funding program.

Education

A degree in the appropriate area of the arts or a related field is necessary. Special education in administration is also a plus. Any training in the use of computers or secretarial skills is also an advantage.

Experience and Skills

Anyone who works in a funding agency must be sensitive to following the procedures which it dictates. This is especially true for an Assistant Program Specialist, who must have both an excellent head for detail and efficient organization. Excellent communications skills are a must, as is a good knowledge of the area of the arts within which he or she will work. The ability to work with budgets is invaluable.

PROGRAM SPECIALIST

CAREER PROFILE

Duties: Manage a funding agency program

Salary Range: $28,000 to $65,000

Employment Prospects: Fair

Advancement Prospects: Good

Prerequisites:

    Education—Undergraduate degree in the arts or related field

    Experience—Background in arts administration, preferably in a government setting

    Special Skills—Expert knowledge of the arts in special field; ability to work with a constituency; political acumen; excellent writing and speaking skills

CAREER LADDER

```
┌─────────────────────────────────┐
│      Program Coordinator        │
└─────────────────────────────────┘

┌─────────────────────────────────┐
│      Program Specialist         │
└─────────────────────────────────┘

┌─────────────────────────────────┐
│   Assistant Program Specialist  │
└─────────────────────────────────┘
```

Position Description

Under supervision of the program coordinator, Program Specialists are responsible for the planning, management, and representation of a particular granting program. In general, this includes regular contact with a constituency, administration of day-to-day operations for the program, working with staff in other departments as needed, and supervising tasks performed by the assistant program specialist. Responsibilities include administering the budget for this area, including monitoring current expenditures and anticipating future needs.

Most funding agencies try to tailor their programs to the needs which exist in the field. For that reason, the Program Specialist spends a good deal of time assessing needs and trends. He or she must evaluate the accomplishments of the program and propose changes to address its shortcomings. When new initiatives are proposed, the Program Specialist must assess the budget implications and constituency effectiveness of all changes. If, for instance, the Program Specialist manages a section of the funding agency which gives money to museum exhibitions, he or she will spend a good deal of time on the phone with museum curators, hearing about the projects they wish to propose and advising them how to apply successfully.

The decisions to give away money, however, are not made by the staff of the funding agency itself, but by a panel of experts in the field, which changes each year. The Program Specialist must choose these panelists and organize their review and discussion of all proposals. Before these panels meet, the Program Specialist, often with the assistance of the assistant program specialist, must review applications to make sure they fit the funding agency's guidelines and include all of the information necessary.

Once funding decisions have been made the Program Specialist must notify all applicants, answering the questions of those who did not receive a grant, and explaining the terms of the gift to those who did. The Program Specialist supervises the disbursement of funds to grant recipients, and solicits final reports on all projects funded.

In addition, the Program Specialist may:

- assist organizations which need special help in writing grants
- recruit applications from the field
- communicate the goals of his or her program to other Program Specialists, and perhaps jointly plan special initiatives

Salaries

The average salary for a Program Specialist is between $28,000 to $65,000 largely depending upon the scale of the funding agency. Usually federal salaries are higher than those of state arts councils.

Employment Prospects

Since Program Specialists work directly with artistic projects, and often with artists, it is a desirable position, and is usually quite difficult to obtain. Experience in a museum or other art institution, as well as administrative expertise, is invaluable.

Advancement Prospects

Advancement prospects for Program Specialists are quite good. If they show talent in running their programs, they will have a good chance to advance to the position of assistant program coordinator or program coordinator.

Education

An undergraduate degree in the arts or in education or a related field is required, and a graduate degree in a similar field may be an advantage. Formal training in administration could also be a plus.

Experience and Skills

The Program Specialist must have experience in planning for and managing a major arts program, preferably with broad and varied experience in arts presentation. He or she must be able to identify needs, opportunities, and trends that relate to the creation of art appropriate to their program. Since a great part of this job is communicating with an arts constituency, the Program Specialist's communication skills, as well as his or her written skills, must be outstanding. The ability to manage a budget effectively is necessary, as are efficiency and the ability to get along in a bureaucratic environment.

ASSISTANT PROGRAM COORDINATOR

CAREER PROFILE

Duties: Assist program coordinator in managing an agency department or cluster of programs

Alternate Title: Assistant Director of Department

Salary Range: $25,000 to $38,000

Employment Prospects: Fair to good

Advancement Prospects: Fair

Prerequisites:
Education—Undergraduate degree in the arts or art administration
Experience—Background in administration and management, preferably arts related
Special Skills—Sensitivity to art; excellent organizational and management skills; writing and speaking ability

CAREER LADDER

```
┌─────────────────────────────────┐
│      Program Coordinator         │
└─────────────────────────────────┘

┌─────────────────────────────────┐
│  Assistant Program Coordinator   │
└─────────────────────────────────┘

┌─────────────────────────────────┐
│  Assistant Program Specialist or │
│            College               │
└─────────────────────────────────┘
```

Position Description

Whereas the program coordinator undertakes the program-related and budget planning for a particular department of the funding agency, the Assistant Program Coordinator is responsible for the day-to-day execution of these policies. This involves a great deal of administrative work, and coordination of the department's staff of program specialists.

The Assistant Program Coordinator is responsible for managing the flow of information within his or her department. This might mean setting up meetings with the staff, working with individual program specialists to monitor their budgets, allocating clerical and secretarial help to the particular individuals who need it, or creating and managing computer systems or other special office systems for the department.

The program coordinator may ask the Assistant Program Coordinator to undertake the nuts-and-bolts planning for a particular issue. For instance, if the program coordinator for art education feels that rural and inner-city school systems need more attention from the agency, the Assistant Program Coordinator would be dispatched to meet with school officials and with legislators; he or she would also read the literature on the issue and synthesize the attitudes of the program specialists into a report, which would then be evaluated departmentwide and eventually be presented to the deputy director and executive director. The Assistant Program Coordinator is also intimately involved in the construction of the department's budget. He or she collects information from each specialist and assists the program coordinator in developing a proposal for the deputy director for budget and administration.

The level of responsibility of the Assistant Program Coordinator varies from agency to agency. In a large organization he or she may have significant planning responsibility, whereas in a smaller agency the job may be similar in status to that of an administrative aide.

In addition, the Assistant Program Coordinator may:

• personally run one or more programs within his or her area
• prepare and distribute memos about the department's activities to the rest of the agency staff

Salaries

Salaries range from $25,000 to $38,000.

Employment Prospects

This position can be an entry-level job for applicants with degrees in the arts or arts administration; in a larger agency, it could be quite competitive. It is often possible to rise to this position from the post of program specialist or assistant program specialist.

Advancement Prospects

If this job is mostly administrative, advancement prospects are only fair; but if one is able to undertake a good deal of management planning, then it is possible to advance to the position of program coordinator.

Education

An undergraduate degree in the field served by the agency department is necessary, and an advanced degree in this area or in arts administration is desirable.

Experience and Skills

Above all, the Assistant Program Coordinator must have exceptional organizational and administrative skills. The ability to undertake a complex research project, drawing from several types of sources, is also important. Knowledge of government agencies and the way they work is an advantage. The Assistant Program Coordinator must be able to work with many staff members and help to communicate their attitudes to his or her direct superiors and to the top management of the agency.

PROGRAM COORDINATOR

CAREER PROFILE

Duties: Manage cluster of related programs in the funding agency

Alternate Title: Director of an agency division

Salary Range: $28,000 to $65,000

Employment Prospects: Poor to fair

Advancement Prospects: Fair to good

Prerequisites:

Education—Undergraduate degree in the arts or related field

Experience—Background in arts administration, preferably in a government setting

Special Skills—Political acumen; ability to communicate, write well, and respond to the arts community

CAREER LADDER

```
┌─────────────────────────────────────┐
│  Deputy Director for Programming     │
└─────────────────────────────────────┘

┌─────────────────────────────────────┐
│       Program Coordinator            │
└─────────────────────────────────────┘

┌─────────────────────────────────────┐
│        Program Specialist            │
└─────────────────────────────────────┘
```

Position Description

A Program Coordinator manages a cluster of related activities within the agency—for instance, programs relating to museum education or contemporary art. With the deputy director for programming or the deputy director for budget and administration, Program Coordinators lead planning, policy development, and evaluation within the area they are responsible for.

The Program Coordinator manages a group of program specialists who are directly responsible for a single granting category. For instance, the Program Coordinator managing grants for art education might supervise program specialists who offer grants to high schools, to museums or to artists who work with children directly. The Program Coordinator is responsible for developing and maintaining meaningful cooperation among these related program specialists. If the Program Coordinator learns of a special need in the field, he or she might make available a grant category composed of individual programs under his or her supervision.

The Program Coordinator develops budget plans within his or her area, allocates staff resources, monitors budget expenditures, and makes decisions concerning shifts in emphasis within the area. For instance, the Program Coordinator for art education may decide to increase funding opportunities for inner-city and rural school systems which have the fewest art-related programs. Although any changes must be approved by

a deputy director, Program Coordinators generate most planning proposals since they are more aware than anyone else of the changing needs in the areas they serve.

In addition, the Program Coordinator must serve as a spokesperson for the agency within a particular area. He or she must shape the tone and presentation of information about his or her programs and solicit comment and response from the field on the effectiveness of the agency's activities. All programs must be evaluated by the coordinator and his or her staff. Ultimately these studies are presented to the deputy and executive directors.

In addition the Program Coordinator may:

- run one or more specific programs personally
- attend professional meetings and conferences in his or her field
- publish articles on funding strategies for art-related publications

Salaries

Salaries for Program Coordinators range from $28,000 to $65,000.

Employment Prospects

The position of Program Coordinator is a dynamic job filled with the satisfaction of serving the arts. It is therefore a position quite difficult to get. Successful applicants should prove an extensive knowledge of a particular program area, experience in the field, and excellent administrative abilities. Previous experience in government would improve one's chances.

Advancement Prospects

It is possible that the Program Coordinator can advance to the position of deputy director. However, it is unlikely that this promotion would take place before several years of distinguished service as a coordinator.

Education

An undergraduate degree in the appropriate program area—for instance, art education—and an advanced degree in that area or in administration are typically required.

Experience and Skills

The Program Coordinator must have excellent knowledge of the field he or she is working in and must know how to communicate with the constituency served through personal contacts, professional meetings, and art publications. The Program Coordinator must be well versed in the methods of gathering information and proposing programs to address a particular need. He or she must be capable of managing a budget of as much as several million dollars. Since the Program Coordinator is the field representative for an area of the agency's activity, he or she must have excellent speaking and writing skills.

DEPUTY DIRECTOR FOR PROGRAMMING

CAREER PROFILE

Duties: Manage policy making and personnel related to the funding programs of the agency

Salary Range: $45,000 to $90,000

Employment Prospects: Poor to fair

Advancement Prospects: Good

Prerequisites:

Education—Undergraduate degree in arts or art administration; graduate degree an advantage

Experience—Background in arts administration in a government or museum setting

Special Skills—Excellent policy making skills and management capacity; ability to work with people; excellent writing and speaking skills

CAREER LADDER

```
┌─────────────────────────────────────┐
│         Executive Director          │
└─────────────────────────────────────┘

┌─────────────────────────────────────┐
│  Deputy Director for Programming    │
└─────────────────────────────────────┘

┌─────────────────────────────────────┐
│        Program Coordinator          │
└─────────────────────────────────────┘
```

Position Description

Since the executive director spends a good deal of his or her time out of the office representing the funding agency, the day-to-day administration of the organization is left to the deputy directors. The Deputy Director for Programming is responsible for managing policy making as well as the personnel related to the funding programs of the agency. He or she also supervises the dissemination of information about the agency's programs to the public as well as to relevant government officials.

One of the most important goals of an arts funding agency is to apply its allotted money to the most productive possible uses—whether directly to artists or to organizations which serve them. The Deputy Director for Programming undertakes an ongoing evaluation of need in the field, and devises appropriate responses on the part of the funding agency. For instance, in order to develop a new funding initiative—like a program to support the creation of new works by artists—the Deputy Director identifies the key issues and assesses the need for, and potential efficacy of, this program by assigning staff members to undertake research in the field. The Deputy Director then evaluates this research and makes recommendations to the executive director. If the recommendation is accepted the Deputy Director must assign or hire the required personnel to manage the new initiative.

The Deputy Director for Programming directly manages the program coordinators in each area of the agency's activity, as well as the public information government relations officer. He or she must monitor the procedures and programs in each of these areas and discuss future plans with these staff members. The Deputy Director must anticipate the need for human and financial resources in the areas he or she manages and articulate these needs to the executive director as well as the deputy director for budget and administration.

Although the executive director is the primary representative of the agency in the community, the Deputy Director for Programming must also occasionally play a role in the articulation of the goals and programs of the agency.

In addition the Deputy Director for Programming might:

- have considerable responsibility in creating the annual budget
- participate in the establishment of a personnel policy
- lobby government officials in particular program areas the agency serves

Salaries

Salaries vary from state to state and in federal agencies, but they typically range from $45,000 to $90,000.

Employment Prospects

Competition is tough for this position. It is necessary for the applicant to have several years of experience in arts management and the proven ability to plan and articulate community needs in the arts.

Advancement Prospects

The chances are very good that a Deputy Director for Programming could advance to the position of executive director, either in the agency he or she works for, or in another similar organization. Prospects are better if the Deputy Director has demonstrated an excellent ability to lobby with the government and articulate the goals of the agency to the public and the arts community.

Education

An undergraduate degree in an area of the arts or the humanities, in addition to a graduate degree in a similar area, or management-related studies, is usually required.

Experience and Skills

The Deputy Director for Programming must have an outstanding ability to understand the needs of a community and create programs which serve those needs. This requires an excellent grasp of the steps required to plan new programs, as well as a sensitivity to artists and the arts. This job involves a great deal of personnel management, so the Deputy Director must be good with people and be able to understand and counsel them on their career goals. The Deputy Director must have an expert knowledge of at least one area of the arts, as well as excellent writing and speaking skills. He or she should also have experience dealing with the government, and have the capacity to lobby effectively.

PUBLIC INFORMATION OFFICER

CAREER PROFILE

Duties: Communicates goals and activities of the agency to the general public and the government

Alternate Title: Director of Public Relations

Salary Range: $35,000 to $75,000

Employment Prospects: Fair

Advancement Prospects: Fair

Prerequisites:

Education—Undergraduate degree in journalism, public relations, or political science

Experience—Extensive background in public relations and government; press connections or experience

Special Skills—Excellent writing and speaking skills; political acumen, computer literacy, Internet proficiency

CAREER LADDER

```
┌─────────────────────────────┐
│     Deputy Director for      │
│   Budget and Administration  │
└─────────────────────────────┘

┌─────────────────────────────┐
│  Public Information Officer  │
└─────────────────────────────┘

┌─────────────────────────────┐
│         Journalist/          │
│ Public Relations Professional│
└─────────────────────────────┘
```

Position Description

The Public Information Officer seeks to communicate the goals and activities of the funding agency, both to the general public, particularly through the press, and to the government bodies, like state legislatures, which oversee the funding agency. For this reason the Public Information Officer must have an excellent knowledge of politics and public relations, and also a total grasp of the kinds of grants the funding agency disperses.

In most cases the Public Information Officer produces the program guidelines for particular granting programs together with a program specialist. He or she must take copy from the program specialist, edit it for publication, and coordinate the design and production of guidelines. The Public Information Officer must also prepare and distribute press releases on the activities of the funding agency, publish a newsletter in order to publicize particular programs and overall goals, and produce an annual report which summarizes the funding agency's accomplishments. For agencies that have created and maintain their own web site, Public Information Officers may be responsible for the content and design for these pages. All of these tools are used to increase awareness of the funding agency among the general public as well as among government officials.

Representatives of a funding agency are often asked to speak to community groups or special-interest arts organizations. The Public Information Officer lectures regularly, and

may help coach other funding agency staff members in public speaking. The person in this position may also write important speeches for the executive director, especially when they are delivered to an audience of government officials.

The Public Information Officer may sometimes write articles about the funding agency to be published in an outside publication, or hold press conferences to make important policy announcements. He or she must stay in close touch with the funding agency's administrative and program staff in order to be aware of the ongoing goals and programs of the organization, and to receive their input into his or her public relations efforts.

In addition the Public Information Officer may:

- write special evaluation reports on funding agency programs
- maintain a photographic file of funding agency activities
- seek interviews in the press for the executive director or other funding agency staff

Salaries

The salary ranges between $35,000 to $75,000.

Employment Prospects

This is a highly sensitive position requiring political savvy, strategic thinking, and excellent writing skills. Competition is therefore quite brisk for the position and requires a good deal of previous experience in the areas of public relations or government.

Advancement Prospects

Advancement to the position of deputy director of planning is possible, but likely only if the Public Information Officer has become intimately involved with policy issues at the funding agency.

Education

An undergraduate degree in journalism, public relations, political science, or the arts is necessary. Graduate work in any of these areas is an advantage.

Experience and Skills

Like all public relations professionals, the Public Information Officer should have a wide network of contacts in the press, excellent writing skills, and superior public speaking ability. A background in journalism or television news would be a great advantage. In communicating with government officials, the Public Information Officer must have excellent interpersonal and negotiation skills. He or she must be aware of the processes of producing publications, and must have a great sensitivity to the arts and particularly the goals of the funding agency itself.

DEPUTY DIRECTOR FOR BUDGET AND ADMINISTRATION

CAREER PROFILE

Duties: Manage the personnel and financial policy issues in the agency

Salary Range: $45,000 to $90,000

Employment Prospects: Fair

Advancement Prospects: Fair

Prerequisites:

Education—Undergraduate or graduate degree in business administration or arts administration

Experience—Extensive background in financial and personnel management, preferably in a government setting

Special Skills—Ability to plan budgets; administer accounting and other financial systems; knowledge of personnel standards; ability to work well with people, computer literacy, Internet proficiency

CAREER LADDER

```
┌─────────────────────────────────────┐
│         Executive Director           │
└─────────────────────────────────────┘

┌─────────────────────────────────────┐
│        Deputy Director for           │
│     Budget and Administration        │
└─────────────────────────────────────┘

┌─────────────────────────────────────┐
│            Accountant                │
└─────────────────────────────────────┘
```

Position Description

The Deputy Director for Budget and Administration manages the financial and personnel policy issues within the funding agency. He or she is supervised by the executive director, but works in tandem with the deputy director for programming to run the agency day to day. Since the major objective of an arts funding agency is the dispersal of money, the management of budgets and contracts with grant recipients is a central activity for someone in this position.

The Deputy Director for Budget and Administration constructs the agency's budget by collecting information from program and administrative staff, as well as from the legislators who fund the agency. He or she plans the sequence of budget negotiations with staff members and then monitors money spent. In most funding agencies recipients of grants are required to submit substantial documentation of how they spend public funds. This documentation must be reviewed by the deputy director for budget and administration. He or she must also be available to answer questions from grant applicants with regard to budgets and the timetable for receiving funds.

This position also includes the planning and implementation of personnel policies, including the establishment of salary levels, undertaking staff evaluations, and designing benefit packages. Since funding agencies are part of the government, rigorous personnel standards typically apply to its employees. The Deputy Director must be aware of these policies and be sure they are implemented agencywide. He or she is also responsible for the process of hiring new employees and planning staff training and orientation programs.

There are many administrative tasks that fall to the Deputy Director for Budget and Administration. He or she may regularly supervise the administrative staff of the agency, from secretaries to accountants. The responsibility for maintenance of the offices of a building may also fall on the shoulders of the Deputy Director. He or she may submit an annual financial report to the legislature, or be called into hearings or negotiations of a financial nature.

In addition the Deputy Director for Budget and Administration may:

• plan and implement a schedule of staff meetings for the entire agency

- manage the purchase and utilization of office equipment and other capital expenditures

Salaries
Salaries range from $45,000 to $90,000 but may be significantly higher in a national or large state agency.

Employment Prospects
Competition is fairly difficult for this position. An applicant needs solid experience—usually several years—in administration for nonprofit organizations, and significant experience managing personnel. The position might attract applicants from the private sector or non-art-related government agencies, as well as people interested in the arts.

Advancement Prospects
Unless the Deputy Director for Budget and Administration has an excellent ability to articulate the agency's goals publicly, it is unlikely that he or she will advance to the position of executive director. However, the administrative experience gained in this position is rigorous and impressive and might prepare the Deputy Director for a government job with more authority, or a position in a major museum as director of finance.

Education
This position requires a financial background with a sensitivity to the arts. Although an undergraduate degree in the humanities might be attractive, an advanced degree in business, personnel management, or nonprofit administration is usually required.

Experience and Skills
The Deputy Director for Budget and Administration must have a thorough grasp of accounting, budget making and the legal aspects of disbursing public funds. He or she must have some experience working with federal or state legislatures. An excellent grasp of personnel management procedures is necessary, as are the ability to work well with people and the capacity to settle disputes among employees and clarify agency policies. An enthusiasm for the agency's art-related mission is an advantage, as are public speaking and writing skills.

EXECUTIVE DIRECTOR

CAREER PROFILE

Duties: Direct programmatic and financial policy of the agency; represent its programs to the public and the government

Salary Range: $65,000 to $150,000

Employment Prospects: Poor

Advancement Prospects: Good

Prerequisites:

Education—Undergraduate degree in the arts or humanities; graduate degree in the humanities or business administration

Experience—Extensive background in arts administration, preferably in a government setting

Special Skills—Excellent policy making skills; superior communications skills; political acumen

CAREER LADDER

```
┌─────────────────────────────┐
│     Executive Director      │
└─────────────────────────────┘

┌─────────────────────────────┐
│      Deputy Director        │
└─────────────────────────────┘

┌─────────────────────────────┐
│    Program Coordinator      │
└─────────────────────────────┘
```

Position Description

Public funding agencies, like federal endowments for the arts or state councils on the arts, are an important source of monies for most arts organizations. Although many have endowments which cover the expenses of building operation and other forms of overhead, public funds are often crucial for the execution of special projects or programs. The National Endowment for the Arts and the National Endowment for the Humanities, as well as most state arts councils, fund arts of all media from theater and music to every area of the visual arts, including individual artists. Since these funding agencies are government bodies, the Executive Director spends a good deal of time communicating with state or federal legislatures about the condition of the arts in the areas he or she serves. The Executive Director is the primary lobbyist for the arts and for the agency's funding allocation. The Executive Director must be able to maintain a high profile in the arts community: By speaking with its leaders, he or she is able to develop the kind of policies which will best serve the field.

The Executive Director is also the leader within the agency and must set programmatic goals as well as agency standards for dispensing funds to artists and arts organizations. By dispensing federal or state funds, these agencies enter into many types of contracts with those who receive money. The Executive Director works with his or her staff to structure these rela-

tionships to ensure that government funds have been spent as they should, and that the process of calling for, receiving, and documenting the use of funds by the funded organizations is as smooth and expeditious as possible.

The Executive Director must also answer to the steering committee of the funding agency. Often, grant awards are not final until this advisory body approves each decision. The Director may also have some direct responsibility for managing personnel.

In addition, the Executive Director might:

- spearhead a special arts initiative in any of the areas the agency serves
- organize symposia on the arts or other major public information events
- make formal reports to government officials about the status of the arts in a particular community or area

Salaries

Depending upon the pay scales of different cities, states, or the federal government, the Executive Director may make between $65,000 and $150,000.

Employment Prospects

The position of Executive Director of a funding agency is very competitive and difficult to obtain. The applicant must combine experience and expertise in political lobbying with a solid knowledge of a wide range of the arts and an excellent grasp of the role that they play in the community. Few people combine those qualities well. In some cases, especially in the federal government, this position is a political appointment.

Advancement Prospects

As the head of a funding agency, the Executive Director has nowhere to advance within the organization. However, he or she may go on to direct another government agency in either the arts or a related area.

Education

The Executive Director should have an undergraduate degree in one area of the arts or in a related humanities field. An advanced degree in business or management or in the arts is also required.

Experience and Skills

Above all the Executive Director must be a skillful representative of the arts within government, and of government within the arts. This requires a great deal of tact, eloquence, and political know-how. The Executive Director must be a person who knows how to get things done in the midst of bureaucracy. He or she must also be able to understand and articulate the various and sometimes contradictory goals of the arts community. The Executive Director must be able to evaluate areas of need and interest, and to use this information to lead an effective planning process.

ART JOURNALISM

PRODUCTION ASSISTANT

CAREER PROFILE

Duties: Assist in technical production of magazine design

Salary Range: $18,000 to $30,000

Employment Prospects: Fair to good

Advancement Prospects: Poor to fair

Prerequisites:
  Education—Undergraduate degree in graphic design
  Experience—Background in technical design and computer layout
  Special Skills—Excellent organizational ability and attention to detail; knowledge of a graphic design program like Quark or PageMaker

CAREER LADDER

```
┌─────────────────────────────┐
│          Designer           │
└─────────────────────────────┘

┌─────────────────────────────┐
│     Production Assistant     │
└─────────────────────────────┘

┌─────────────────────────────┐
│    Graphic Design School     │
└─────────────────────────────┘
```

Position Description

The Production Assistant helps the designer with the technical aspects of putting together a magazine. The process of preparing the periodical for publication includes many steps, and in a magazine which comes out frequently, there is always great pressure to meet deadlines. The position of Production Assistant has changed drastically since magazines have started to operate their production departments electronically. Instead of archaic methods that involve typesetting and page paste-ups, magazine pages are being produced in graphic design programs like Quark or PageMaker which merge copy and layout into computerized files. After the designer chooses the different typefaces and images that will appear on the page, dummy type is set in position where the actual copy will appear. The page is sent electronically to the Production Assistant who will clean up the page and make it fit perfectly within the magazine's specs. Then, the page is sent to the editorial side of the magazine so the appropriate editor can input the real copy and back to the production assistant who is responsible for the finishing touches, such as cutting words, incorporating captions and sidebars, and making sure images are transposed, cropped, and positioned accurately. The design department will then have a chance to approve the color separation and ensure that the film which will accompany the electronic file actually shows the true colors of the images on the page. Once the design department, production department, editorial department, and managing editor approve the pages, they are ready to be shipped to the printer electronically.

On a small magazine the Production Assistant may be hired on a part-time basis only, whereas on a major publication with a more complex graphic identity, he or she may be a very busy, full-time employee who grows to have significant input into certain aspects of the magazine's design.

In addition the Production Assistant may:

- coordinate design-related bills
- do research on graphic styles
- provide occasional secretarial support for the editorial staff

Salaries

The Production Assistant may make as little as $10 to $15 per hour on a part-time basis, or from $18,000 to $30,000 full time.

Employment Prospects

Since the Production Assistant works primarily on the technical design of the publication and has relatively little input into a graphic concept, it is possible to enter this position with little more experience than a proficiency in computer layout and knowledge of graphic design programs. Magazines often work with a pool of freelance Production Assistants.

Advancement Prospects

Unless the Production Assistant demonstrates excellent conceptual design skills in the process of his or her technical work, it is unlikely that he or she will advance to the position of designer. However, being a Production Assistant in a creatively designed publication can prepare one for further education, or a better job elsewhere.

Education

A degree in graphic design or other training in the technical processes of design is required. Coursework in art or art history is an advantage.

Experience and Skills

The position of Production Assistant requires familiarity with a computer layout program and the ability to create eye-catching, easy-to-read designs electronically. Since the Production Assistant must follow the instructions of the designer carefully, he or she must be an organized, hardworking person who is able to meet strict deadlines.

DESIGNER

CAREER PROFILE

Duties: Responsible for conceptual and technical design of the magazine

Salary Range: $22,000 to $55,000

Employment Prospects: Fair

Advancement Prospects: Fair to good

Prerequisites:

Education—Undergraduate or graduate degree in graphic design

Experience—Significant experience in conceptual and technical design

Special Skills—Sensitivity to art, and the ability to create a framework for the fine arts; superior conceptual design skills; knowledge of a graphic design program like Quark or PageMaker

CAREER LADDER

```
┌─────────────────────────────────┐
│             Editor              │
└─────────────────────────────────┘

┌─────────────────────────────────┐
│            Designer             │
└─────────────────────────────────┘

┌─────────────────────────────────┐
│       Production Assistant       │
└─────────────────────────────────┘
```

Position Description

An art magazine's design can be a fundamental expression of its editorial policy. Some magazines favor straightforward layouts, whereas others employ special graphic techniques which can convey specific messages about the magazine's point of view, such as a sense of contemporaneity or the desire to reach a broad public. Not only is the Designer responsible for preparing the magazine for publication, but with the editor he or she is involved with creating a design identity for the publication.

Some major magazines change their graphic design conventions annually or every few years, but usually maintain a consistent look throughout a single year. In order to develop a design concept, the Designer must be aware of other periodicals serving similar audiences as well as the types of articles that will be published in the magazine. With this background knowledge, he or she works closely with the editor, making proposals of alternative design concepts, one of which will ultimately win approval.

Within established design guidelines for a publication, there is always a significant amount of flexibility. Therefore, for every issue of the periodical the Designer must assess the material to be included and organize it visually. This includes choosing different typefaces, illustrations, and special graphic elements, if desired or necessary. The Designer should stay true to the look of the magazine, but he or she may also come up with creative new solutions for presenting the changing content from issue to issue. One of the most important elements of any magazine is its cover, and the Designer must devote a good deal of time and energy to choosing photos, illustrations, and/or graphics that will make it eye-catching and unique.

In addition to his or her considerable work in creating design concepts with the editorial staff, the Designer has a large amount of layout design to do for every issue. Smaller art magazines may be quite low on support staff so that the Designer must supervise the typography and the positioning of images from which the printer works. Usually the Designer coordinates negotiations with the printer, and he or she is always on hand during the actual printing to ensure that color illustrations are accurate and all other specifications are followed.

In addition the Designer may:

- engage a photographer to make special pictures for the publication
- design promotional materials for the periodical
- assist advertisers in designing their ads

Salaries

Depending upon the size of the magazine, the Designer makes between $22,000 and $55,000.

Employment Prospects

Since art magazine editors are visually oriented, they are usually very particular about the person they choose to design their publication. Although salaries tend to be lower than in a corporate design setting, competition can be intense, and an extensive background in publishing, with a distinguished portfolio of art-related projects, is usually necessary for a major publication. In a smaller art magazine, chances are better that one may be employed with only moderate experience.

Advancement Prospects

Most art magazines have a single Designer, so there is little room to grow within the publication itself. However, association with a prestigious art magazine can prepare one for greater challenges in other organizations, whether they be art-related or not.

Education

The Designer should have a degree in graphic design, with training in both design conception and computer layout skills. Any additional art or art history-related training can be an advantage.

Experience and Skills

The Designer of an art magazine must have a great sensitivity to art and art history. There is a delicate balance between the photographs of works of art and the design into which they fit. The Designer must be able to strike a balance between his or her concept and the works of art published. Knowledge of art history and art criticism is invaluable in this position. The Designer must be able to establish a good rapport with the editor and the writers for the magazine. Excellent technical and conceptual design skills are necessary, as is considerable experience in producing periodicals.

CRITIC

CAREER PROFILE

Duties: Review exhibitions; write feature articles about art and artists

Salary Range: 0 to $40,000+

Employment Prospects: Poor

Advancement Prospects: Fair

Prerequisites:

Education—Undergraduate or graduate degree in art history

Experience—Extensive background in writing about art

Special Skills—Superior writing ability; excellent knowledge of art and art history; ability to conceptualize critically

CAREER LADDER

```
+----------------------------------+
|              Editor              |
+----------------------------------+

+----------------------------------+
|        Contributing Editor       |
+----------------------------------+

+----------------------------------+
|              Critic              |
+----------------------------------+
```

Position Description

Working as an art Critic is one of the most difficult positions in the arts. Not only is it hard to get your work into print, but even if you do, the pay is usually very low. Most critics start by writing reviews or short articles for small publications, either for a very small fee or for no money at all. Once a Critic has built up a significant body of writing, he or she can then approach major or intermediate publications. It may take several years before one can actually make a living from writing about art, and there are few who succeed.

Art Critics write for newspapers, art magazines, general-interest magazines, and museum publications. Many Critics supplement their writing activity with teaching, curatorial work, or some other form of regular employment. Although working for a metropolitan newspaper or general-interest magazine can be lucrative and prestigious, the work one can do in this context is limited by the necessity of writing for a general-interest audience. Most art magazines have a group of freelance Critics whose reviews or feature articles they regularly publish. Although art magazines offer Critics the opportunity to delve more deeply into ideas about art, these publications may not be able to offer work as regular or profitable as a staff position on a newspaper or general-interest publication. Once an art Critic establishes a reputation through hard work, talent, and persistence, he or she may be offered opportunities to lecture or contribute essays to museum catalogues. Most art Critics balance their activi-

ties between regular relationships with publications and one-time freelance opportunities.

There are many attitudes about how one should discuss art, and most Critics have developed a point of view. Some Critics are very interested in describing what artwork looks like and the emotions it illicits; others are more concerned with the ideas that artists use to conceive their work. Art Critics who are known for strong and reasoned positions usually have greater success in the field of art publishing than those with a journalistic bent, who are more suited to working for newspapers or general-interest magazines.

In addition a Critic may:

- undertake book-length projects
- curate exhibitions on a freelance basis
- edit anthologies of critical writing

Salaries

At the beginning of a Critic's career he or she may make nothing, or next to nothing. Feature articles may bring fees ranging from less than $100 to thousands of dollars. A staff writer for a major general-interest magazine can make $40,000 or more.

Employment Prospects

Without years of experience, an impressive record of publications and an expert knowledge of one or several areas of art, art history, or critical theory, it is highly unlikely that one can obtain a position as an art Critic. In journalistic settings, such as a metropolitan newspaper, or in a small, locally focused art magazine, it is easier to get a first break, but even in these areas excellent writing skills and expert knowledge are required.

Advancement Prospects

For an art Critic, advancement means writing more extensively and for better publications. Professional growth may occur very slowly for an art Critic, requiring years of writing for minor or local publications. The best way of advancing is to keep thinking, writing, and learning about one's field.

Education

Education can vary greatly for art critics. Some have no formal training in the field of art history; they know what they do through independent research and reading. Others have participated in formal degree programs in art history, art, or criticism. Some art Critics have been trained in journalism. Ultimately, what counts is the quality of the writing and the Critic's judgments.

Experience and Skills

In addition to excellent writing skills and the ability and desire to stay abreast of a field of art history or critical theory, the good art Critic must have a skill which is difficult to qualify—the ability to elucidate works of art in an interesting way. The art Critic should have as much experience as possible working with or speaking to artists, and must have written a great deal, since this is often the best way of perfecting one's critical skills. To succeed as an art Critic one must be persistent and resourceful. No matter how small a publication, the chance to publish a piece of writing is an important opportunity for the beginning art Critic.

TRANSLATOR

CAREER PROFILE

Duties: Translate reviews and articles from a foreign language to English

Salary Range: $20 to $100 per hour, or fee may be paid by the word

Employment Prospects: Fair

Advancement Prospects: Fair

Prerequisites:

Education—Undergraduate or graduate degree in art history or languages

Experience—Extensive translation experience, preferably in the context of the arts

Special Skills—Superior knowledge of one or more foreign languages, and excellent technical skills in English; editorial and writing skills

CAREER LADDER

```
┌─────────────────────────────┐
│           Editor            │
└─────────────────────────────┘

┌─────────────────────────────┐
│       Assistant Editor      │
└─────────────────────────────┘

┌─────────────────────────────┐
│          Translator         │
└─────────────────────────────┘
```

Position Description

The art world has become more and more international, increasing the pressure on American art magazines to include significant coverage of work that is happening in Europe, as well as in South America and other parts of the world. Often, however, it is difficult or impossible to find an English-speaking critic who knows enough about the work in these areas to write about them authoritatively. For this reason most art magazines with even a minor international focus employ part-time Translators. Although it is unlikely that one could work as an art magazine Translator full time, it is a viable way for a multilingual critic to supplement his or her income.

As in all types of translation, the Translator who works for an art magazine must have a good general knowledge of, and sensitivity to, the articles he or she is translating. Often, a critic who has a good knowledge of another culture and an expert grasp of its language fills this position. When an article or review needs translation an editor at the art magazine contacts the Translator, who reads it, makes a draft translation which is sent to the author for comments, and then delivers the finished copy to the magazine. Because deadlines are always tight in a periodical, the Translator will probably have to complete his or her job quickly without sacrificing accuracy.

Although any one art magazine may have only a small volume of translation to do per issue, the number of people

with sufficient language skills and knowledge of the arts to perform this function well is extremely small, so a Translator may be able to establish a good reputation and receive work from several sources. Working on an art magazine as a Translator may lead to other projects, such as foreign art book translation.

In addition the Translator may:

- do editorial work for the magazine, especially with foreign authors
- write reviews in English for the magazine
- do special research in areas of foreign art for the magazine

Salaries

A Translator may make $20 to $100 per hour, or more, or may be paid by the word.

Employment Prospects

There are limited opportunities for the Translator at art magazines, yet work is available for highly qualified candidates—those who combine an excellent knowledge of art with expert knowledge of at least one foreign language. As with all freelance positions, the Translator must make his or her qualifications and potential services known to the magazine's editor, and perhaps work on a trial project before being formally hired.

Advancement Prospects

It is possible that a Translator who is a skilled writer or experienced editor may advance to a critic's position or an editorial post in the magazine, after trust has been established through translation jobs.

Education

An undergraduate degree in the arts or languages is necessary, and a graduate degree in the study of a foreign language may also be required.

Experience and Skills

The Translator must have experience making translations, preferably in the area of the arts. He or she must have an excellent grasp of English and be aware of the kinds of art criticism or historical writing which the art magazine publishes. Editorial experience or background as a critic are invaluable in this position.

CONTRIBUTING EDITOR

CAREER PROFILE

Duties: Write and suggest articles for the art magazine

Salary Range: $5,000 to $50,000

Employment Prospects: Poor

Advancement Prospects: Fair

Prerequisites:

Education—Undergraduate or graduate degree in art history

Experience—Extensive background in critical writing; editorial experience

Special Skills—Superior writing skills; excellent knowledge of art in the field of the magazine

CAREER LADDER

```
┌─────────────────────────────┐
│            Editor           │
└─────────────────────────────┘

┌─────────────────────────────┐
│     Contributing Editor     │
└─────────────────────────────┘

┌─────────────────────────────┐
│            Critic           │
└─────────────────────────────┘
```

Position Description

A Contributing Editor does not work at the art magazine on a daily basis, but is usually a freelance writer or critic who regularly writes articles for the publication. Instead of waiting to be asked by an editor to write a particular piece, the Contributing Editor suggests his or her own topics for approval by the editor. The Contributing Editor may also suggest other writers or topics for coverage in the magazine, while not writing them personally, and in such cases may have primary editorial responsibility for working with the author.

Since most art magazines must operate on a limited budget, working with Contributing Editors is a good way to expand editorial capacity without paying full-time salaries. Contributing Editors are especially effective for magazines that wish to cover regions or countries far from their editorial offices. A large American art magazine, for example, may have one or more Contributing Editors working in Europe who will suggest stories or exhibitions for review. Smaller magazines whose editorial offices are in one city may have Contributing Editors in other cities. Such an editor not only writes but also often coordinates a small group of freelance writers.

Contributing Editors may also attend regular editorial meetings with the magazine's full-time staff. This is an important function, for they bring a fresh, "outsider" point of view into the inner circle of the publication. Often, because they have fewer administrative responsibilities than other editors, Contributing Editors are able to stay more aware of new developments or artists who warrant coverage.

Contributing Editors are usually writers first and editors second, so, like art critics, they must assiduously attend art exhibitions, visit artists, and stay current with reading in the field. In most cases a critic must attain a broad and impressive reputation before he or she is asked to contribute to an art publication in this way. For many critics, though, it is a good way to maintain some degree of security while having the freedom to take outside jobs.

In addition the Contributing Editor may:

- write a regular column or correspondence for the magazine
- hire and dispatch freelance writers in other cities or countries
- meet regularly with the editor

Salaries

Depending upon the extent of the Contributing Editor's involvement in the magazine, he or she may make as little as $5,000 or as much as $50,000. In some cases, the Contributing Editor is paid directly for articles or reviews.

Employment Prospects

Generally to be offered a position as a Contributing Editor for a major art magazine, one must have established an impressive reputation and publication record as a critic. Competition is very brisk, and opportunities are limited. There are also logistical limitations in some cases: For instance, if a magazine needs a Contributing Editor to cover a certain country or region, only people who know that area well are considered.

Advancement Prospects

The prestige of being a Contributing Editor at a major art publication can greatly enhance one's reputation as an art critic. In addition, chances are good for a Contributing Editor to advance to the position of staff editor. However, bear in mind some Contributing Editors prefer not to be on staff because that may reduce the time they could devote to actual writing.

Education

There is no standard education requirement, though in most cases an undergraduate degree in art history is necessary, and a graduate degree desirable. The Contributing Editor's writing skills and knowledge of the field are more important than formal education.

Experience and Skills

The Contributing Editor must be an experienced art critic or writer who has written widely and well in the areas of the art magazine's interest. An impressive publication record is necessary, as are good connections among writers and artists in one's field. Editorial skills and experience are usually required, though in most cases the Contributing Editor is valued primarily for his or her writing skills and ability to recognize important artists or movements which warrant coverage.

ASSISTANT EDITOR

CAREER PROFILE

Duties: Assist editor in preparing copy and illustrations for the magazine

Salary Range: $18,000 to $40,000

Employment Prospects: Poor to fair

Advancement Prospects: Fair to good

Prerequisites:

Education—Undergraduate or graduate degree in art history

Experience—Background in writing about art; some editorial skills

Special Skills—Excellent writing ability; knowledge of art and art history; good organizational and clerical talents

CAREER LADDER

```
┌─────────────────────────────────┐
│      Editor/Managing Editor      │
└─────────────────────────────────┘

┌─────────────────────────────────┐
│        Assistant Editor          │
└─────────────────────────────────┘

┌─────────────────────────────────┐
│      Editorial Assistant or      │
│           College or             │
│         Graduate School          │
└─────────────────────────────────┘
```

Position Description

There are hundreds of details associated with publishing a magazine, and small mistakes can translate into embarrassment for the publication. Working in tandem with the editor or managing editor, the Assistant Editor helps to bring the publication through the manuscript phase to a finished periodical. The specific duties may vary greatly depending upon the size of the magazine and the way its staff is organized. However, most art magazine staffs are small enough so that the Assistant Editor may become involved in every aspect of editorial activity.

The Assistant Editor may spend a great deal of time proofreading manuscripts. Usually any piece of writing needs to be checked several times: before going to the typesetter, afterwards, and then once more after the author has looked over the typeset copy. He or she may also assist in checking the accuracy of the author's factual assertions, or be asked to research the availability of photographs for the issue.

The Assistant Editor may be expected to read and respond to reader mail, and to read unsolicited manuscripts to find promising articles for the magazine. He or she may also be asked to read and sort out press releases from galleries, museums, and artists in order to assist the editor or managing editor in making decisions about what exhibitions to review.

Most art magazines are low on secretarial support. The Assistant Editor may provide typing, filing, and other clerical assistance for the senior editorial staff. He or she may also be responsible for coordinating headlines or photo cap-

tions. The Assistant Editor may undertake research projects on art-historical or critical issues and maintain a library of source books or an archive of the magazine's back issues.

Like all members of an editorial staff, the Assistant Editor is often a jack-of-all-trades who may be writing a review of a gallery exhibition one day and typing the manuscript of another author the next.

In addition an Assistant Editor may:

- receive and route bills such as requests for writers' fees
- communicate with regular columnists or reviewers
- organize editorial meetings

Salaries

Depending upon the size of the art magazine, an Assistant Editor may make between $18,000 and $40,000.

Employment Prospects

Since the Assistant Editor is a junior member of the editorial staff, it can be an entry-level position. However, even with relatively little experience required, competition for this position can be intense. A distinguished educational record or a background in writing about art is usually necessary.

Advancement Prospects

The prospects for promotion are fair to good for an Assistant Editor. If he or she has been able to work directly with authors and to write a good deal on his or her own, or has become involved with forging an editorial policy for the magazine through working closely with the editor, chances are better for advancement. However, to rise to the position of editor at a major art magazine, one must have built a considerable reputation in the field.

Education

An undergraduate degree in art history or journalism may be sufficient for an Assistant Editor, though an advanced degree may be an advantage.

Experience and Skills

The Assistant Editor must have an excellent technical grasp of English and be proficient at proofreading. He or she should have a great sensitivity to art, art history and critical issues, and a lively curiosity about the field. Experience as a writer about art is invaluable, as are excellent research skills. The Assistant Editor must also be computer literate (ie: word processing, web skills, database and search skills, page editing skills, etc.). Experience in producing a publication is also an advantage.

MANAGING EDITOR

CAREER PROFILE

Duties: Manage day-to-day editorial activity of the magazine

Salary Range: $35,000 to $75,000+

Employment Prospects: Poor

Advancement Prospects: Good to excellent

Prerequisites:

Education—An undergraduate or graduate degree in art history, English, or journalism

Experience—Extensive editorial experience, preferably on an art magazine

Special Skills—Excellent knowledge of magazines; superior grasp of English; good knowledge of art history; management skills

CAREER LADDER

```
┌─────────────────────────────┐
│          Editor             │
└─────────────────────────────┘

┌─────────────────────────────┐
│      Managing Editor        │
└─────────────────────────────┘

┌─────────────────────────────┐
│      Assistant Editor       │
└─────────────────────────────┘
```

Position Description

In association with the editor, the Managing Editor is responsible for the day-to-day editorial activity of the magazine. Although the Managing Editor is typically consulted on editorial policies, he or she is primarily responsible for the nuts-and-bolts activities of bringing articles in and getting the publication ready to go to press. Most editorial staffs work collaboratively, so the editor and Managing Editor may share responsibilities almost equally on some periodicals.

The Managing Editor usually has responsibility for ongoing activities at the magazine. For instance, he or she may be charged with determining what exhibitions to review each issue, and what artists to ask to review them. This involves sifting through vast amounts of information in the form of press releases or photographs in order to decide what shows are significant and warrant coverage.

The Managing Editor may also supervise the processing of articles once they are received from writers. Like the editor, he or she may give suggestions with regard to grammar and content to the author and would also be responsible for overseeing the layout of the magazine, making sure the copy is properly proofread, reviewed with the writer, then dispatched to the designer. The Managing Editor may also work directly with the designer to ensure that he or she has manuscripts and photographs when necessary, and that the magazine is proceeding through production on schedule.

In a large magazine where several editors are commissioning articles and working with writers, the Managing Editor must coordinate this activity, making sure that a particular issue has all of its articles, reviews, or illustrations in order. In this context, he or she may also be responsible for the orderly management of office systems, including policies on answering correspondence from readers, or on reading and replying to unsolicited manuscripts.

The Managing Editor may supervise the magazine's editorial budget. He or she must work with the editorial staff to assess costs, plan a workable budget, and then supervise expenditures throughout the year. His or her financially related activity may also include working closely with advertisers. Art magazines are a primary means for art galleries and museums to get the word out about their exhibitions. Often these ads require special design or other individual treatment which may fall into the province of the Managing Editor.

Although the specific duties of a Managing Editor may vary depending upon the structure of the publication, he or she is the person who makes sure that the complex process of publishing a magazine proceeds efficiently and smoothly.

In addition the Managing Editor may:

- write articles for the magazine
- write grants

Salaries

Depending on the size of the magazine, the Managing Editor may make between $35,000 and $75,000+.

Employment Prospects

All art magazine editorial positions are difficult to get. Depending upon the structure of the publication, the Managing Editor may have less to do with artistic direction than with the editorial and financial management of the magazine. In that case, magazine experience may be more important than an expert knowledge of art. When the Managing Editor is deeply involved in editorial policy, he or she must have an impressive publications and editorial record.

Advancement Prospects

In most art magazines, the editorial staff remains quite stable. Advancement may be difficult, but it also may be irrelevant in a major publication where the Managing Editor grows to have an important editorial voice. Only if the person in this position has been deeply involved in editorial policy is he or she likely to advance to the position of editor.

Education

The Managing Editor should have a degree in art history, journalism, or English. Depending upon the level of scholarly content in the publication, he or she may need an advanced degree in art history.

Experience and Skills

The Managing Editor must have extensive experience in producing a periodical publication. He or she must be aware of the steps necessary for processing a manuscript, designing a publication, and printing it. In addition, this person must be able to manage people as well as budgets. An excellent knowledge of art is a great asset, if not absolutely necessary. The ability to make decisions about editorial direction and artistic quality is also an important skill. Even more than the editor, the Managing Editor must be an excellent administrator who is thorough, careful, and able to work under pressure.

EDITOR

CAREER PROFILE

Duties: Design and execute magazine's editorial policy

Alternate Title: Executive Editor

Salary Range: $38,000 to $85,000+

Employment Prospects: Poor

Advancement Prospects: Fair to good

Prerequisites:

Education—Undergraduate or graduate degree in art history

Experience—Extensive editorial or writing background in the area of art covered by the magazine

Special Skills—Superior editorial and writing ability; the talent of accurately observing and predicting the art world's trends; good rapport with writers and artists

CAREER LADDER

```
┌─────────────────────────────┐
│           Editor            │
└─────────────────────────────┘

┌─────────────────────────────┐
│       Managing Editor       │
└─────────────────────────────┘

┌─────────────────────────────┐
│       Assistant Editor      │
└─────────────────────────────┘
```

Position Description

Art magazines are one of the primary means of communication among artists, museums, galleries, and the other institutions of the art world. They range from inexpensive tabloids primarily focused on a regional community to vividly colored international journals which combine ideas from several nations. No matter what the scale of the magazine, its Editor is responsible for providing the publication with an appropriate focus on art-historical or critical issues.

The Editor must determine the magazine's overall policy, which includes deciding what critical or art-historical issues it will consistently cover, and what attitudes it will espouse openly, if any. The Editor is responsible for commissioning specific articles from appropriate writers. This means that the art magazine Editor must have an expert knowledge of the community his or her publication serves; this expertise is gained by visiting exhibitions and artists and through talking to art critics about the issues which interest them. Some art magazines are very close to being academic journals, and their activity is closely associated with a particular group of writers or artists. Other magazines provide "news" about the art scene. Most combine some of both.

Once the Editor commissions an article from a writer, he or she continues to work with that person, first during the phase of conception and research and finally when the manuscript is submitted to the magazine. After reviewing the writer's draft, the Editor suggests grammatical or content changes for the author to consider. In a small magazine or tabloid the Editor may work with every writer directly, whereas in a larger magazine he or she may work with only a few authors, or only make final editorial decisions. In either case, the Editor has ultimate responsibility for the content of the publication.

In addition to working with writers, the Editor guides the designer in establishing the look of the periodical. Especially in an art magazine, the design concept can say a lot about editorial policies and beliefs: Finding the right design language is an important editorial issue. As the artistic chief of the magazine, the Editor must represent his or her publication in the community, and may be involved in soliciting advertising revenues or grants if the publication is organized as a nonprofit venture.

In addition the Editor may:

- manage all personnel issues at the publication
- commission special works by artists for the magazine
- write articles for the publication

Salaries

Depending upon the size of the publication, the Editor may make between $38,000 and $85,000+.

Employment Prospects

There are very few art magazines, and consequently editorial positions are scarce—but highly desired for their excitement, prestige, and the opportunity to affect what the world thinks about a particular artist or art movement. Competition is extremely brisk, and it is unlikely that one can enter a responsible editorial position without considerable experience in writing about art or organizing exhibitions. As with museum work, a good reputation and publications record is essential.

Advancement Prospects

The Editor is the top artistic post in a magazine. In a major publication, the Editor may stay in the position for several years, finally advancing to another job in publishing or in an arts organization. For an Editor of a smaller publication, chances are fair for advancement, though it is unlikely that someone managing a locally directed publication would advance to one with national scope.

Education

An undergraduate degree in art history or a related field is necessary. For a publication with a strongly theoretical or art-historical focus an advanced degree is necessary. A degree in journalism may be sufficient for some art magazine jobs.

Experience and Skills

A good Editor must combine an intelligent, well-thought-out point of view with a rigorous knowledge of language and excellent writing skills. The Editor must be able to assess how the practice of art or art history is developing, through close observation and extensive reading of the important current writing in his or her field. He or she must be able to establish good working relationships with artists and writers. Visual sensitivity, excellent interpersonal skills, and the ability to work under a great deal of pressure are all necessary. An extensive background in critical or art-historical writing is invaluable.

AUCTION GALLERIES

INFORMATION COORDINATOR

CAREER PROFILE

Duties: Respond to journalists' inquiries; assist with special events; handle faxes; arrange tours

Alternate Title: Assistant Publicist

Salary Range: $18,000 to $25,000

Employment Prospects: Fair

Advancement Prospects: Fair to good

Prerequisites:
Education—Bachelor's degree required; background in art and/or public relations helpful
Experience—None
Special Skills—Writing ability; typing

CAREER LADDER

```
┌─────────────────────────────────┐
│          Publicist              │
└─────────────────────────────────┘

┌─────────────────────────────────┐
│    Information Coordinator       │
└─────────────────────────────────┘

┌─────────────────────────────────┐
│      Student or Secretary        │
└─────────────────────────────────┘
```

Position Description

The Information Coordinator assists the publicist in the day-to-day operations of the public relations department and assists with any special events undertaken to publicize the auction gallery. Ordinary duties include answering any questions for journalists writing about the gallery; handling faxes and other special communications; arranging tours upon request; and helping to prepare press releases.

The special events responsibilities of the Information Coordinator may include helping to arrange teas or cocktail parties for people who can publicize the auction house. Such events are likely to fall outside the usual nine-to-five working hours.

Salaries

The Information Coordinator can expect a salary of between $18,000 and $25,000 per year.

Employment Prospects

There is a fair chance of finding a position as an Information Coordinator. There are not many such jobs, but the turnover is fairly rapid as people move on to other jobs inside or outside of the auction house.

Advancement Prospects

The Information Coordinator has a reasonable chance of moving up within the auction gallery. He or she could be promoted to the position of publicist or could move to a different administrative or expert department.

Education

A bachelor's degree is required for this job, preferably with some background in art and/or public relations.

Experience and Skills

No particular experience is necessary for this position, but any writing experience will be useful. The clerical duties of the Information Coordinator make good typing skills a must. In addition, excellent communications and writing skills are important.

Tips for Entry

Personal contacts are extremely helpful in obtaining a job as an Information Coordinator. Working as an intern or a secretary in an auction house can provide the opportunity to make such contacts.

PUBLICIST

CAREER PROFILE

Duties: Write and distribute press releases; liaison with expert departments; handle press relations; plan special events

Alternate Title: Public Relations Director

Salary Range: $20,000 to $35,000

Employment Prospects: Fair

Advancement Prospects: Poor

Prerequisites:

Education—Bachelor's degree; art and public relations background preferred

Experience—Previous work as an information coordinator or elsewhere in public relations

Special Skills—Writing ability, communications skills

CAREER LADDER

```
+-------------------------------+
|           Publicist           |
+-------------------------------+


+-------------------------------+
|    Information Coordinator     |
+-------------------------------+
```

Position Description

The Publicist at an auction gallery is responsible for publicizing the gallery and its auctions. The Publicist stays closely in touch with the various expert departments and prepares publicity for upcoming sales. This may involve press releases on important works that will be on sale, on the famous collectors who are selling the works, or on the prices expected for artwork at a certain auction.

The Publicist normally supervises a staff of information coordinators or assistants who handle routine press inquiries and perform the day-to-day functions of the department.

The Publicist must also have good contacts in the press in order to obtain editorial coverage for the auction house in newspapers and magazines. This publicity attracts customers to the auction gallery. Special events such as teas, cocktail parties, and exhibition openings are also designed to bring the potential buyers into the auction house and make them aware of the works for sale.

Auctions may be geared to different suggested price ranges, so the Publicist has to target the right audience for the auction gallery's publicity. Information on an auction of major Impressionist paintings must be placed in upscale publications; details on a print auction will likely be targeted to a wider readership.

Salaries

A Publicist will be paid approximately $20,000 to $35,000 per year.

Employment Prospects

A qualified candidate has a fair chance of obtaining a Publicist position at an auction gallery. There are few such jobs, but the turnover is relatively great, making openings available.

Advancement Prospects

It is difficult to advance from the position of Publicist within an auction gallery. Many Publicists leave the auction gallery business to seek employment as Publicists for art galleries or in public relations firms.

Education

The Publicist must have a bachelor's degree, preferably with some background in art or art history and in public relations.

Experience and Skills

Previous work in public relations—either within the auction gallery field or outside it—is essential.

Writing is the most important skill for a Publicist. In addition, the Publicist should have strong interpersonal skills in order to deal effectively with members of the press and with department managers within the auction gallery.

CUSTOMER SERVICE ASSISTANT

CAREER PROFILE

Duties: Answer customer questions, take phone bids, assist clients

Alternate Title: Administrative Assistant

Salary Range: $18,000 to $25,000

Employment Prospects: Fair

Advancement Prospects: Fair

Prerequisites:
　　Education—Bachelor's degree; some art background necessary
　　Experience—None
　　Special Skills—Communication skills; tact; typing

CAREER LADDER

```
┌─────────────────────────────────┐
│   Customer Service Manager      │
└─────────────────────────────────┘

┌─────────────────────────────────┐
│   Customer Service Assistant    │
└─────────────────────────────────┘

┌─────────────────────────────────┐
│    Student or Secretary         │
└─────────────────────────────────┘
```

Position Description

The Customer Service Assistant is a jack-of-all-trades who works to help customers of the auction house. This entails answering customer service queries, taking sealed and telephone bids, assisting with details of credit or shipping, and so on.

It is important for the Customer Service Assistant to get to know the auction house's regular clientele. Serious buyers expect special service, and the Customer Service Assistant is responsible for providing extra help to important clients.

The Customer Service Assistant performs various clerical duties as directed by the department manager, and spends considerable time on the telephone in performing his or her duties. Evening work may be required, as many major auctions are held at night.

This is a good entry-level position for persons interested in the auction gallery business.

Salaries

Customer Service Assistants generally make between $18,000 and $25,000 per year.

Employment Prospects

Chances for a job as a Customer Service Assistant are fair. The number of such positions is limited, but the turnover is relatively rapid.

Advancement Prospects

Opportunities for advancement are also fair. The Customer Service Assistant can move up within the administrative sphere of the auction house or laterally into one of the expert departments.

Education

The Customer Service Assistant must have a bachelor's degree, with at least some background in art. An art or art history major may be preferred, but not required.

Experience and Skills

There are no particular experience requirements for this position, but any work with the public will be useful. A person who has served an internship in an auction gallery will have an advantage in obtaining a job as a Customer Service Assistant.

The clerical duties of the job make it necessary for the Customer Service Assistant to have good typing skills. In addition, the Customer Service Assistant should have excellent communications skills and the ability to deal helpfully and courteously with the public.

CUSTOMER SERVICE MANAGER

CAREER PROFILE

Duties: Manage customer service department; prepare seating plans for major auctions; know clientele; take bids; provide information to customers

Salary Range: $22,000 to $35,000

Employment Prospects: Fair

Advancement Prospects: Fair

Prerequisites:
  Education—Bachelor's degree; art background required
  Experience—Previous work in an administrative department at an auction gallery
  Special Skills—Communications skills; tact; typing

CAREER LADDER

> **Customer Service Manager**

> **Customer Service Assistant**

Position Description

The Customer Service Manager has an important position within the administration of the auction gallery. The customer service department is responsible for customer relations, for keeping both the regular clientele and the occasional buyer happy. The Customer Service Manager supervises a staff that takes care of the routine duties of the department, such as taking bids, giving information, answering questions, and so on.

The Customer Service Manager also has responsibility for becoming familiar with the regular clientele of the gallery and being sensitive to their needs. The Manager must be able to discern which buyers are serious and which are not, and must be able to handle the politics of seating customers at important auctions. The actions of the Customer Service Manager can have a great influence on attracting and retaining regular clientele for the gallery by making each customer feel well taken care of.

Salaries

Customer Service Managers can expect to make a salary of between $22,000 and $35,000 per year.

Employment Prospects

There is a fair chance of a qualified individual's being able to find a position as a Customer Service Manager. Such positions are not numerous, but the turnover is fairly steady.

Advancement Prospects

The Customer Service Manager has a fair opportunity to advance to another position within the auction house, particularly if he or she is interested in making a lateral move to another administrative department or to an expert department.

Education

The Customer Service Manager must have a bachelor's degree and should have either a major or a minor in art or art history.

Experience and Skills

It is necessary for the aspiring Customer Service Manager to have had previous experience as an assistant in the customer service department of an auction gallery, or in a related department, such as advertising or public relations.

The Customer Service Manager must have excellent communications skills and should work well with the public. It is important to be tactful and to have strong social skills. Because of the clerical duties of the position, it is also necessary to have good typing ability.

DEPARTMENT ASSISTANT

CAREER PROFILE

Duties: Perform appraisals; locate artwork for sale; research artwork; assist in arranging sales

Salary Range: $18,000 to $25,000

Employment Prospects: Fair

Advancement Prospects: Fair

Prerequisites:
   Education—Bachelor's degree; art background preferred
   Experience—None
   Special Skills—Communications skills; ability to work well with people

CAREER LADDER

```
┌─────────────────────────────┐
│     Department Manager      │
└─────────────────────────────┘

┌─────────────────────────────┐
│     Department Assistant    │
└─────────────────────────────┘

┌─────────────────────────────┐
│     Student or Secretary    │
└─────────────────────────────┘
```

Position Description

A Department Assistant works in an expert department (e.g., contemporary art, American paintings, or prints) acquiring items for sale, arranging auctions, appraising pieces, preparing catalogues, and working with important customers.

The position of Department Assistant is really a training job. The assistant works closely with the department manager, learning how to find and appraise a specialized type of artwork and how to locate and cultivate potential buyers for that kind of work. This involves interaction with art dealers and collectors as well as estates and trusts.

The position may require some travel and will most likely entail night work, as many important auctions are held in the evening.

Salaries

Salaries for Department Assistants are generally in the $18,000 to $25,000 range.

Employment Prospects

Aspiring Department Assistants have a fair chance of landing such a job. There are usually many applicants for the assistant position, but the turnover tends to be rapid, making openings available.

Advancement Prospects

Advancement opportunities are fair for a Department Assistant. Chances for promotion are particularly good when the business climate is good and, conversely, poor when there is a downturn in the economy. A Department Assistant may be promoted to department manager or move into an administrative department within the auction house. Work as a Department Assistant can also be good experience for someone who wishes to work at an art gallery.

Education

The Department Assistant should have a bachelor's degree, with some background in art or art history.

Experience and Skills

There is no particular experience required of a Department Assistant.

Good communications skills are important in this position, and it is important for the jobholder to be able to deal comfortably with collectors and art dealers. Sales skills can be helpful, and a good eye for art is most valuable.

Tips for Entry

Some of the larger auction galleries offer courses in art; these can be a good background, and they present an opportunity to make contacts within the auction house. A few auction galleries offer internships, which can also get your foot in the door. Finally, an individual may be able to find a secretarial position at an auction house and work his or her way up from there.

DEPARTMENT MANAGER

CAREER PROFILE

Duties: Supervise expert department; find artwork to sell; perform appraisals; research important pieces; arrange sales; cultivate clientele

Alternate Titles: Vice president; Department Head

Salary Range: $22,000 to $40,000+

Employment Prospects: Fair

Advancement Prospects: Poor

Prerequisites:

Education—Bachelor's degree required; art background helpful

Experience—Work as an assistant in an expert or administrative department

Special Skills—Expert knowledge appropriate to the department; ability to deal with the public

CAREER LADDER

```
┌─────────────────────────────┐
│        Gallery Owner        │
└─────────────────────────────┘

┌─────────────────────────────┐
│     Department Manager      │
└─────────────────────────────┘

┌─────────────────────────────┐
│    Department Assistant     │
└─────────────────────────────┘
```

Position Description

A Department Manager runs an expert department at an auction gallery. Examples of expert departments are American paintings, contemporary art, Asian art, Impressionist paintings, Old Master paintings, prints, sculpture, and so on. The Department Manager is an expert at locating artwork for his or her department to sell and at appraising such artwork. This expertise is usually gained on the job while working as an assistant in the department.

The Manager generally is responsible for preparing several sales each year. This involves acquiring items to sell by researching, talking to collectors, and traveling to see particular works; supervising the logistics of the sale; helping to prepare catalogues, advertising, and press releases; appraising items for sale; and nurturing contacts with important collectors and dealers.

Many Department Managers, though not all, are licensed auctioneers. The licensing procedure, usually administered by the state involved, entails the submission of affidavits of good character, but does not usually require any particular educational background.

The Department Manager can make the department successful by carefully cultivating the important buyers in his or her field of expertise. Hence, social skills, communications skills, and sales ability are important.

Salaries

The Department Manager can expect to make a salary of between $22,000 and $40,000 per year, with even higher salaries available to those with more experience or special expertise.

Employment Prospects

A qualified applicant for the position of Department Manager has a fair chance of winning the job. There are few such positions, but the turnover in them is relatively rapid, making openings available.

Advancement Prospects

The opportunities for the Department Manager to advance are limited. Only a handful of senior positions exist in auction galleries. Some Department Managers may, however, move on to open their own auction houses or to work in the art gallery business.

Education

The prospective Department Manager must have a bachelor's degree with some background in art and art history.

Experience and Skills

On-the-job training is the most important preparation an individual can have for this post. Most of the knowledge one needs in order to appraise artwork is acquired while he or she works as an assistant in an expert department.

The Department Manager must have strong communications skills in order to assist with publicity, advertising, and catalogue preparation. It is also critical for him or her to have developed an eye for good artwork and for what will sell, and to be able to deal easily with important customers.

Organizations and Associations

There are no organizations specifically for auction gallery employees. The National Auctioneers Association (NAA) (see Appendix V) might be useful to Department Managers who are also auctioneers.

ART-RELATED BUSINESSES

ARTIST AGENT

CAREER PROFILE

Duties: Solicit work for illustrators; handle promotion, negotiation, billing, traffic, quality control

Alternate Titles: Illustrator's Representative; Artist Representative; Photographer's Representative

Salary Range: 25% commission

Employment Prospects: Fair

Advancement Prospects: Fair

Prerequisites:
   Education—College-level coursework in art, art history, and business
   Experience—Sales and general business experience; familiarity with commercial art
   Special Skills—Communication skills, negotiation skills

CAREER LADDER

```
┌─────────────────────────────┐
│   Independent Artist Agent   │
└─────────────────────────────┘

┌─────────────────────────────┐
│        Artist Agent          │
└─────────────────────────────┘

┌─────────────────────────────┐
│   Assistant to Artist Agent  │
└─────────────────────────────┘
```

Position Description

An Artist Agent works on a commission basis to get work for freelance graphic artists, photographers, and illustrators. Functioning as an artist's marketing arm, the Artist Agent handles many business aspects of the artist's work. Typically, the Agent will promote the artist's work to art directors and others in a position to give out assignments; then, when an assignment is secured, the Agent will negotiate the price, deadline, etc., handle the artist's rights, send out the bill for the job, track the work, handle the transmission of the work, collect the artist's payment, and distribute the money as appropriate.

The Agent helps the artist to build his or her portfolio in order to advance in a particular direction. For example, if an artist wishes to work at illustrating children's books, the Agent will seek jobs of that kind and help the artist build a body of work that will help get more assignments in that field.

Interpersonal skills are important to an Artist Agent because he or she often needs to negotiate as much with the client as with the hiring art director. Some artists are resentful of having to pay the Agent's commission; some art directors enlist the Agent to deal with the artist regarding missed deadlines or unsatisfactory work. This is all part of the Agent's job and requires patience and diplomacy.

Similarly, an artist client may be dissatisfied with the amount or type of work the Agent offers him or her, and these matters must be worked out for the artist/Agent relationship to succeed.

Salaries

This is strictly a commission job, with the Agent receiving 25% to 30% of the artist's fee. Thus yearly income is dependent on how hard the Agent works and how many sales he or she is able to make. Realistically, a newcomer to this field might make $20,000 the first year, but that income should grow as more contacts are made and more assignments are completed successfully.

Employment Prospects

A newcomer to the field has a fair chance of finding employment. Competition in this area has increased markedly in recent years.

Advancement Prospects

Chances for advancement as an Artist Agent are largely self-determined, as the main way to move up in this field is to go out on one's own as an independent Artist Agent. Once you have some strong experience in the field and you determine that you can sell enough business to keep yourself going, you can set up your own agency. Strong contacts in the field and an excellent track record are extremely helpful.

Education

There are no specific educational requirements for an Artist Agent, though most firms would expect candidates to have completed coursework in art history and business or sales.

Experience and Skills

Sales experience is extremely valuable to an Artist Agent. The best preparation for someone hoping to enter this field is to work as an assistant to an Artist Agent.

All business and sales skills are important, and negotiation skills are essential. A thorough knowledge of commercial art is very helpful, and the ability to communicate with others is invaluable.

Organizations and Associations

Networking is an important element of this job, so organizational affiliations are very useful. Prospective Artist Agents should join the Graphic Artists Guild, the Society of Illustrators and the Society of Photography and Artists representatives in order to make contacts and gain professional support (see Appendix V).

Tips for Entry

Look for a job as assistant to a top-notch Artist Agent. Cultivate your instincts; there are no set rules in this business.

PRINT PUBLISHER

CAREER PROFILE

Duties: Confer with artist, choose print medium, select publisher, sell prints

Alternate Title: Print Edition Producer

Salary Range: $25,000 to $100,000+

Employment Prospects: Poor

Advancement Prospects: Poor

Prerequisites:

Education—Most have college degree, though no degree is required

Experience—Work in fine art book publishing or art gallery

Special Skills—Business ability, artistic taste, familiarity with techniques of printmaking

CAREER LADDER

```
┌─────────────────────────────┐
│      Print Publisher         │
└─────────────────────────────┘

┌─────────────────────────────┐
│    Gallery Position or       │
│    Publishing Position       │
└─────────────────────────────┘
```

Position Description

A Print Publisher produces prints—for example, lithographs, serigraphs, or etchings—of an artist's work. The Publisher generally compiles a portfolio of the prints of the various artists with whom he or she works, then sells the portfolio to galleries and collectors.

The Publisher usually selects an artist with whom he or she would like to work on the basis of the artist's work and the Publisher's sense of whether prints of such work will sell. Depending on the way the Publisher prefers to work, the actual ideas regarding the project can come from the artist or from the Publisher. It may take weeks or months to develop an artistic concept for a print series.

Once the artwork is completed, the Publisher works as the liaison with the printer who will be making the prints. It is not necessary for the Publisher to have printmaking skills, but it is important that he or she is well versed in the printmaking process, so that he or she can evaluate different printers and assure high-quality work.

The completed prints are owned by the Publisher, who retains financial responsibility throughout the entire process. The Publisher makes arrangements to pay the artist and the printer according to an agreed-upon formula. It is then the function of the Print Publisher to market the prints to galleries and collectors. This can be done in person, through a sales force or through catalogues. When selling prints personally, the Publisher will find that it is important to have extensive contacts in the art world, so that he or she can locate and target potential customers.

This is essentially an entrepreneurial job for a person with previous experience as an art dealer, a fine-art book publisher, or a gallery salesperson.

Salaries

It is difficult to determine what initial compensation would be for a Print Publisher, but a moderately successful person just starting out might expect to earn from $25,000 to $70,000 a year. As the business grows, profits might increase to $100,000 per year or more. The amount of money earned as a print publisher is a direct result of how much effort you put into your career. There are many different arrangements that can be made financially with clients. Sometimes fees are split, and other times the publisher gives the artist fees. Sometimes a museum does the public relations. All terms are negotiable.

Employment Prospects

It is fairly difficult to get started as a Print Publisher, as this is generally a self-employed position requiring start-up capital. Few Print Publishers employ assistants.

Advancement Prospects

As this is an entrepreneurial job, most Print Publishers regard it as a lifetime goal and do not expect to advance beyond it. Increased income and profitability might be regarded as a form of advancement.

Education

Though there are no formal educational requirements, most people in this work have college degrees.

Experience and Skills

It is essential for a Print Publisher to have worked in an art gallery, in fine-art book publishing, or as an art dealer in order to have the basic tools necessary to succeed.

The Publisher should be familiar with the printmaking process, though he or she need not actually have printmaking skills. In addition, a thorough understanding of business administration is very important.

Tips for Entry

The more experience and contacts one has in the art world, the better. In addition, a few large Print Publishers do hire assistants; working in this capacity could be very helpful in learning the business.

CORPORATE CURATOR

CAREER PROFILE

Duties: Acquire and place artwork for corporate collection; record keeping

Salary Range: $30,000 to $75,000

Employment Prospects: Good

Advancement Prospects: Fair

Prerequisites:
   Education—Bachelor's degree in art or art history; master's degree preferred
   Experience—Gallery or museum work
   Special Skills—Artistic taste; understanding of corporate climate; ability to deal with all kinds of people; interpersonal skills

CAREER LADDER

```
┌─────────────────────────────┐
│   Corporate Art Director     │
└─────────────────────────────┘

┌─────────────────────────────┐
│      Corporate Curator       │
└─────────────────────────────┘

┌─────────────────────────────┐
│          Registrar           │
└─────────────────────────────┘
```

Position Description

A Corporate Curator works within a corporation's art program. Such programs generally are started when the corporation moves into a new building; important individuals within the firm see a need for an organized way to decorate the new surroundings while enriching the environment for employees and supporting the art community. Thus a formal program is begun to acquire artwork, place it in appropriate settings within the physical environment, and undertake the necessary record keeping to keep track of the growing collection.

The Corporate Curator is involved with the purchase of artwork based on guidelines set down by the corporation. Many corporations form advisory boards of art professionals to guide them in their art acquisitions. The Curator is responsible for working within the given budget and for registrar-type tracking of the pieces within the collection, so a strong detail orientation and administrative skills are important.

This position is a unique one in the art world, in that the employees of the corporation who come into contact with the artwork may not be receptive to it. Some corporations purchase artwork that might be considered challenging to the workers—that is, not just a kind of pretty wallpaper—and the Corporate Curator must be sensitive to this. Therefore, the Curator should have strong communications skills and the ability to deal with all kinds of people, such as artists, corporate executives, clerical workers.

Companies like Art Assets are trying to go beyond the norm to provide innovative services and work with emerging artists.

Salaries

Entry-level salaries for Corporate Curators range from about $30,000 to $60,000 and can go higher for those with strong registrar experience. As one progresses within the field, salaries continue to range upward to about $75,000 per year.

Employment Prospects

Because this is an expanding area, with more companies starting formal art programs each year, employment prospects are good and continually growing.

Advancement Prospects

Advancement prospects for Corporate Curators are fair. There are usually two or more Curators working for an art program director, so upward movement is somewhat limited, but experience in this position is also good preparation for careers in gallery or museum work.

Education

A bachelor's degree in art or art history is essential, and a master's degree in art history, fine arts, or arts administration is strongly preferred.

Experience and Skills

Any kind of art experience is helpful to those wishing to enter this field. Experience requirements tend to be less formal and rigorous for Corporate Curators than for their museum counterparts. Record keeping and registrar experience, though, is especially valued in the corporate setting.

Though artistic taste is hard to define, it is a valuable asset for a Corporate Curator. In addition, it is important for the aspiring Curator to have a strong ability to communicate with very different people—both artists and corporate executives, for example.

Organizations and Associations

The organization for Corporate Curators is the Association of Professional Art Advisors (APAA) (see Appendix V).

Tips for Entry

Any experience in registrar work—perhaps volunteering in a local museum—will be helpful in gaining entry to this field.

ART CONSULTANT

CAREER PROFILE

Duties: Keep current on art trends; establish contacts with artists, galleries, and clients; market consulting services

Salary Range: $25,000 to $150,000+

Employment Prospects: Fair

Advancement Prospects: Poor

Prerequisites:

Education—No degree required, but most have college degrees

Experience—Extensive familiarity with the art world; art gallery experience is especially useful

Special Skills—Sales skills, organizational ability, outgoing nature

CAREER LADDER

```
┌─────────────────────────────────┐
│   Independent Art Consultant    │
└─────────────────────────────────┘

┌─────────────────────────────────┐
│         Art Consultant          │
└─────────────────────────────────┘

┌─────────────────────────────────┐
│        Gallery Position         │
└─────────────────────────────────┘
```

Position Description

An Art Consultant is a person, usually self-employed, who assists people in buying artwork. Because buying art can be an important investment, and because the art world seems complex and unfamiliar to some people, potential art buyers may wish to call on the services of someone who is more familiar with various kinds of artwork, artists, and galleries to help them make a purchase decision.

Generally, Art Consultants have had a lifelong interest in art and spend a great deal of time and energy learning about different styles and trends in the art world. They may have majored in art or art history in college. They may have volunteered or been employed by a local art museum. They may have worked in one or more art galleries. Most typically, art is both an occupation and a hobby for them, and as Art Consultants they find enjoyment in bringing their own love of art to others.

To get started, one may go to work for one of the few large art consulting firms. Such firms generally work on a contract basis to assist corporations in decorating their offices with art, or to help builders to design art into their new office complexes to make them more attractive. In such a consulting firm one can get a good feel for the business and for the delicate skills needed to match art to a client's taste.

Alternatively, someone with experience in gallery or museum work and a large number of potential clients can go into business for him or herself as an Art Consultant. Such a person would select galleries and artists with whom to work, creating a good mix of styles and prices, and then go about attracting clients. The Consultant may initiate monthly events, such as bus tours to nearby museums, visits to artists' studios or lectures at certain galleries. He or she will publicize these events through regular mailings to a client list. Compensation will come from commissions on gallery purchases by clients and/or flat fees on top of the price of clients' purchases directly from artists.

Salaries

A self-employed Consultant can earn from $25,000 to $150,000+ a year, depending on the number and prestige of his or her clients. Payment can either be a set fee for a specified period of time or 5% to 10% of the purchase. A Consultant who is employed by a large art consulting firm will earn about $30,000 to $75,000.

Employment Prospects

It is fairly easy to obtain employment with an art consulting firm if you have a degree in art or art history and some sales and interpersonal skills. To be an independent Art Consultant, you must have extensive contacts in the art world and some start-up capital.

Advancement Prospects

Independent Consultants generally view this work as a lifelong goal. Increased earnings may thus be viewed as a kind of advancement. Art Consultants working for consulting firms have limited opportunities for advancement, and they may wish to go out on their own as Consultants or to move into gallery work. They may also work for corporations, but this can be limiting.

Education

Art consulting firms generally require bachelor's degrees, and most independent Consultants have such degrees as well.

Experience and Skills

There are no specific requirements, but any experience in gallery or museum work will be useful. Sales and marketing experience is helpful as well.

A successful Art Consultant is likely to have spent a great deal of free time learning about art through such means as lectures, courses, talking to artists, and poking around museums. The more outgoing and curious one is, and the more contacts he or she has in the art world, the better his or her chances of success.

Organizations and Associations

An Art Consultant should be a member of any art museum in his or her area for networking.

Tips for Entry

This is a job in which volunteer work at a museum can be helpful. Giving tours, helping to arrange lectures, assisting curators—anything that increases your knowledge of art and your contacts within the art world—will help prepare you for working as an Art Consultant. This can sometimes be done in return for low pay or college credits.

ART TRANSPORTER

CAREER PROFILE

Duties: Coordinating traveling art exhibits; consolidating works; overseeing transportation arrangements; liaison with lenders, institutions, and local carriers

Alternate Title: Traffic Manager—This is more of a business term. Art Handler is more common.

Salary Range: $18,000 to $30,000, $50,000 for department managers

Employment Prospects: Good

Advancement Prospects: Good

Prerequisites:
  Education—Bachelor's degree in art or art history, with some business coursework. Most have Master's Degrees, but this isn't necessary.
  Experience—Exposure to transportation and freight industry
  Special Skills—Administrative ability, detail orientation, typing

CAREER LADDER

```
+-------------------------------+
|     Sales Representative       |
+-------------------------------+

+-------------------------------+
|       Art Transporter          |
+-------------------------------+

+-------------------------------+
|      Warehouse Manager         |
+-------------------------------+
```

Position Description

An Art Transporter is a key person in the moving of artwork for exhibition—an important and growing aspect of the art and museum worlds. This is also done for galleries, collectors, and corporate collections. Art transportation includes the packing, shipping, and tracking of individual pieces of art; it is a specialized business because of the value of the goods being transported and the special care the works require. But a major part of the art transportation business is the coordination of the moving of entire exhibits from city to city and museum to museum, often over great distances and lengthy periods of time.

The Art Transporter is responsible for the smooth movement of such exhibits. The Art Transporter deals with museum registrars, local freight carriers, lenders of artwork, and others, in the consolidation, packing, dispatching, and moving of works. As a traffic manager, the Art Transporter will be given a complete itinerary for an exhibit before it begins and will be responsible for monitoring all the details of its delivery to each museum in a timely fashion.

Salaries

Art Transporters can expect to start at around $18,000 per year. Those with more experience and those who work for larger art transportation firms can make up to $30,000 per year.

Employment Prospects

Art transportation is a fairly open field in which to find employment. Because the field is not well known to the public, competition for positions is less intense than in other art-related careers. Also, there is less competition because of lack of applicants with art knowledge.

Advancement Prospects

Chances for advancement in art transportation are good, particularly for those who wish to move into the sales area. There are frequent openings for representatives to sell art transportation services to galleries and museums; experience in traffic management will enable a sales-oriented person to make an easy transition into an outside sales position.

Very few companies have full-time salespeople. Mostly management handles sales as well.

Education

A bachelor's degree in art or art history is good preparation for a career in art transportation. Business courses should supplement the liberal arts or fine arts background in order to provide some practical training.

Experience and Skills

The best possible practical experience for someone wishing to enter this field is to work for a gallery or as summer help in a museum. Art shuttles are better than van lines, as only a small percentage of van lines do business in art. Other positions that might help get a foot in the door include installer, packer, and crater. Familiarity with transportation procedures—and, in particular, with bills of lading—is valuable to potential employers in this business.

A detail orientation is important for the successful Art Transporter, who may have to track several important exhibits. Any business, administrative, or commercial skills will be valuable. Typing is an important skill for an art transporter, and he or she should be articulate in order to deal effectively with museum personnel, art lenders, freight carriers, and others.

This is a deadline-oriented, high-pressure business, and the ability to deal with stress is valuable to those working in it.

Tips for Entry

Art transportation is a business in which one can truly work up the ladder. Full- or part-time warehouse work can lead to on-the-job training for a career in this business. In addition, any contacts with museum registrars and/or fine-art packers would be useful.

FRAMING TECHNICIAN

CAREER PROFILE

Duties: Cutting, mounting, joining, blocking, stretching, and assembling framing materials

Alternate Title: Framing Apprentice

Salary Range: $16,000 to $25,000

Employment Prospects: Good

Advancement Prospects: Good

Prerequisites:
Education—High school; may be a part-time job for high school student
Experience—None
Special Skills—Manual dexterity, eye for design

CAREER LADDER

```
┌─────────────────────────────┐
│    Framing Salesperson      │
└─────────────────────────────┘

┌─────────────────────────────┐
│    Framing Technician       │
└─────────────────────────────┘

┌─────────────────────────────┐
│         Student             │
└─────────────────────────────┘
```

Position Description

A Framing Technician is the junior employee of a frame shop. He or she is in a training position in which all the skills of framing are learned. The Technician will become familiar with the materials used in framing and the methods by which a frame is assembled.

Under the supervision of a framer, the Technician will learn to cut glass, mats, and frames; how to block, stretch, and dry-mount materials that are to be framed; how to join frames; and how to assemble the various materials for a completed frame.

Once these skills have been learned, the Technician will execute the frame designs created by the salespeople in the frame shop. It is expected that the Technician will work with care and that he or she will have some understanding of the design elements of the custom frame.

Salaries

The Framing Technician usually works for an hourly wage that ranges from $8.00 for a beginner to $12.00 for more experienced personnel.

Employment Prospects

It is fairly easy to obtain a position as a Frame Technician. This entry-level job is a good part-time occupation for a high school or college student who is taking art courses.

Advancement Prospects

A Frame Technician who learns quickly and performs diligently has a good chance of being promoted to framing salesperson.

Education

A high school diploma is a general requirement for a Framing Technician, but a high school student may be hired for this position on a part-time or vacation basis.

Experience and Skills

No particular experience is necessary, but a background in art is helpful. This is a training position in which most of the skills of the trade will be learned, but manual dexterity and the ability to work carefully and plan ahead are valuable. An instinct for design would be useful as well.

Organizations and Associations

The Professional Picture Framers Association (see Appendix V) serves people in this field.

Tips for Entry

Check with all the frame shops in your area, and be persistent. Your eagerness to learn could be valuable to a potential employer.

FRAMING SALESPERSON

CAREER PROFILE

Duties: Assisting customers in selecting custom framing; preparing and assembling custom frames; training framing technicians

Alternate Title: Senior Framing Technician

Salary Range: $16,000 to $25,000

Employment Prospects: Good

Advancement Prospects: Fair

Prerequisites:
    Education—High school; art background; framing apprenticeship; art school experience
    Experience—Work in frame shop
    Special Skills—Framing skills; people skills

CAREER LADDER

```
┌─────────────────────────────┐
│       Custom Framer         │
└─────────────────────────────┘

┌─────────────────────────────┐
│    Framing Salesperson      │
└─────────────────────────────┘

┌─────────────────────────────┐
│      Frame Technician       │
└─────────────────────────────┘
```

Position Description

Framing Salespeople are the helpful counter people at a frame shop. They assist customers by displaying various framing materials and making suggestions as to the design of a custom frame.

This is a challenging position, because customers bring a wide variety of items in for framing, and the Salesperson must try to help the customer create a frame that will suit both the artwork and the environment in which it will eventually be displayed. This is a matter of taste and design, and the Salesperson must learn when to lend his or her expertise and when to tactfully bow to the customer's preferences. Thus, this job requires design skills, knowledge of the materials available, communications ability, and the technical framing skills to bring it all together.

The Framing Salesperson is also responsible for writing orders carefully and correctly, so that the frame will be assembled properly, and for calculating the price of the finished frame. In addition, the Salesperson may have to instruct or assist one or more technicians in constructing frames.

Salaries

Framing Salespeople are usually paid by the hour, generally in a range from $8.00 to $15.00. More qualified salespeople will be paid more.

Employment Prospects

It is relatively easy for a framer with some experience to get a job as a Framing Salesperson. There are many frame shops, and turnover is fairly high.

Advancement Prospects

Advancement from this position is only fair. To advance, one may become a frame shop manager, a job in which there is considerably less turnover. Or a Framing Salesperson may open his or her own frame shop, which requires capital and some business administration skills.

Education

A high school diploma is generally required, and a framing apprenticeship is a must. This is not an entry-level position. It is also good to have passed the Certified Picture Framer exam given by the Professional Picture Framers Association.

Experience and Skills

A Framing Salesperson should have one to two years of experience as a framing technician. It is necessary for a Framing Salesperson to have a full range of framing skills, which are usually acquired through an informal framing apprenticeship.

Organizations and Associations

Framing salespersons may wish to join the Professional Picture Framers Association (see Appendix V).

Tips for Entry

It is often possible to obtain employment as a Framing Salesperson on a part-time basis. This can lead to full-time employment later.

CUSTOM FRAMER

CAREER PROFILE

Duties: Managing frame shop, designing frame jobs, hiring, training, sales

Alternate Titles: Framer, Frame Shop/Gallery Manager

Salary Range: $25,000 to $75,000

Employment Prospects: Fair

Advancement Prospects: Poor

Prerequisites:
    Education—Art background; bachelor's degree helpful; business courses useful
    Experience—Framing apprenticeship; sales; business administration
    Special Skills—Framing skills, customer relations

CAREER LADDER

```
┌─────────────────────────────┐
│      Frame Shop Owner        │
└─────────────────────────────┘

┌─────────────────────────────┐
│       Custom Framer          │
└─────────────────────────────┘

┌─────────────────────────────┐
│     Framing Salesperson      │
└─────────────────────────────┘
```

Position Description

The Custom Framer manages a store that specializes in custom frame work. Many such stores also house small galleries, with which the Custom Framer may be involved. In general, however, the Custom Framer is responsible for assisting customers in selecting framing materials, designing the framing, and executing the framing or directing others to do so.

The framer hires and trains sales clerks, designers, and technicians to assist him or her in performing these tasks. He or she will be involved in business administration activities as well, such as bookkeeping, advertising, and purchasing of materials.

Some Custom Framers own their own shops; others manage such shops for their owners. Store owners are generally more involved with the business aspects of the shop than are Custom Framers, who are usually working for others. A frame shop owner may see this entrepreneurial position as his or her ultimate goal, not wishing to advance further. A Custom Framer who is working for somebody else is unlikely to advance unless he or she opens a frame shop of his or her own.

Salaries

Salaries for people in this position range from about $25,000 for the manager of a small frame shop to about $75,000 for the person who manages a larger, more prestigious shop. The owner of a custom frame house in a large art market such as New York may make upwards of $100,000 if the store is especially profitable.

Employment Prospects

It is fairly easy for someone who has served a framing apprenticeship to become a Custom Framer once he or she has some experience. There are many frame shops, and experienced personnel are hard to find. For an owner, it requires capital to start up or purchase a framing business.

Advancement Prospects

Custom Framers find it difficult to advance in the field without opening their own businesses. An owner may consider advancement to mean increased profitability of his or her business.

Education

A high school diploma is a standard requirement; an art background is helpful, and any business courses would be useful. For an upsale custom shop, a higher education degree may be necessary.

Experience and Skills

A Custom Framer should have several years of experience in framing. It is necessary for a Custom Framer to have served an apprenticeship in framing. This is not a formal program, but a period of training in mounting, cutting, blocking, stretching, joining, and designing of framing materials. Most Framers acquire this training by working in sales and technician positions at frame shops.

Organizations and Associations

A Custom Framer may wish to join the Professional Picture Framers Association (see Appendix V).

Tips for Entry

Any employment experience in a frame shop—even part time—will be useful.

ART SUPPLY SALESPERSON

CAREER PROFILE

Duties: Assist customers, take inventory, reorder items, make sales

Alternate Title: Art Supply Salesclerk

Salary Range: $7.00 to $12.00 per hour

Employment Prospects: Good

Advancement Prospects: Good

Prerequisites:
Education—High school diploma
Experience—Previous sales experience preferred but not mandatory
Special Skills—Dependability, honesty, willingness to learn and to work hard, friendliness

CAREER LADDER

```
┌─────────────────────────────────┐
│   Art Supply Store Manager      │
└─────────────────────────────────┘

┌─────────────────────────────────┐
│   Art Supply Salesperson        │
└─────────────────────────────────┘

┌─────────────────────────────────┐
│          Student                │
└─────────────────────────────────┘
```

Position Description

An Art Supply Salesperson is the customer contact person in an art supply store. The job's duties include helping customers to find the items they need; assisting customers with information about art supplies; ringing up sales; inventorying items in the store; reordering items as needed; and performing other tasks the manager may require, such as stocking shelves or dusting merchandise.

An art supply store usually has one or more Salespersons working for a store manager. Hours generally follow the normal retail times, with some evening hours available, as well as weekend hours.

Salaries

Most Art Supply Salespersons are paid on an hourly basis, with rates running from $7.00 to $12.00 per hour depending on experience. A full-time Salesperson would earn about $14,000 to $25,000 a year.

Employment Prospects

There are good opportunities for young people to get into this job. Many high school and college students find part-time work in art supply stores.

Advancement Prospects

The chances for advancement in this field are good. A hard-working, capable employee can work his or her way up to become an assistant store manager or a store manager.

Education

There is no particular educational requirement for Art Supply Salespeople. A high school or college student can qualify for this position.

Experience and Skills

Most store managers are willing to hire inexperienced people for this job, but they generally prefer people with some previous experience in sales.

Personal qualities are more important than experience for a beginning Art Supply Salesperson. It is imperative that the Salesperson be dependable and honest. Friendliness and courteousness are key attributes. Finally, a willingness to learn and to work hard is valuable to potential employers.

Tips for Entry

Though there are no special educational requirements for this job, any art courses and business courses—high school or college—will be beneficial.

ART SUPPLY STORE MANAGER

CAREER PROFILE

Duties: Supervise employees, handle accounting, assist customers, oversee advertising, order merchandise

Salary Range: $20,000 to $40,000

Employment Prospects: Good

Advancement Prospects: Poor

Prerequisites:
   Education—Bachelor's degree preferred
   Experience—Previous sales experience
   Special Skills—Organization, detail orientation, management ability, sales skills

CAREER LADDER

```
┌─────────────────────────────────┐
│    Art Supply Store Manager      │
└─────────────────────────────────┘

┌─────────────────────────────────┐
│     Art Supply Salesperson       │
└─────────────────────────────────┘

┌─────────────────────────────────┐
│            Student               │
└─────────────────────────────────┘
```

Position Description

An Art Supply Store Manager is responsible for the smooth functioning of an art supply store. This includes the hiring and training of employees; ordering merchandise and monitoring sales; handling or overseeing the bookkeeping and accounting; making sure the store is clean and orderly; and performing the same customer assistance and sales duties as the art supply salespeople.

The Manager should be prepared to work long hours, since he or she cannot normally perform all of these functions between nine and five. Evening and weekend work are usually required to keep the store running smoothly.

Salaries

Salaries for Art Supply Store Managers generally range from $20,000 to $40,000 per year.

Employment Prospects

There are good opportunities for people with experience in this field to move up to store management. Since there is high turnover on the salesclerk level, there is limited competition for management positions.

Advancement Prospects

Opportunities to advance in this field are poor. Store management is the highest position available, though an individual may wish to open his or her own store or to find work with an art supply manufacturer.

Education

Not all art supply stores require their Managers to have college degrees, but such degrees are helpful.

Experience and Skills

Art Supply Store Managers should have previous experience as art supply salespersons. In addition, an art background and familiarity with art supplies is important.

The Store Manager should have supervisory skills, general business and sales skills, and such qualities as dependability, honesty, willingness to work hard, and friendliness.

Organizations and Associations

The organization for the art supply business is the National Art Materials Trade Association (see Appendix V).

Tips for Entry

The combination of experience in business and art is valuable to employers in this field.

APPENDIXES

APPENDIX I
EDUCATIONAL INSTITUTIONS

UNDERGRADUATE PROGRAMS

The great majority of colleges and universities offer degree programs in art and art history, so we have not listed them here; a general college guide such as *Barron's* or *Fiske's* will provide you with listings of these common majors. Be sure to look under different headings—for example, those interested in fine art should check such majors as art, ceramic art, crafts, drawing, fiber/textiles, illustration, painting, printmaking, sculpture, studio art and visual art. Similarly, those interested in graphics should check commercial art, computer graphics, design, graphic design, and illustration design. Majors like advertising, architecture, art education, art history, fashion design, interior design, jewelry design, and photography are listed separately.

Since programs of study in art therapy and arts administration are less common, a listing of schools providing these majors is presented here to make the information more readily available.

Art Therapy

ARKANSAS

University of Central Arkansas
Conway, AR 72035
www.uca.edu

ILLINOIS

Barat College
Lake Forest, IL 60045
www.barat.edu

INDIANA

Marian College
Indianapolis, IN 46222
www.marian.edu

KANSAS

Emporia State University
Emporia, KS 66801
www.emporia.edu

MASSACHUSETTS

Anna Maria College
Paxton, MA 01612
www.annamaria.edu

Elms College
Chicopee, MA 01013
www.elms.edu

Emmanuel College
Boston, MA 02115
www.emmanuel.edu

Springfield College
Springfield, MA 01109
www.spfld.edu

NEW MEXICO

College of Santa Fe
Santa Fe, NM 87505
www.csf.edu

NEW YORK

Russell Sage College
Troy, NY 12180
www.sage.edu

OHIO

Bowling Green State University
Bowling Green, OH 43403
www.bgsu.cdu

Capital University
Columbus, OH 43209
www.capital.edu

Ursuline College
Pepper Pike, OH 44124
www.ursuline.edu

PENNSYLVANIA

Carlow College
Pittsburgh, PA 15213
www.carlow.edu

Mercyhurst College
Erie, PA 16546
www.mercyhurst.edu

Seton Hill College
Greensburg, PA 15601
www.setonhill.edu

Arts Administration

CALIFORNIA

University of the Pacific
Stockton, CA 95211
www.uop.edu

GEORGIA

Georgia College
Milledgeville, GA 31061
www.gac.peachnet.edu

Wesleyan College
Macon, GA 31210
www.wesleyan-college.edu

ILLINOIS

Columbia College
Chicago, IL 60605
www.colum.edu

Illinois Wesleyan University
Bloomington, IL 61702
www.iwu.edu

INDIANA

Butler University
Indianapolis, IN 46208
www.butler.edu

KENTUCKY

University of Kentucky
Lexington, KY 40506
www.uky.edu

LOUISIANA

Southeastern Louisiana University
Hammond, LA 70402
www.selu.edu

MASSACHUSETTS

Anna Maria College
Paxton, MA 01612
www.annamaria.edu

Elms College
Chicopee, MA 01013
www.elms.edu

Simmons College
Boston, MA 02115
www.simmons.edu

MISSOURI

Culver-Stockton College
Canton, MO 63435
www.culver.edu

NEW MEXICO

College of Santa Fe
Santa Fe, NM 87505
www.csf.edu

NEW YORK

Wagner College
Staten Island, NY 10301
www.wagner.edu

GRADUATE PROGRAMS

As with undergraduate majors, graduate programs in such areas as applied arts and design, art and art history, and architecture are too numerous to list here; a guide to graduate schools such as *Peterson's* can provide this information. However, museum studies is a program offered at only a few dozen schools; the following listing is provided for your convenience.

Museum Studies

ARIZONA

Arizona State University
Tempe, AZ 85287
www.asu.edu

CALIFORNIA

California State University/Long Beach
Long Beach, CA 90840
www.csulb.edu

John F. Kennedy University
Orinda, CA 94563
www.jfku.edu

San Francisco State University
San Francisco, CA 94132
www.sfsu.edu

University of California/Riverside
Riverside, CA 92521
www.ucr.edu

University of Southern California
Los Angeles, CA 90089
www.usc.edu

COLORADO

Colorado State University
Fort Collins, CO 80523
www.colostate.edu

University of Colorado at Boulder
Boulder, CO 80309
www.colorado.edu

University of Denver
Denver, CO 80210
www.du.edu

DELAWARE

University of Delaware
Newark, DE 19717
www.udel.edu

DISTRICT OF COLUMBIA

George Washington University
Washington, DC 20052
www.gwis.circ.gwu.edu

FLORIDA

University of Florida
Gainesville, FL 32611
www.ufl.edu

IOWA

University of Iowa
Iowa City, IA 52240
www.uiowa.edu

LOUISIANA

Southern University at New Orleans
New Orleans, LA 70126
www.suno.edu

MARYLAND

Morgan State University
Baltimore, MD 21251
www.morgan.edu

MASSACHUSETTS

Boston University
Boston, MA 02215
web.bu.edu

Framingham State College
Framingham, MA 01701
www.framingham.edu

Tufts University
Medford, MA 02155
www.tufts.edu

MICHIGAN

University of Michigan
Ann Arbor, MI 48109
www.umich.edu

NEBRASKA

University of Nebraska/Lincoln
Lincoln, NE 68588
www.unl.edu

NEW JERSEY

Seton Hall University
South Orange, NJ 07079
www.shu.edu

NEW YORK

Bank Street College of Education
New York, NY 10025
www.bnkst.edu

Bard Graduate Center
New York, NY 10021
www.bard.edu

College of New Rochelle
New Rochelle, NY 10805
www.cnr.edu

Fashion Institute of Technology (SUNY)
New York, NY 10001
www.fitnyc.suny.edu

New York University
New York, NY 10003
www.nyu.edu

State University of New York at Oneonta
Cooperstown, NY 13326
www.oneonta.edu

Syracuse University
Syracuse, NY 13244
cwis.syr.edu

OHIO

Case Western Reserve University
Cleveland, OH 44106
www.cwru.edu

PENNSYLVANIA

Duquesne University
Pittsburgh, PA 15282
www.duq.edu

University of the Arts
Philadelphia, PA 19102
www.uarts.edu

TEXAS

Baylor University
Waco, TX 76798
www.baylor.edu

Texas Tech University
Lubbock, TX 79409
www.ttu.edu

VIRGINIA

College of William and Mary
Williamsburg, VA 23187
www.wm.edu

Hampton University
Hampton, VA 23668
www.hamptonu.edu

WASHINGTON

University of Washington
Seattle, WA 98195
www.washington.edu

APPENDIX II
TRADE, INDUSTRIAL
AND VOCATIONAL SCHOOLS

The following is a list of schools that offer training in art—generally career-oriented and geared to aspiring commercial, graphic, and fine artists. They range from public vocational high schools to private instructional studios and profit-making trade schools. For additional possibilities, check into the community colleges in your area.

ALABAMA

ITT Technical Institute
500 Riverhills Business Park
Birmingham, AL 35242
(205) 991-5410
www.itt-tech.edu

ARIZONA

Scottsdale Artists' School
3720 N. Marshall Way
Scottsdale, AZ 85251
(602) 990-1422 or (800) 333-5707
www.scottsdaleartschool.org

ARKANSAS

Arkansas Arts Center
P.O. Box 2137
Little Rock, AR 72203
(501) 372-4000
www.arkarts.com

University of Arkansas Community College/Hope
P.O. Box 140
Hope, AR 71802
(870) 777-5722
www.uacch.cc.ar.us

CALIFORNIA

Academy of Art College
79 New Montgomery St.
San Francisco, CA 94105
(415) 274-2222 or (800) 544-ARTS
www.academyart.edu

Art Center College of Design
1700 Lida St.
Pasadena, CA 91103
(626) 396-2373
www.artcenter.edu

California College of Arts & Crafts
450 Irwin St.
San Francisco, CA 94107
(800) 447-1-ART
www.ccac-art.edu

California Institute of the Arts
24700 McBean Pkwy.
Valencia, CA 91355-2340
(805) 253-7863
www.calarts.edu

California Institute of Technology
1201 E. California Blvd.
Pasadena, CA 91125-0001
(626) 395-6346
www.caltech.edu

Hollywood Art Center School
2025 N. Highland Ave.
Los Angeles, CA 90068
(323) 851-1103

Otis College of Art & Design
9045 Lincoln Blvd.
Los Angeles, CA 90045
(310) 665-6800 or (800) 527-OTIS
www.otisart.edu

Richmond Art Center
2540 Barrett Ave.
Richmond, CA 94804
(510) 620-6772
www.therac.org

San Francisco Art Institute
800 Chestnut St.
San Francisco, CA 94133
(415) 771-7020
www.sanfranciscoart.edu

COLORADO

Aurora Schools Technical Center
500 Airport Blvd.
Aurora, CO 80011
(303) 344-4910

Colorado Institute of Art
200 East Ninth Ave.
Denver, CO 80203-2903
(303) 837-0825 or (800) 275-2420
www.cia.aii.edu

Washington Heights Art Center
6375 W. First Ave.
Lakewood, CO 80226
(303) 237-7407

CONNECTICUT

Art Guild
P.O. Box 1482
Farmington, CT 06034
(860) 677-6205

Connecticut Institute of Art
581 W. Putnam Ave.
Greenwich, CT 06830
(203) 869-4430
www.artinstitute.com

Lyme Academy of Fine Arts
84 Lyme St.
Old Lyme, CT 06371
(860) 434-5232 x122
www.lymeacademy.edu

Paier College of Art
20 Gorham Ave.
Hamden, CT 06514
(203) 287-3031
www.Paierart.com

DELAWARE

Delaware Art Museum School
2301 Kentmere Pkwy.
Wilmington, DE 19806
(302) 571-9594
www.delart.mus.de.us

DISTRICT OF COLUMBIA

Corcoran School of Art
500 17th St. NW
Washington, DC 20006
(202) 639-1814
www.corcoran.org

FLORIDA

Dunedin Fine Arts & Cultural Center
1143 Michigan Blvd.
Dunedin, FL 34698
(727) 298-3322
www.flamuseums.org/fam/flamuseums/
     pages/030.htm

**Lindsey Hopkins Technical Education
     Center**
750 NW 20th St.
Miami, FL 33127
(305) 324-6070
www.dcps.dade.k12.fl.us/lindsey

**Miami Lakes Technical Education
     Center**
5780 NW 158th St.
Miami, FL 33014
(305) 557-1100
www.dade.k12.fl.us/mltec

New World School of the Arts
300 Northeast Second Ave.
Miami, FL 33132-2297
(305) 237-3620
www.mdcc.edu

Tampa Technical Institute
2410 East Bush Blvd.
Tampa, FL 33612
(813) 935-5700

Ringling School of Art & Design
2700 N. Tamiami Trl.
Sarasota, FL 34234
(941) 351-5100
www.tkonet.com

South Technical Education Center
1300 SW 30th Ave.
Boynton Beach, FL 33435
(561) 369-7000

GEORGIA

The Art Institute of Atlanta
6600 Peachtree Dunwoody Rd.
100 Embassy Row
Atlanta, GA 30328
(770) 384-8300 or (800) 274-4242
www.aia.aii.edu

Gertrude Herbert Institute of Art
506 Telfair St.
Augusta, GA 30901
(706) 722-5495

Savannah College of Art & Design
342 Bull St.
Savannah, GA 31401
(912) 525-5100 or (800) 869-SCAD
www.scad.edu

HAWAII

Honolulu Academy of Arts
900 S. Beretania St.
Honolulu, HI 96814
(808) 532-8700
www.honoluluacademy.org

IDAHO

ITT Technical Institute
12302 W. Explorer Dr.
Boise, ID 83713-1529
(208) 322-8844
www.itt-tech.edu

ILLINOIS

American Academy of Art
332 S. Michigan Ave.
Chicago, IL 60604
(312) 461-0600
www.aaart.edu

Art Institute of Chicago
37 S. Wabash
Chicago, IL 60603
(312) 899-5219
www.artic.edu

**The Illinois Institute of Art
     at Chicago**
Apparel Center
350 N. Orleans St. #136
Chicago, IL 60654-1503
www.ilia.aii.edu

Peoria Art Guild
203 Harrison St.
Peoria, IL 61602
(309) 637-2787
www.ilohwy.com/p/peoriaag.htm

INDIANA

J. Everett Light Career Center
1901 E. 86th St.
Indianapolis, IN 46240
(317) 259-5265
www.msdwt.k12.in.us/schools/JELCC/
     JELC.htm

IOWA

Des Moines Art Center School
4700 Grand Ave.
Des Moines, IA 50312
(515) 277-4405

KENTUCKY

ITT Technical Institute
10509 Timberwood Circle
Louisville, KY 40223-5392
(502) 327-7424

LOUISIANA

Sowela Technical Institute
3820 J. Bennett Johnston Ave.
Lake Charles, LA 70615
(318) 491-2688
www.embark.com/details/college/1/40/
     d4_4740.asp

MAINE

Maine College of Art
97 Spring St.
Portland, ME 04101
(800) 639-4808
www.meca.edu

MARYLAND

Maryland Institute College of Art
1300 W. Mt. Royal Ave.
Baltimore, MD 21217
(410) 225-2255
www.mica.edu

Mergenthaler Vocational School
3500 Hillen Rd.
Baltimore, MD 21218
(410) 396-6496

Schuler School of Fine Arts
7 E. Lafayette Ave.
Baltimore, MD 21202
(410) 685-3568
www.auronet.com/schuler/

MASSACHUSETTS

Art Institute of Boston
700 Beacon St.
Boston, MA 02215
(617) 262-1223
www.aiboston.edu

ITT Technical Institute
1671 Worcester Rd., Suite 100
Framingham, MA 01702
(508) 879-6266
www.itt-tech.edu

Massachusetts College of Art
621 Huntington Ave.
Boston, MA 02115
(617) 232-1555 x443
www.massart.edu

Museum of Fine Arts School
230 The Fenway
Boston, MA 02115
(617) 267-6100
www.smfa.edu

New England School of Art & Design
81 Arlington St.
Boston, MA 02116
(617) 536-0383
www.miser.suffolk.edu/nesad/

New Art Center
P.O. Box 600330
Newtonville, MA 02460-0003
(617) 964-3424
www.newartcenter.org

MICHIGAN

Center for Creative Studies
201 E. Kirby
Detroit, MI 48202
(313) 872-3118
www.ccscad.edu

Kendall College of Art & Design
111 Division Ave. North
Grand Rapids, MI 49503-3194
(800) 676-2787
www.kcad.edu

MINNESOTA

Minneapolis College of Art & Design
2501 Stevens Ave. South
Minneapolis, MN 55404
(800) 874-MCAD
www.mcad.edu

MISSOURI

Kansas City Art Institute
4415 Warwick Blvd.
Kansas City, MO 64111
(816) 472-4852
www.kcai.edu

NEBRASKA

ITT Technical Institute
9814 M St.
Omaha, NE 68127
(402) 331-2900
www.itt-tech.edu

NEVADA

ITT Technical Institute
168 Gibson Rd.
Henderson, NV
(702) 558-5404
www.itt-tech.edu

NEW HAMPSHIRE

New Hampshire Institute of Art
148 Concord St.
Manchester, NH 03104
(603) 669-2731

NEW JERSEY

Atlantic County Vocational School
5080 Atlantic Ave.
Mays Landing, NJ 08330
(609) 641-6562

Johnson Atelier Technical Institute
60 Ward Ave. Extension
Mercerville, NJ 08619-3428
(609) 890-7777
www.atelier.org

Mercer County Technical School
1085 Old Trenton Rd.
Trenton, NJ 08690
(609) 586-2121 or (609) 586-5146
www.mccc.edu

Middlesex County Vocational School
112 Rues Lane
East Brunswick, NJ 08816
(732) 257-3300
www.mc-votech.org

Passaic County Vocational School
45 Reinhardt Rd.
Wayne, NJ 07470
(973) 790-6000

NEW MEXICO

ITT Technical Institute
5100 Masthead
Albuquerque, NM 87109
(505) 828-1114
www.itt-tech.edu

Santa Fe Art Institute
1600 St. Michael's Dr.
Santa Fe, NM 87505
(505) 473-6225
www.sfai.org

NEW YORK

Art Students League of New York
215 W. 57th St.
New York, NY 10019
(212) 247-4510
www.metrobeat.com/e/v/nycny/0015/60/95

Chautauqua Institution, School of Art
Box 1098
Chautauqua, NY 14722
(716) 357-6233
www.chautauqua-inst.org

Christie's Education
55 E. 59th St.
New York, NY 10022
(212) 355-1501
www.christes.com/education

Fashion Institute of Technology
Seventh Ave. at 27th St.
New York, NY 10001-5992
(212) 217-7675
www.fitnyc.suny.edu

Island Drafting & Technical Institute
128 Broadway
Amityville, NY 11701
(516) 691-8733
www.islanddrafting.com

National Academy School of Fine Art
5 E. 89th St.
New York, NY 10128
(212) 996-1908
www.nationalacademy.org

New York Academy of Art
111 Franklin St.
New York, NY 10013
(212) 966-0300
www.nyaa.edu

New York Studio School
8 W. 8th St.
New York, NY 10011
(212) 673-6466
www.nyss.org

Parsons School of Design
66 Fifth Ave.
New York, NY 10011
(800) 252-0852
www.parsons.edu

Pratt Institute
  School of Professional Studies
295 Lafayette St. 2nd Floor
New York, NY 10012
(212) 461-6040 x280
www.pratt.edu

School of Visual Arts
209 E. 23rd St.
New York, NY 10010
(212) 592-2100
www.sva.edu

NORTH CAROLINA

Mint Museum of Art
2730 Randolph Ave.
Charlotte, NC 28207
(704) 337-2000
www.mintmuseum.org

Sawtooth Center for Visual Design
226 N. Marshall St.
Winston-Salem, NC 27101
(336) 723-7395
www.sawtooth.org

OHIO

Antonelli College
124 E. 7th St.
Cincinnati, OH 45202
(513) 241-4338
www.antonellic.com

Art Academy of Cincinnati
1125 St. Gregory St.
Cincinnati, OH 45202
(513) 721-5205
www.artacademy.edu

Ashtabula Art Center
2928 W. 13th St.
Ashtabula, OH 44004
(440) 964-3396
www.glenbeigh.com/aac

Cincinnati Academy
2181 Victory Pkwy. Suite 200
Cincinnati, OH 45206
(513) 961-2484

Cleveland Institute of Art
11141 East Blvd.
Cleveland, OH 44106
(800) 223-4700
www.cia.edu

College of Art Advertising
4343 Bridgetown Rd.
Cincinnati, OH 45211
(513) 574-1010

School of Fine Arts
38660 Mentor Ave.
Willoughby, OH 44094
(440) 951-7500

OREGON

ITT Technical Institute
6035 NE 78th Ct.
Portland, OR 97218
(503) 255-6500

PENNSYLVANIA

Art Institute of Philadelphia
1622 Chestnut St.
Philadelphia, PA 19103
(215) 567-7080
www.aiph.aii.edu

Art Institute of Pittsburgh
526 Penn Ave.
Pittsburgh, PA 15222
(412) 263-6600
www.aip.aii.edu

Bok Vocational School
8th & Mifflin Sts.
Philadelphia, PA 19148
(215) 952-6200

**Lancaster Career & Technology Center
  at Brownstown**
Snyder & Metzler Rds.
Brownstone, PA 17508
(717) 859-5100
www2.iul3.k12.pa.us/comrel/lancctc.html

Hussian School of Art
1118 Market St.
Philadelphia, PA 19107-3679
(215) 981-0900
www.hussianart.edu

North Montco Vocational School
1265 Sumneytown Pike
Landsdale, PA 19446
(215) 368-1177

Pennsylvania Academy of Fine Arts
1301 Cherry St.
Philadelphia, PA 19107
(215) 972-7600
www.pafa.org

Pittsburgh Technical Institute
635 Smithfield St.
Pittsburgh, PA 15222
(412) 471-1011
www.pittsburghtechnical.com

Sweetwater Center for the Arts
200 Broad St.
Sewickley, PA 15143
(412) 741-4405
www.artsnet.heinz.cmu.edu

Triangle Tech
P.O. Box 551
DuBois, PA 15801
(814) 371-2090
www.papsa.org/tri1.html

Triangle Tech
222 E. Pittsburgh St.
Greensburg, PA 15601
(724) 832-1050

Triangle Tech
1940 Perrysville Ave.
Pittsburgh, PA 15214
(412) 359-1000

Triangle Tech
2000 Liberty
Erie, PA 16502
(814) 453-6016

RHODE ISLAND

Providence Learning Connection
201 Wayland Ave.
Providence, RI 02906
(401) 274-9330

Rhode Island School of Design
Two College St.
Providence, RI 02903-2791
(410) 454-6300 or (800) 364-7473
www.risd.edu

TENNESSEE

Memphis College of Art
1930 Poplar Ave.
Overton Park
Memphis, TN 38104
(901) 272-5100
www.mca.edu

Memphis Technical School
3225 Walnut Grove
Memphis, TN 38112
(901) 320-6200

Nossi College of Art
907 Two Mile Pkwy.
Goodlettsville, TN 37072
(615) 851-1088

TEXAS

The Art Institute of Dallas
2 North Park East
8080 Park Lane
Dallas, TX 75231
(800) 275-4243
www.aid.aii.edu

ITT Technical Institute
5700 Northwest Pkwy.
San Antonio, TX 78249-3303
(210) 694-4612
www.itt-tech.edu

Lowell Collins School of Art
2903 Saint St.
Houston, TX 77027
(713) 622-6962

UTAH

Salt Lake Art Center
20 South West Temple
Salt Lake City, UT 84101
(801) 328-4201

WASHINGTON

Academy of Realist Art
5004 Sixth Ave. NW
Seattle, WA 98107
(800) 880-3898
www.realistart.com

Bellevue Art Museum
301 Bellevue Sq.
Bellevue, WA 98004
(425) 454-3322
www.bellevuart.org

Pratt Fine Arts Center
1902 S. Main St.
Seattle, WA 98144
(206) 328-2200
www.pratt.org

New School of Visual Concepts
500 Aurora Ave. N.
Seattle, WA 98109
(206) 623-1560
www.svcseattle.com

WISCONSIN

Wustum Museum of Fine Arts
2519 Northwestern Ave.
Racine, WI 53404
(414) 636-9177

APPENDIX III
SCHOLARSHIPS, FELLOWSHIPS, GRANTS, AND LOANS

Following are a number of schools and organizations that offer financial support for students of art, architecture, and design. Amounts listed are per year, and many are renewable. Local organizations such as Rotary or the Lions Club, also offer scholarships—be sure to check into these as well. In addition, ask the financial aid officer of the school you hope to attend for help in applying for aid.

Albion College
Albion, MI 49244
Fine Arts Scholarship, $1,000
www.albion.edu/fac/biol

Alfred University
Alfred, NY 14802
Art Portfolio Scholarship, $3,500–$5,500
www.alfred.edu

**American Association
   of University Women**
1111 Sixteenth St. NW
Washington, DC 20036
Fellowships for women studying
   architecture, $5,000–$12,000
www.aauw.org

American Institute of Architects
1735 New York Ave. NW
Washington, DC 20006
Scholarships and fellowships in
   architecture, $750–$2,500
www.aiaonline.com

Art Libraries Society of North America
3900 E. Timrod St.
Tucson, AZ 85711
Scholarships in art librarianship
www.arlisna.org

Artists Foundation
516 E. 2nd St., #49
Boston, MA 02127
Scholarships in art

**Association for Information and Image
   Management**
1100 Wayne Ave.
Suite 1100
Silver Spring, MD 20910
Scholarships in photography
www.aiim.org

Belhaven College
Jackson, MS 39202
Art Scholarship, $500–$1,000
www.belhaven.edu

Birmingham Southern College
Birmingham, AL 35254
Fine Arts Scholarship, up to $4,000
www.bsc.edu

Bluefield State University
Bluefield, WV 24701
Scholarship for Creative Promise
www.bluefield.wvnet.edu

Boston University
Boston, MA 02215
Arts Scholarship
www.bu.edu

Bradford College
Haverhill, MA 01835
Arts Scholarship, $5,000 average
www.bradford.edu

Cardinal Stritch College
Milwaukee, WI 53217
Art Scholarship, $1,000–full tuition
www.stritch.edu

Carnegie-Mellon University
Pittsburgh, PA 15213
Fine Arts Scholarship, half tuition or more
www.cmu.edu

Chapman University
Orange, CA 92866
Talent/Service Award in art, up to 80%
   of tuition
www.chapman.edu

Chautauqua Foundation
P.O. Box 1098
Chautauqua, NY 14722
Scholarships in art

Coe College
Cedar Rapids, IA 52402
Fine Arts Scholarship, $1,500+
www.coe.edu

College of Notre Dame of Maryland
Baltimore, MD 21210
Art Scholarship, up to $3,000
www.ndm.edu

College of Saint Benedict
St. Joseph, MN 56374
Performing Fine Arts Scholarship,
   up to $2,000
www.csbsju.edu

Colorado State University
Fort Collins, CO 80523
Creative/Performing Arts Award,
   up to $1,500
www.colostate.edu

Columbus State University
Columbus, GA 31907
Fine Arts Scholarship
www.colstate.edu

Concordia College
Ann Arbor, MI 49224
Art Scholarship
www.csp.edu

Concordia College
Portland, OR 97211
Performing Arts Scholarship
www.cu-portland.edu

Conservation Analytical Laboratory
  Smithsonian Institution
Museum Support Center
Washington, DC 20560
Scholarships in art conservation
www.simsc.si.edu/cal

Cooper Union for the Advancement
  of Science and Art
30 Cooper Square
New York, NY 10003
Scholarships in architecture and fine arts
www.cooper.edu

Cornell College
Mount Vernon, IA 52314
Music/Art Scholarship, $5,000–$15,000
www.cornell-iowa.edu

Cumberland College
Williamsburg, KY 40769
Music/Art Scholarship
cc.cumber.edu

Daemen College
Amherst, NY 14226
Visual Arts Scholarship, $5,000
www.daemen.edu

Denison University
Granville, OH 43023
Alumni Award for Leadership and Talent,
  $3,000+
www.denison.edu

Eckerd College
St. Petersburg, FL 33711
Special Talent Scholarship, up to $8,000
www.eckerd.college

Edgewood College
Madison, WI 53711
Fine Arts Grants, $250–$1,500
www.edgewood.edu

Eureka College
Eureka, IL 61530
Fine Arts Scholarship, $1,000–$6,000
www.eureka.edu

Fashion Institute of Technology
227 W. 27th St.
New York, NY 10001
Scholarships in fashion design
www.fitny.suny.edu

Flexographic Technical Association
  Foundation
900 Marconi Ave.
Ronkonkoma, NY 11779
Scholarships in graphic arts, $2,000+;
  Post-graduate research fellowship in
  flexography, $10,000

Florida State University
Tallahassee, FL 32306
Visual Arts Scholarship
www.fsu.edu

Francis Marion University
Florence, SC 29501
Art/Music Scholarship, $100–$500
www.fmarion.edu

Freer Gallery of Art
Harold P. Stern Memorial Fund
Office of the Director
Smithsonian Institution
Washington, DC 20560-0707
Grants in field of Japanese art
www.si.edu/asia

Georgian Court College
Lakewood, NJ 08701
Art Scholarship
www.georgian.edu

Goucher College
Baltimore, MD 21204
Rosenberg Art/Music Scholarship, $5,000
www.goucher.edu

Graphic Arts Technical Foundation
200 Deer Run Rd.
SewicKley, PA 15143
Scholarship in graphic arts
www.gatf.lm.com

Haystack Mountain School of Crafts
Deer Isle, ME 04627
Scholarships in crafts, graphic arts
www.haystack-mtn.org

Home Fashion Products Association
355 Lexington Ave.
New York, NY 10017
Scholarships in interior design and
  fashion design

Hope College
Holland, MI 49422-9000
Distinguished Artist Award, $2,500 average
www.hope.edu

Incarnate Word University
San Antonio, TX 78209
Fine Art Scholarship
www.uiw.edu

Indiana State University
Terre Haute, IN 47809
Creative and Performing Arts Award,
  $1,100 average
www-isu.indstate.edu

Industrial Designers Society of
  America
IDSA
1142 Walker Rd.
Great Falls, VA 22066
Graduate and undergraduate
  scholarships in industrial design,
  $2,000–$2,500
www.idsa.org

Institute of Store Planners
25 N. Broadway
Tarrytown, NY 10591
Scholarships in interior design
www.ispo.org

International Furnishings and Design
  Association
Education Foundation
1200 19th St., NW
Suite 300 Washington, DC 20036
Scholarships in interior design, $1,500+;
  Professional grants, $1,000
www.ifda.com

Iowa Arts Council
600 E. Locust
Capitol Complex
Des Moines, IA 50319
Grants for Iowa art students
www.culturalaffairs.org/iac/

J. Paul Getty Museum
1200 Getty Center Dr.
Los Angeles, CA 90049
Scholarships, fellowships, and research
  grants in art conservation, art history
  and museum studies
www.getty.edu

Jacksonville State University
Jacksonville, AL 36265
Art Scholarship, full tuition
www.jsu.edu

Latino Studies Fellowship Program
Smithsonian Institution
Office of Fellowships and Grants
955 L'Enfant Plaza SW
Suite 7000
Washington, DC 20560-0902
Fellowships in Latino art and culture
webl.si.edu/ofg/

**Ladies Auxiliary to the Veterans of
    Foreign Wars of the United States**
406 W. 34th St.
Kansas City, MO 64111
Patriotic Art Award, $500–$3,000

**Leslie T. Posey & Frances U. Posey
    Foundation**
1800 2nd St., Suite 905
Sarasota, FL 34236
Scholarships in art, $1,000–$4,000

Limestone College
Gaffney, SC 29340
Fine Arts Scholarship, $500–$1,500
www.limestone.edu

LIU-Southampton
Southampton, NY 11968
Art Scholarship, $1,000–$6,000
www.southampton.liu.edu

Long Island Advertising Club, Inc.
34 Richards Rd., Suite 100
Port Washington, NY 11050
Advertising and commercial art
    scholarships, $1,000–$2,000
www.liac.org

Lycoming College
Williamsport, PA 17701
Art/Music Scholarship, $500–$2,500
www.lycoming.edu

MacMurray College
Jacksonville, IL 62650
Fine Arts Scholarship, $2,000
www.mac.edu

Marietta College
Marietta, OH 45750
Fine Arts Scholarship, $1,500–$3,500
www.marietta.edu

Maryville College
Maryville, TN 37801
Art Scholarship, up to $4,000
www.maryvillecollege.edu

Marycrest College
Davenport, IA 52804
Performing/Fine Arts Scholarship
www.mcrest.edu

McMurray University
Abilene, TX 79697
Art, Music Scholarship
www.mcm.edu

Memphis College of Art
Overton Park
Memphis, TN 38104
Scholarships in art and design
www.mca.edu

Metropolitan Museum of Art
1000 Fifth Ave.
New York, NY 10028
Fellowships in art history and art
    conservation
www.metmuseum.org

Michigan State University
East Lansing, MI 48824
Creative Arts Scholarship
www.msu.edu

Minneapolis College of Art & Design
2501 Stevens Ave. South
Minneapolis, MN 55404
Scholarships in fine arts, design and
    media arts
www.mcad.edu

Molloy College
Rockville Center, NY 11571
Fine/Performing Arts Scholarship,
    $500–full tuition
www.molloy.edu

Moore College of Art and Design
Philadelphia, PA 19103
Sarah Peters Scholarship, up to $2,000
www.moore.edu

Mount Mercy College
Cedar Rapids, IA 52402
Music and Art Scholarship, $500–$2,000
www2.mtmercy.edu

Mount Olive College
Mount Olive, NC 28365
Music/Art Scholarship, up to $2,000
www.mountolivecollege.edu

Mount Union College
Alliance, OH 44601
Art/Music/Theater Proficiency Award,
    up to $3,000
www.muc.edu

Muskingum College
New Concord, OH 43762
Performance Scholarship in
    Art/Music/Theater, up to $3,000
www.muskingum.edu

National Association of Black Journalists
8701 Adelphi Rd.
Adelphi, MD 20783
Scholarships in photograph, $2,500
www.nabj.org

**National Foundation for Advancement
    in the Arts**
800 Brickell Ave. Suite 500
Miami, FL 3313
Scholarships for high school seniors,
    $100–$3,000; fellowships in visual
    arts, $1,000 monthly stipend
www.nfaa.org

National Museum of American Art
Smithsonian Institution
Washington, DC 20560-0210
Predoctoral fellowships in art and visual
    culture of the United States, $15,000+;
    Postdoctoral fellowships, $27,000+
www.americanart.si.edu

**National Museum of the American
    Indian**
NMAI Cultural Resources Center
4220 Silver Hill Rd.
Suitland, MD 20746
Graduate and post-graduate fellowships
    in conservation
www.si.edu/nmai

National Roofing Foundation
10255 W. Higgins
Suite 600
Rosemont, IL 60018
Scholarships in architecture
www.nrca.net/about/nrf/

National Scholarship Trust Fund
GATF
4615 Forbes Ave.
Pittsburgh, PA 15213
$100–$1,000 scholarships for students
    of graphic arts

Nazareth College
Rochester, NY 14618
Art/Music Scholarship, up to $2,000
www.naz.edu

North Dakota State University
1301 N. University
Fargo, ND 58105
Scholarships in apparel, textiles, and
    interior design, up to $1,000
www.ndsu.nodak.edu

Northwest University
Kirkland, WA 98083
Fine Arts Festival Scholarship,
    $600–$4,000

Ohio Arts Council
727 E. Main St.
Columbus, OH 43205
Fellowships in art for Ohio residents,
    $5,000–$10,000

Otis School of Art and Design
Los Angeles, CA 90057
Art and Design Scholarship
www.otisart.edu

**Outdoor Writers Association
    of America**
27 Fort Missoula Rd.
Suite #1
Missoula, MT 59804
Scholarships in art $2,500–$3,500
www.owaa.org

Pastel Society of America
15 Gramercy Park So.
New York, NY 10003
Painting Scholarship
www.anny.org/orgs/0150/001p0150.htm

Photographic Society of America
2005 Walnut St.
Philadelphia, PA 19103
Photography Scholarship
www.psa-photo.org

Piedmont College
Demorest, GA 30535
Fine Arts Scholarship, up to $2,000

Rhythm & Hues
5404 Jandy Place
Los Angeles, CA 90066
Attn: Scholarship

Scholarships in computer modeling,
    computer character animation, digital
    cinematography
www.rhythm.com

Salem State College
Salem, MA 01970
Arts Scholarships, up to full tuition
www.salem.mass.edu

Scholastic, Inc.
555 Broadway
New York, NY 10012
Scholarships for high school seniors
    talented in art or photography, up to
    $20,000
www.scholastic.com

Seattle Pacific University
Seattle, WA 98119
Arts Scholarship
www.spu.edu

Seton Hill College
Greensburg, PA 15601
Fine Arts Scholarship, $1,000 average
www.setonhill.edu

**Smithsonian Institution Fellowship
    Program**
Office of Fellowships and Grants
955 L'Enfant Plaza SW
Suite 7000
Washington, DC 20560-0902
Fellowships supporting research in
    residence at Smithsonian facilities,
    including:
  • Archives of American Art
  • Cooper-Hewitt, National Design
    Museum
  • Freer Gallery of Art/Arthur M.
    Sackler Gallery
  • Hirshhorn Museum and Sculpture
    Garden
  • National Museum of African Art
  • National Museum of American Art
  • National Museum of American
    History
  • National Museum of the American
    Indian
  • National Portrait Gallery
  • National Postal Museum
Postdoctoral and senior fellowships,
    $27,000+; predoctoral fellowships,
    $15,000+; and graduate student
    fellowships, $3,500+.

Society of Illustrators
128 E. 63rd St.
New York, NY 10021
Scholarships in illustration and graphic arts
www.societyillustrators.org

Southwestern University
Georgetown, TX 78626
Fine Arts Scholarship, $1,000–$3,000
www.southwestern.edu

St. Francis College
Fort Wayne, IN 46808
Art Scholarship, $1,000–$2,000
www.sfcpa.edu

St. Mary-of-the Woods College
St. Mary-of-the-Woods, IN 47876
Creative Arts Scholarship, up to $2,000
www.smwc.edu

Stratton Arts Festival
PO Box 2728
Manchester Center, VT 05255
Awards for fine arts, crafts and
    photography displayed by Vermont
    residents at the festival, $250–$1,500
www.strattonartsfestival.org

Swann Foundation Fund
Library of Congress
Prints & Photographs Division
Washington, DC 20540-4730
Post-grad fellowship in
    Cartoon/Caricature, $15,000 average
www.loc.gov/rr/print/swann/
    swann-apply.html

Texas A & M University/Corpus Christi
Corpus Christi, TX 78412
Fine Arts scholarship
www.tamucc.edu

Texas Christian University
Fort Worth, TX 76129
Fine Arts scholarship, up to $4,000
www.tcu.edu

Truman State University
Kirksville, MO 63501
Scholarships in art, music, and theater
www.Truman.edu

Unitarian Universalist Association
25 Beacon St.
Boston, MA 02108
Fine Arts Scholarship
www.uua.org

University of Massachusetts
Amherst, MA 01003
Chancellor's Talent Award/Arts, full
  tuition
www.umass.edu

University of Mississippi
University, MS 38677
Fine Arts Scholarship, $100–$2,282
www.olemiss.edu

University of North Carolina
Greensboro, NC 27402
Creative Arts Scholarship, $100–$1,500
www.uncg.edu

University of South Carolina
Aiken, SC 29801
Fine Arts Scholarship
www.sc.edu

University of Texas
Austin, TX 78713
Arts and Talent Scholarship, $1,000
www.utexas.edu

Ursuline College
Pepper Pike, OH 44124
Art Scholarship
www.ursuline.edu

Virginia Museum of Fine Arts
2800 Grove Ave.
Richmond, VA 23221
Fellowships in art, art history and
  photography
www.vmfa.state.va.us

Viterbo College
La Crosse, WI 54601
Fine Arts Scholarship
www.viterbo.edu

Wabash College
Crawfordsville, IN 47933
Fine Arts Fellowship, up to $11,000
www.wabash.edu

Waverly Community House Inc.
Main St. Waverly, PA 18471
Scholarships in art, architecture and
  photography

Wesleyan College
Macon, GA 31210
Fine Art Talent Scholarship, up to $5,000
www.wesleyan-college.edu

West Virginia University
Morgantown, WV 26506
Creative Arts Music and Theater
  Scholarships
www.wvu.edu

Western Montana College
Dillon, MT 59725
Art Scholarship, $1,000
www.wmc.edu

Western Oregon University
Monmouth, OR 97361
Creative Arts Scholarship, $200–$1,500
www.wosc.osshe.edu

Whitney Museum of American Art
945 Madison Ave.
New York, NY 10021
Scholarships in art criticism, art history
  and museum studies
www.whitney.org

Yale Center for British Art
1080 Chapel St.
P.O. Box 208280
New Haven, CT 06520-8280
Visiting fellowships in art, art history,
  and related fields
www.yale.edu/ycba/

APPENDIX IV
INTERNSHIPS

Working as an intern in your intended career field can be an invaluable kind of education. Not only will you have an opportunity to see what the day-to-day routine is like, but you will also function almost as an apprentice, learning from experienced workers. You'll have a chance to make personal contacts as well—your coworkers can help you with information on how to get a job, suggest alternate careers for someone with your skills, and advise you on pitfalls to watch out for.

The following list, arranged by state, includes organizations that offer internships—paid and unpaid—followed by the specific art-related career areas they offer. But don't stop here! If you think an internship is right for you, check with the professional organizations in your field of interest for other possibilities. Browsing career sites on the Internet or searching the Yellow Pages can help you find companies that might be willing to hire you on a temporary or no-pay basis. Also, many local newspapers regularly hire interns, so don't hesitate to check with any that appeal to you, even if they're not listed here.

ALASKA

Anchorage Daily News
P.O. Box 149001
Anchorage, AK 99514-9001
(907) 257-4275
adn.com/adn./job_info.html
www.adn.com
Photography

CALIFORNIA

Contra Costa Times
2640 Shadelands Dr.
Walnut Creek, CA 94596
(925) 935-2525
www.contracostatimes.com
*Minority Internship Program:
Photography, News Art*

J. Paul Getty Museum
Education Department
1200 Getty Center Dr.
Suite 1000
Los Angeles, CA 90049
(310) 440-7383
www.getty.edu/museum/
*Administration, Conservation, Curatorial,
Exhibition Design, etc.*

Landor Associates
1001 Front St.
San Francisco, CA 94111
(415) 365-4882
www.landor.com
Design

Los Angeles Times
Times Mirror Square
Los Angeles, CA 90053
(213) 237-5000
www.latimes.com
Photography, Graphics

San Francisco Chronicle
Internship Programs
Editorial Hiring & Development
901 Mission St.
San Francisco, CA 94103
(415) 777-7100
sfgate.com/chronicle/jobs
www.sfgate.com/chronicle
Graphics, News Art, Photography

San Francisco Museum of Modern Art
151 Third St.
San Francisco, CA 94103
(415) 357-4170
www.sfmoma.org
Marketing, Communications

Valley Times
127 Spring St.
Pleasanton, CA 94566
(925) 935-2525
*Minority Internship Program:
Photography, News Art*

CONNECTICUT

Yale Center for British Art
Box 208820
New Haven, CT 06520-8280
(203) 432-2800
www.yale.edu/ycba
Museum Studies

DISTRICT OF COLUMBIA

Smithsonian Institution
Center for Museum Studies
Arts & Industries Bldg.
900 Jefferson Dr. SW
Room 2235
Washington, D.C. 20560-0427
(202) 357-3102
siintern@cms.si.edu
www.si.edu
*Art History, Museum Studies,
Exhibit Design, Membership &
Development, etc.*

The Washington Times
3600 New York Ave. NE
Washington, D.C. 20002
(202) 636-3000
www.washtimes.com
Photography

FLORIDA

M & M Creative Services
P.O. Box 2457
Tallahassee, FL 32316
(888) 224-1169
Graphic Design

Orlando Sentinel
Employment Center
M.P. 57
633 N. Orange Ave.
Orlando, FL 32801
(407) 420-5000
www.orlandosentinel.com
Photography

ILLINOIS

Contemporary Art Workshop
542 W. Grant Pl.
Chicago, IL 60614
(773) 472-4004
Sculpture, Arts Administration

Sessions Inc.
1500 North LaSalle, #1D
Chicago, IL 60610
(312) 642-8558
Graphic Design

KENTUCKY

Courier-Journal
525 W. Broadway
Louisville, KY 40202
(502) 582-4616
www.courier-journal.com
Art, Photography, Design

MARYLAND

The Sun
501 N. Calvert St.
Baltimore, MD 21278
(410) 332-6000
News Art, Photography

MASSACHUSETTS

The Boston Globe
Summer Intern Program
P.O. Box 2378
Boston, MA 02107-2378
(617) 929-3120
www.boston.com/globe
Graphics, Photography

Boston Magazine
300 Massachusetts Ave.
Boston, MA 02115

(617) 262-9700
www.bostonmagazine.com
Art, Production

Franklin Advertising Associates Inc.
51 Winchester St.
Newton, MA 02461
(617) 244-8368
Art

MICHIGAN

Detroit Free Press
600 W. Fort St.
Detroit, MI 48226
(313) 222-6490
www.freep.com
Graphics, Photography

MINNESOTA

The Duluth News-Tribune
424 W. First St.
Duluth, MN 55802
(218) 723-5308
www.duluthnews.com
Photography

MISSISSIPPI

The Sun Herald
P.O. Box 4567
Biloxi, MS 39535
(228) 896-2100
www.sunherald.com
Page Design, Graphics

MISSOURI

Hallmark Cards, Inc.
Creative Staffing & Development -#444
    Visual Internship Program
2501 McGee
P.O. Box 419580
Kansas City, MO 64141-6580
(816) 274-5111
www.hallmark.com
Art, Design

NEVADA

Las Vegas Review-Journal
P.O. Box 70
Las Vegas, NV 89125
(702) 383-0211
www.lvrj.com
Photography

NEW YORK

American Association of Advertising
    Agencies
405 Lexington Ave.
18th Floor
New York, NY 10174
(212) 682-2500
www.aaaa.org
Multicultural Advertising Intern
    Program: Art Direction

Brooklyn Museum of Art
200 Eastern Pkwy.
Brooklyn, NY 11238
(718) 638-5000 x230
www.brooklynart.org
Museum Work

The Center for Photography
59 Tinker St.
Woodstock, NY 12498
(914) 679-9957
www.cpw.org
Photography, Arts Administration

Cooper-Hewitt National Design
    Museum
2 E. 91st St.
New York, NY 10128
(212) 849-8400
www.si.edu/ndml
Art, Design, Architecture, Museum Studies

Harper's Magazine
Internship Program
666 Broadway
New York, NY 10012
(212) 614-6500
www.harpers.org
Art

MAD Magazine
Art Intern Program
1700 Broadway
New York, NY 10019
(212) 506-4880
www.dccomics.com/mad/
Magazine Production

Museum of Modern Art
11 W. 53rd St.
New York, NY 10019
(212) 708-9893
www.moma.org
Arts Administration, Museum Studies, etc.

Penguin Putman
375 Hudson St.
New York, NY 10014
(212) 366-2003
Design

Siano & Spitz Advertising
936 N. Clinton St.
Syracuse, NY 13204
(315) 479-5581
Art

Simon & Schuster
1230 Ave. of the Americas
New York, NY 10020
(212) 698-7000
www.simonandschuster.com
Art & Design

Solomon R. Guggenheim Museum
1071 Fifth Ave.
New York, NY 10128
(212) 423-3500
www.guggenheim.org
Arts Administration, Art History

Women's Studio Workshop
P.O. Box 489
Rosendale, NY 12472
(914) 658-9133
www.wsworkshop.org
Art

NORTH CAROLINA

Greensboro News & Record
News Director/
    Recruitment Coordinator
200 E. Market St.
Greensboro, NC 27420
(336) 412-5919
www.thedepot.com
Photography

NORTH DAKOTA

Grand Forks Herald
375 Second Ave. N
P.O. Box 6008
Grand Forks, ND 58206-6008

(701) 780-1130
www.gfherald
Photography

OHIO

Cincinnati Enquirer
312 Elm St.
Cincinnati, OH 45202
(513) 768-8392
enquirer.com/today/
Photography, Graphics

Cleveland Plain Dealer
1801 Superior Ave.
Cleveland, OH 44114
(216) 999-4103
www.cleveland.com
Graphics, Photography

Columbus Dispatch
34 S. 3rd St.
Columbus, OH 43215
(614) 461-5000
www.dispatch.com
News Art, Photography

F & W Publications, Inc.
1507 Dana Ave.
Cincinnati, OH 45207
(513) 531-2690 x589
Editorial for Art Books and Magazines

Intermuseum Conservation Association
Allen Art Building
Oberlin, OH 44074
*Internships (pre-graduate, graduate and
    post-graduate) in art conservation*

OKLAHOMA

Ackerman, Hood & McQueen, Inc.
1601 NW Expressway
Suite 1100
Oklahoma City, OK 73118
(405) 843-7777
www.am.am.com
Art, Photography

PENNSYLVANIA

Fernhill Press
1901 North Penn Rd.
Hatfield, PA 19440

(215) 997-5900
www.fernhillpress.com
Desktop Publishing

Lieberman Appalucci
4635 Crackerspot Rd.
Allentown, PA 18104
(610) 395-7111
www.lieb-app.com
Advertising Art

Philadelphia Daily News
P.O. Box 7788
Philadelphia, PA 19101
(215) 854-5879
www.web.philly.com/daily-news
Photography, Graphics

Philadelphia Inquirer
400 N. Broad St.
Philadelphia, PA 19130
(610) 313-8104 (Graphics)
(215) 854-5045 (Photo)
web.philly.com/inquirer
Graphics, Photography

Pittsburgh Post-Gazette
34 Blvd. of the Allies
Pittsburgh, PA 15222
(412) 263-1100
www.post-gazette.com
Graphics, Photography

Rodale Inc.
33 E. Minor St.
Emmaus, PA 18098
(610) 967-5171
Art, Photography

SOUTH DAKOTA

Aberdeen American News
124 S. Second St.
Aberdeen, SD 57401
(605) 225-4100
www.aberdeenews.com
Art, Photography

TEXAS

Austin American-Statesman
Summer Internship Program
305 S. Congress Ave.
Austin, TX 78704

(512) 445-3662
austin360.com
Graphics, Photography

Temerlin McClain Advertising
Internship Coordinator
P.O. Box 619200
Dallas/Fort Worth Airport, TX 75261
(972) 556-1100
www.temmc.com
Art Direction

VIRGINIA

The Virginian-Pilot
150 W. Brambleton Ave.
Norfolk, VA 23510
(757) 446-2390
www.pilotonline.com
Photography

WISCONSIN

Kohler Company
444 Highland Dr.
Kohler, WI 53044
(920) 457-4441 x72197
Industrial Design Coop

APPENDIX V
ORGANIZATIONS AND ASSOCIATIONS

Listed below are some major organizations and associations for persons interested in careers in art. These groups can be extremely useful resources for the individual, providing information, contacts, and support.

Keep in mind, however, that there are hundreds of local and regional art groups that might be equally helpful to peo-ple interested in art and art careers—museum associations and auxiliaries, city art leagues, state and county art guilds, and the like. Be sure to check into such organizations in your area.

Advertising Club of New York
235 Park Ave. So.
New York, NY 10003
(212) 533-8080

**Advertising Production Club
of New York**
60 E. 42nd St
New York, NY 10165
(212) 983-6042

American Advertising Federation
1101 Vermont Ave. NW, Suite 500
Washington, DC 20005
(202) 898-0089
www.aaf.org

American Art Therapy Association
1202 Allanson Rd.
Mundelein, IL 60060
(847) 949-6064
www.arttherapy.org

American Artists Professional League
47 Fifth Ave
New York, NY 10003
(212) 645-1345

**American Institute for Conservation
of Historic and Artistic Works**
1717 K St. NW, Suite 200
Washington, DC 20006
(202) 452-9545

American Institute of Architects
1735 New York Ave. NW
Washington, DC 20006
(202) 626-7300
www.aiaonline.com

American Institute of Graphic Arts
164 Fifth Ave.
New York, NY 10010
(212) 807-1990
www.aiga.org

American Library Association
50 E. Huron St.
Chicago, IL 60611
(312) 944-6780
www.ala.org

American Society of Artists
PO Box 1326
Palatine, IL 60078
(312) 751-2500

American Society of Interior Designers
608 Massachusetts Ave. NE
Washington, DC 20002
(202) 546-3480
www.asid.org

**American Society of Psychopathology
of Expression**
74 Lawton St.
Brookline, MA 02146
(617) 738-9821

**Art and Antique Dealers League
of America**
353 E. 78th St.
New York, NY
(212) 879-7558
www.dir-dd.com/aadla.html

Art Dealers Association of America
575 Madison Ave.
New York, NY 10022
(212) 940-8590
www.artdealers.org

Art Directors Club
104 W. 29th St.
New York, NY 10001
(212) 643-1440
www.adcny.org

Art Information Center
280 Broadway
New York, NY 10007
(212) 227-0282

Association of Art Museum Directors
41 E. 65th St.
New York, NY 10021
(212) 249-4423
www.aamd.org

College Art Association
275 Seventh Ave.
New York, NY 10001
(212) 691-1051
www.collegeart.org

Graphic Artists Guild
90 John St., Suite 403
New York, NY 10038
(212) 791-3400
www.gag.org

Independent Curators International
799 Broadway, Suite 205
New York, NY 10003
(212) 254-8200
www.ici-exhibitions.org

**National Antique and Art Dealers
Association of America**
220 E. 57th St.
New York, NY 10022
(212) 826-9707
www.naadaa.org

National Art Education Association
1916 Association Dr.
Reston, VA 20191
(703) 860-8000
www.naea-reston.org

National Association of Women Artists
41 Union Square West
New York, NY 10003
(212) 675-1616

National Auctioneers Association
8880 Ballentine
Overland Park, KS 66214
(913) 541-8084
www.auctioneers.org

National Council of Architectural Registration Boards
1735 New York Ave. NW
Suite 700
Washington, D.C. 20006
(207) 783-6500
www.ncarb.org/
www.exittech.com

National Organization of Minority Architects
1020 Ralph Abernathy Blvd.
Atlanta, GA 30310
(404) 753-4129
www.noma.net

Professional Picture Framers Association
4305 Sarellen Rd.
Richmond, VA 23231
(804) 226-0430
www.ppfa.com

Public Relations Society of America
33 Irving Pl.
New York, NY 10003
(212) 995-2230
www.research-umbc.edu

Society of Illustrators
128 E. 63rd St.
New York, NY 10021
(212) 838-2560
www.societyillustrators.org

Society of Publication Designers
60 E. 42nd St.
New York, NY 10165
(212) 983-8585
www.spd.org

Typophiles
300 Jay St.
A 543
Brooklyn, NY 11201
(718) 260-5131

Visual Artists and Galleries Association
350 Fifth Ave. Suite 6305
New York, NY 10118
(212) 736-6666

Women in Production
347 Fifth Ave.
New York, NY 10016
(212) 481-7793
www.wip.org

APPENDIX VI
BIBLIOGRAPHY

SELECTED PERIODICALS

**Advertising and Graphic Arts
  Techniques**
246 Fifth Ave. Suite 300
New York, NY 10001
(212) 889-6500

African Arts
University of California, Los Angeles
African Studies Center
Box 951310
Los Angeles, CA 90095
(310) 825-1218

Afterimage
Visual Studies Workshop
31 Prince St.
Rochester, NY 14607
(716) 442-8676
www.rit.edu/~vswwww/afterindex.html

AHA Hispanic Arts News
Association of Hispanic Arts
250 W. 26th St. 4th Floor
New York, NY 10001
(212) 727-7227
www.latinoarts.org

American Art Review
P.O. Box 480500
Kansas City, MO 64148
(913) 451-8801

American Artist
1515 Broadway
New York, NY 10036
(212) 764-7300

American Craft
72 Spring St.
New York, NY 10012
(212) 274-0630
www.craftcouncil.org

American Indian Art
7314 East Osborn Dr.
Scottsdale, AZ 85251
(480) 994-5445

**American Institute for Conservation
  Journal**
American Institute for Conservation of
  Historic and Artistic Works
1717 K St. NW, Suite 200
Washington, DC 20006
(202) 452-9545
www.palimpset.stanford.edu/aic/

American Journal of Art Therapy
Vermont College of Norwich University
Montpelier, VT 05602
(802) 828-8810

Americans for the Arts
1 E. 53rd St.
New York, NY 10022
(800) 321-4510
www.artusa.org

Applied Arts
18 Wynford Drive
Suite 411
Toronto, Ontario
Canada
M3C 3S2
(416) 510-0909
www.imagesite.com/muse/archart

Archives of American Art Journal
Smithsonian Institution
Archives of American Art
901 D St. SW, Suite 704
Washington, DC 20560-0937
(202) 314-3900

Art and Auction
Auction Guild
11 E. 36th St.
New York, NY 10016
(212) 447-9555

Art Bulletin
College Art Association
275 Seventh Ave.
New York, NY 10001
(212) 691-1051

Art Calendar
P.O. Box 199
Upper Fairmount, MD 21867
(410) 651-9150
www.artcalendar.com

Art in America
575 Broadway
New York, NY 10021
(212) 941-2800

**Art Institute of Chicago Museum
  Studies**
Art Institute of Chicago
111 S. Michigan Ave.
Chicago, IL 60603
(312) 443-3540
www.artic.edu/aic/index.html

Art Journal
College Art Association
275 Seventh Ave.
New York, NY 10001
(212) 691-1051
www.collegeart.org

Art New England
425 Washington St.
Brighton, MA 02135
(617) 782-3008
www.artnewengland.com

Art Now
97 Grayrock Rd.
P.O. Box 5541
Clinton, NJ 08809
(908) 638-5255

Art on Paper
39 E. 78th St.
Suite 501
New York, NY 10021
(212) 988-5959

Art Students League News
215 W. 57th St.
New York, NY 10019
(212) 247-4510
www.artincontext.org

Artbyte
39 E. 78th St.
Suite 501
New York, NY 10021
(212) 988-5959
www.artbyte.com

Artforum
350 Seventh Ave.
New York, NY 10001
(212) 475-4000

Artnews
48 W. 38th St.
New York, NY 10018
(212) 398-1690
www.artnewsonline.com

Arts Education Policy Review
Heldref Publications
1319 18th St., NW
Washington, DC 20036
(202) 296-6267
www.heldref.org/html/body_aper.html

Arts of Asia
1309 Kowloon Centre
29–39 Ashley Rd.
Kowloon, Hong Kong
852-23762228
www.asianart.com

Arts Quarterly
New Orleans Museum of Art
Box 19123
New Orleans, LA 70179
(504) 488-2631
www.noma.org

Artweek
2149 Paragon Drive Suite 100
San Jose, CA 95131
(408) 441-7065
www.artweek.com

Bomb
New Art Publications
594 Broadway Suite 905
New York, NY 10012
(212) 431-3943
www.bombsite.com

CAA Newsletter
College Art Association
275 Seventh Ave.
New York, NY 10001
(212) 691-1051
www.collegeart.org

Clay Times
15481 Second St.
P.O. Box 365
Waterford, VA 20197
(540) 882-3576
www.claytimes.com

Cleveland Museum of Art Bulletin
11150 East Blvd.
Cleveland, OH 44106
(216) 421-7340
www.clemusart.com

Communication Arts
110 Constitution Dr.
Menlo Park, CA 94025
(650) 326-6040

Curator
Altamira Press
1630 N. Main St.
Walnut Creek, CA 94596

Design Issues
MIT Press Journals
5 Cambridge Center
Cambridge, MA 02142
(617) 253-2889
www.mitpress.mit.edu

Detroit Institute of Arts Bulletin
5200 Woodward Ave.
Detroit, MI 48202
(313) 833-7961
www.dia.org

Dialogues
Box 2572
Columbus, OH 43216
(614) 621-3704

Digital Publishing Design Graphics
A.C.N. 005 987 922
6 School Road, Ferny Creek
Victoria 3786
Australia
61-3-9755-1149

Empirical Study of the Arts
Baywood Publishing Co.
26 Austin Ave.
Box 337
Amityville, NY 11701
(516) 691-1270
www.baywood.com

Fiberarts
50 College St.
Asheville, NC 28801
(828) 253-0467

Folk Art
Museum of American Folk Art
555 W. 57th St., Suite 1300
New York, NY 10019
(212) 977-7170

Graphic Design USA
AIGA 164 Fifth Ave.
New York, NY 10010
(212) 255-4004

IFAR Journal
International Foundation for Art Research
500 Fifth Ave., Suite 1234
New York, NY 10010
(212) 391-6234
www.ifar.org

Interior Design
345 Hudson St. 4th floor
New York, NY 10014
(212) 519-7200

International Center of Medieval Art Newsletter
The Cloisters
Fort Tryon Park
New York, NY 10040
(212) 928-1146
www.cityinsights.com

Master Drawings
29 E. 36th St.
New York, NY 10016
(212) 685-0008

Metropolitan Museum of Art Bulletin
1000 Fifth Ave.
New York, NY 10028
(212) 535-7710
www.metmuseum.org

Museum News
1575 I St. NW
Suite 400
Washington, DC 20005
(202) 289-1818

New Art Examiner
Chicago New Art Association
314 W. Institute Pl.
Chicago, IL 60610
(312) 649-9900
www.newartexaminer.com

October
MIT Press
5 Cambridge Center
Cambridge, MA 02142-1407

(617) 253-2889
www.mitpress.mit.edu

Oz Graphics
Design Graphics Pty. Ltd.
A.C.N. 005 987 922
6 School Rd., Ferny Creek
Victoria 3786
Australia
61-3-9755-1149

Philadelphia Museum of Art Bulletin
Box 7646
Philadelphia, PA 19101
(215) 763-8100
www.philamuseum.org

Praxis: A Journal of Cultural Criticism
Dickson Art Center
UCLA
Los Angeles, CA 90024
(310) 206-6905
www.arts.ucla.edu

St. Louis Art Museum Bulletin
1 Fine Arts Dr.
St. Louis, MO 63110
(314) 721-0067
www.slam.org

Sculpture Review
National Sculpture Society
1177 Ave. of the Americas
New York, NY 10036
(212) 764-5645
www.nationalsculpture.org

Sotheby's Newsletter
1334 York Ave.
New York, NY 10021
(212) 606-7000
www.sothebys.com

Southwest Art
5444 Westheimer Suite 1440
Houston, TX 77056
(713) 296-7900

Virginia Museum of Fine Arts Bulletin
2800 Grove Ave.
Richmond, VA 23221

(804) 257-0534
www.vmfa.state.va.us

Walters Art Gallery Bulletin
600 N. Charles St.
Baltimore, MD 21201
(410) 547-9000
www.thewalters.org

Watercolor
1515 Broadway
New York, NY 10036
(212) 764-7300

Winterthur Portfolio
University of Chicago Press
5720 S. Woodlawn Ave.
Chicago, IL 60637
(773) 702-7700

World Art
2 Gateway Center
11th Floor
Newark, NJ 07102
(973) 643-7500 (U.S. editorial offices)

BOOKS

Abbott, Robert J., *Art & Reality: The New Standard Reference Guide and Business Plan for Actively Developing Your Career as an Artist.* Santa Ana, CA: Seven Locks Press, 1997.

Ball, Victoria Kloss, *Opportunities in Interior Design and Decorating Careers.* Lincolnwood, IL: NTC Publishing Group, 1995.

Blakeslee, Carolyn, Barb Dougherty and Drew Steis, eds., *Making a Living as an Artist.* New York, NY: The Lyons Press, 1998.

Boldt, Laurence G., *Zen and the Art of Making a Living: A Practical Guide to Creative Career Design,* revised edition. New York, NY: Penguin Books, 1999.

Bowen, Linda Cooper, *The Graphic Designer's Guide to Creative Marketing.* New York, NY: John Wiley & Sons, Inc., 1999.

Brommer, Gerald F., and Joseph A. Gatto, *Careers in Art: An Illustrated Guide,* second edition. Worcester, MA: Davis Publications, 1999.

Camenson, Blythe, *Careers for Introverts & Other Solitary Types.* Lincolnwood, IL: NTC Publishing Group, 1998.

Caplin, Lee E., ed., *The Business of Art,* third edition. Paramus, NJ: Prentice Hall Press, 1998.

Fernandes, Teresa, and Steven Heller, *Becoming a Graphic Designer: A Guide to Careers in Design.* New York, NY: John Wiley & Sons, Inc., 1999.

Field, Shelly, *100 Best Careers for Writers and Artists.* New York, NY: Simon & Schuster Trade, 1997.

Field, Shelly, *Career Opportunities in Theater and the Performing Arts.* New York, NY: Checkmark Books, 1999.

Foote, Cameron S., *The Business Side of Creativity.* New York, N.Y: W.W. Norton & Company, Inc., 1996.

Ganim, Barbara A., *Approach an Advertising Agency And Walk Away With the Job You Want.* Lincolnwood, IL: NTC Publishing Group, 1998.

Gardner, Elizabeth B., *Arts and Crafts Careers.* Lincolnwood, IL: NTC Publishing Group, 1998.

Gillette, J. Michael, *Theatrical Design and Production: An Introduction to Scene Design and Construction, Lighting, Sound, Costume, and Makeup,* fourth edition. Mountain View, CA: Mayfield Publishing Co., 1999.

Goldfarb, Roz, *Careers by Design,* revised edition. New York, NY: Allworth Press, 1997.

Gordon, Barbara, *Opportunities in Commercial Art and Graphic Design Careers.* Lincolnwood, IL: NTC Publishing Group, 1997.

Grant, Daniel, *How to Start and Succeed as an Artist.* New York, NY: Allworth Press, 1997.

Grant, Daniel, *The Artist's Resource Handbook,* revised edition. New York, NY: Allworth Press, 1997.

Grant, Daniel, *The Fine Artist's Career Guide.* New York, NY: Allworth Press, 1998.

Haines, Lurene, *The Business of Comics.* New York, NY: Watson-Guptill Publications, 1998.

Harris, Michael G., *Professional Architectural Photography.* Woburn, MA: Butterworth-Heinemann, 1998.

Henderson, Harry, *Career Opportunities in Computers and Cyberspace.* New York, NY: Facts on File Publications, 1999.

Johnson, Maurice J., and Evelyn C. Moore, *So You Want to Work in the Fashion Business?: A Practical Look at Apparel Product Development and Global Manufacturing.* Upper Saddle River, NJ: Prentice Hall, 1998.

Kotler, Neil G., *Museum Strategy and Marketing: Designing Missions, Building Audiences, Generating Revenue and Resources.* San Francisco, CA: Jossey-Bass Publishers, 1998.

Lang, Cay, *Taking the Leap: Building a Career as a Visual Artist.* San Francisco, CA: Chronicle Books, 1998.

Lewis, Roger K., *Architect? A Candid Guide to the Profession,* revised edition. Cambridge, MA: MIT Press, 1998.

Mauro, Lucia, *Careers for Fashion Plates & Other Trendsetters.* Lincolnwood, IL: VGM Career Books, 1996.

McDonald, Tom, *The Business of Portrait Photography.* New York, NY: Amphoto Books, 1996.

McHugh, Kenna, *Breaking into Film: Making Your Career Search a Blockbuster.* Princeton, NJ: Peterson's, 1998.

Meyers, Herbert M., *The Marketer's Guide to Successful Package Design.* Lincolnwood, IL: NTC Business Books, 1998.

Michels, Caroll, *How to Survive and Prosper as an Artist: Selling Yourself Without Selling Your Soul,* fourth ed. New York, NY: Henry Holt and Company, Inc., 1997.

Minsky, Laurence, *How to Succeed in Advertising When All You Have Is Talent: Today's Top Creatives Show You How (Careers for You).* Lincolnwood, IL: VGM Career Horizons, 1996.

Morgan, Jim, *Management for the Small Design Firm: Handling Your Practice, Personnel, Finances and Projects.* New York, NY: Watson-Guptill Publications, 1998.

Naftali, Lee, *You're Certifiable: The Alternative Career Guide to More Than 700 Certificate Programs, Trade Schools, and Job Opportunities.* New York, NY: Fireside Books, 1999.

Newberry, Betsy, *Designer's Guide to Marketing.* Cincinnati, OH: North Light Books, 1997.

———, *Peterson's Professional Degree Programs in the Visual and Performing Arts 1999,* fifth edition. Princeton, NJ: Peterson's Guides, 1998.

Pressman, Andy, *Professional Practice 101: A Compendium of Business and Management Strategies in Architecture.* New York, NY: John Wiley & Sons, 1997.

Reno, Kelly, *The 101 Best Freelance Careers.* New York, NY: Berkley Books, 1999.

Shaw, John, *John Shaw's Business of Nature Photography: A Professional's Guide to Marketing and Managing a Successful Nature Photography Business.* New York, NY: Amphoto Books, 1997.

Silber, Lee, *Career Management for the Creative Person.* New York, NY: Three Rivers Press, 1999.

Sint, Steve, *Wedding Photography: Art, Business, and Style.* Rochester, NY: Silver Pixel Press, 1998.

Smith, Constance, *Art Marketing 101: A Handbook for the Fine Artist,* updated edition. Penn Valley, CA: ArtNetwork, 1998.

Smith, Jeanette, *Breaking into Advertising: How to Market Yourself Like a Professional* Princeton, NJ: Peterson's, 1998.

Stasiowski, Frank A., *Starting a New Design Firm, or Risking It All!* New York, NY: John Wiley & Sons, 1994.

Swirsky, Judith, *On Exhibit 2000: Art Lover's Travel Guide to American Museums.* New York, NY: Abbeville Press Publishers, 1999.

Vitali, Julius, *The Fine Artist's Guide to Marketing and Self-Promotion: Innovative Techniques to Build Your Career as an Artist.* New York: NY: Allworth Press, 1996.

WEB SITES

www.adcny.org—Art Directors Club web site: job bank and information on visual communications

www.amn.org—Art Museum Network

www.art.net—Internet art gallery

www.artresources.com – Internet Art Resources

www.artwalker.com—Visit artists' renditions of locations around the world

www.artsednet.getty.edu/—The Getty Museum's Art Education Web Site

www.artseek.com—Art news, artists' directory, and Internet art resources www.artsedge.kennedy-center-org—Kennedy Center's Arts Edge

www.artswire.org/kenroar/—Arts Wire (New York Foundation for the Arts): A full pallette of art news, job information, web recourses, etc.

www.ci.nyc.ny.us/html/home.html—New York City Art Commission

www.creativeassets.com—Creative Assets Talent Network: job listings and art news

www.fisk.edu/vl/Literature/Overview.html—Links to art web sites

www.gaes.com—Graphic Arts Employment Specialists: recruiting service for printing, publishing, and graphic arts industries

www.gallerynow.com—Online art gallery

www.heritagepreservation.org/abouthp/preslink.htm—Links to museums and other art-related web sites

www.metmuseum.org—Metropolitan Museum of Art

www.mikesart.com—Art and design links and magazine

www.moma.org—Museum of Modern Art

www.nypl.org/research/chss/spe/art/artarc/artarch.html—New York Public Library Art and Architecture collection

www.servtech.com/~mvail/art.html—Digital Libraian: Best of the Web (art-related sites)

www.snd.org—Society for News Design: job bank, competitions, workshops, etc.

www.world-arts-resources.com—World Wide Arts Resources

www.xensei.com/adl/—Art Deadlines: newsletter listing opportunities for artists and art students

INDEX